BRADFORD CORPORATION MOTORBUSES

by

J. S. King

Venture *publications*

ISBN 1 898432 51 1

Front Cover Illustration

Bradford City Transport No. 220 – an AEC Regent V with a Metropolitan-Cammell-Weymann body – may not have been the author's favourite type of bus, but as part of the largest group of vehicles ever purchased by Bradford it worked hard for its owners and was to be seen on most routes in and around the city.
After precisely ten years' service for Bradford Corporation it passed to the West Yorkshire Passenger Transport Executive, and is now an active member of the fleet of 'Transperience' – the West Yorkshire Transport Museum at Low Moor, Bradford.

[Photo: John A. Senior

Produced in the United Kingdom

CONTENTS

FOREWORD

by
Bernard B. Browne,
C.Eng., F.I.Mech.E., M.I.R.T.E.

1952-56 Yorkshire Woollen District Transport Company
1956-59 Technical Assistant, Bolton Corporation Transport
1959-62 Technical Assistant, Liverpool Corporation Transport
1962-65 Rolling-Stock Engineer, Wallasey Corporation Transport
1965-74 Rolling-Stock Engineer, Bradford City Transport
1974-82 Development Engineer, West Yorkshire Passenger Transport Executive
1982-87 Chief Engineer, Blackpool Borough Transport

I was delighted when I was asked by the author to write a few words for this excellent book. By a coincidence I had just read his book *The Bradford Trolleybus* which had awakened many memories of the happy and satisfying years I spent at Bradford City Transport.

Stanley King and I have known each other for nearly thirty years, and he has never failed to impress me with the dedication he gives to serving the City of Bradford as an elected member of the Council, and the time he devotes to membership of national bodies. His knowledge of and enthusiasm for the world of passenger transport is well known, and never better expressed than in this book on the Bradford bus fleet.

Bradford City Transport, through the foresight of the Transport Committee and the officers of the Department was in the vanguard of British municipal bus fleets during the middle of this century. From the development of the early Leyland buses through the mid 1930s with the AEC 'Q' type until the last Bradford order for all-alloy bodied Daimler 'Fleetline' double-deckers, the fleet was always guaranteed to induce much favourable comment and respect from the British bus industry, and perhaps more importantly, the passengers it carried in the West Riding.

For those of us who lived close to Bradford the sight of the blue and cream fleet excited an affection and interest whether they were running on the level of Manningham Lane or climbing hard to Queensbury. The Bradford bus never had it easy !

For me that affection deepened with the chance to influence the fleet's future as trolleybus operation declined and eventually ceased. To my mind this book serves as a fitting tribute to the elected members, officers and staff whose hard work and dedication, often in far from ideal circumstances, produced a municipal bus fleet that served the passengers and citizens well for half a century.

I commend this book to you in the knowledge that it will be interesting, informative and most enjoyable. It is bound to become a reference work and a great success for the author. Surely an era of which the good folk of Bradford may be justly proud.

Bernard B. Browne
Fleetwood,
Lancashire
February 1995

INTRODUCTION

by
Henry A. Sissling

Bradford City Councillor 1955-1969
and Alderman 1969-1972
Deputy Chairman of the Transport Committee 1960-62
and Chairman 1962-63, 1967-68.

Bradford Corporation was always a leader in Municipal undertakings and there is no doubt that Bradford Corporation Passenger Transport was one of the largest and most successful of all.

Transport throughout the ages has always shown an ever-changing picture, and transport in Bradford was no exception. During the 76 years of its existence many challenges were faced. Two World Wars, the growth of motor cars for personal transport plus the huge housing estates in many cases situated at the limits of the City boundaries, placed a heavy burden on both management and staff. They responded to this challenge with enthusiasm and dedication, providing public transport service of a very high standard.

As an ex-chairman of the Bradford Transport Committee I remember with pride the excellent managers and indeed all employees of the undertaking.

Councillor King has already told the story of Bradford trolleybuses and now in this new book he continues the epic with fascinating detail and pictures of the Bradford motorbus undertaking.

I thank and commend him for his contribution to Bradford history, and know that the book will provide pleasure and information both now and in future years.

H. A. Sissling
Guiseley
February 1995

AUTHOR'S PREFACE AND ACKNOWLEDGEMENTS

Although the motorbuses operated by Bradford Corporation from 1926 to 1974 were less well-known than the tramcars or trolleybuses, it must be remembered that they played a vital role in the life and work of the City and its people, and ultimately constituted the only form of road passenger transport available in the area.

Municipal transport, now regrettably only a memory, provided an efficient, popular and cheap public facility controlled by a down-to-earth management directly responsible to the locally-elected City Council. Although modern private bus companies or operations controlled by large joint authorities all have their distinct merits, nevertheless detailed local knowledge, first-hand experience, ability to react immediately to everyday events and a policy of 'running a tight ship' were a combination hard to beat.

Bradford City Transport's remaining archives contain no lengthy reports, verbose analyses or tedious consultants' documents – only brief, to-the-point statements of actions taken and proposed. I am therefore deeply grateful to colleagues past and present who have assisted and advised, in particular Messrs J. Copland, A. Feather, C. Wright, J. H. Cheetham, G. Lumb, G. B. Lodge, M. Peck, G. Welburn, A. A. Townsin, M. Hampson, A. R. Whitaker, G. H. F. Atkins, R. Marshall, Dr M. Harrison, the Reverend Eileen Routh, Mrs J. B. Ball, the Bradford Industrial Museum, Bradford City Libraries, West Yorkshire Archives, West Yorkshire PTE, the Omnibus Society, the 'Telegraph and Argus' (Mr Perry Austin-Clark, Mr S. Homer and Mrs F. Wood), the late C. T. Humpidge, E. Deakin, J. A. Pitts and J. S. Cockshott, my old colleagues Alderman H. A. Sissling and Mr B. B. Browne for contributing the Introduction and Foreword respectively and Venture Publications for their suggestions, patience, diligence and precision.

Having recorded the story of the trolleybuses and now the motorbuses, I hope to complete the trilogy with a history of the tramways in due course.

Stanley King
Heaton, Bradford
March 1995

Bradford City Councillor since 1970;
Shadow Chairman of West Yorkshire PTA since 1986;
Currently member of the Association of Metropolitan
Authorities (AMA) Public Transport Committee..

1 FIRST GEAR

In the year 1807, when George III was King, Bradford was a pleasant market town picturesquely settled in a tranquil dale in the West Riding of Yorkshire.

Northwards the trout-filled Bradford Beck and the neighbouring canal wandered slowly towards the Aire Valley at Shipley; on all other sides the encircling foothills shielded the inhabitants from the extremes of the Northern climate. To the west an extensive rural parish reached towards high Pennine moors; southward and eastward turnpike roads, mail coaches and stage waggons gave access to Halifax, Brighouse, Huddersfield, Leeds and Wakefield.

The town's fame and fortune lay not in agricultural pursuits but in wool, and the advent of steam power and railways transformed the whole district within a few generations into a borough, the fastest-growing municipality in England and the wool capital of the world.

'We hear that steps are to be taken to start an omnibus to run several times a day between Bradford and Great Horton by way of Little Horton,' the *Bradford Observer* commented approvingly on 4th March 1847. It was a false start, however, and despite other launchings it was probably not until 22nd December 1864 that a permanent horse-bus service was established by the Bradford Livery Stable Co Ltd, which also began to operate horse-drawn and steam-worked tramways in 1882.

A time-table published about 1888 listed the following horse-bus services:–

Midland Station to Bolton Woods – Monday, Thursday and Saturday;
Darley Street top to Lister Park – Monday to Saturday (Sunday if fine);
Darley Street top to Carlisle Hotel – Monday to Saturday;
Pack Horse Inn to Thornton – Monday to Saturday;
Pack Horse Inn to Denholme – Tuesday, Thursday and Saturday;
Pack Horse Inn to Wilsden – Monday, Thursday and Saturday;
New Inn to Wilsden – Sunday;
St. George's Hall to Dudley Hill (Imperial Hotel) – daily;
Town Hall to West Bowling (Gaythorne Road) – Monday to Saturday;
Town Hall to Queensbury (Granby Inn) – daily;
Town Hall to Listerhills – Monday to Saturday;
Midland Station to Saltaire – Sunday if fine;
Midland Station to Bolton and Eccleshill – Monday to Saturday.

'J. Ballard's Penny Bus' seen at Fairmount, North Park Road, circa 1881   [BCT

The Eccleshill bus, a 22-seater pulled by three black horses, was driven by 'Old Bill', a ruddy-faced individual who found driving thirsty work and had to resort to a wine and spirit shop at each end of the journey. The West Bowling conveyances – smart 3-horse vehicles and the only double-deckers in the town – were considered the best of their kind, although the Bradford Tramways and Omnibus Company's buses which served Listerhills, the Lower Globe and Oak Lane were always well turned out, with red plush curtains and cushions and bright harness.

Very different were the Carlisle Road and Westgate services which were provided by a jumble of individually-owned waggonettes – shabby contraptions hauled by hungry horses – which observed no time-table but set off when all seats were occupied and all fares paid. However, it was the tramcars, larger and better-equipped to tackle the gradients, that carried the greatest number of passengers.

For Bradford, now rapidly approaching the peak of its prosperity, 1897 was a year to remember. On 10th July Queen Victoria raised it to the proud rank of City in honour of her Diamond Jubilee, and the ever-progressive Corporation promptly unveiled plans for ambitious projects such as electric tramways, stately art galleries and vast waterworks in distant Nidderdale. Such was the pace of civic progress that two noteworthy private transport ventures came and went almost unnoticed, overshadowed by more momentous events.

In the previous year Mr James Edward Tuke had driven the first car – a 3½ hp Arnold-Benz – through the streets of Bradford, and had used it in the municipal elections. On securing an agency for Arnold-Benz cars he founded a Yorkshire Motor Car Co Ltd, based at Albert Buildings, 6 Great Horton Road. Next he bought a covered Daimler waggonette and boldly advertised in the *Bradford Observer* on 25th September, 1897, that he was operating a 'Motor Omnibus Daily from Town Hall to Four Lane Ends'.

The venture was brief – probably only a few days – as the feeble, fitful machinery was ill-suited to the rigours of continuous running, and with a 6d fare the 'bus' could not compete with the penny steam-tram ride. Nevertheless in that age of eager innovation the idea was not forgotten.

The 'bus' had been maintained and garaged at the Belle Vue Drill Hall by Mr Albert House, cycle-maker, of Hustlergate, who in 1900 bought a 6½ hp two-cylinder Daimler resembling a 'governess-cart' and capable of seating ten passengers. The mechanism was simple and primitive with chain-drive and a gear-change controlled by a horizontal handle working round a slotted sector-plate; the driver lifted it out of one slot and dropped it into the next.

In August 1900, Mr House used the Daimler to launch a daily service along Manningham Lane in competition with the Rawson Square to Lister Park horse-trams. The trams scarcely noticed their rival; indeed, they actually passed it as it struggled in bottom gear up the imperceptible gradient at Belle Vue. Undaunted, his son, Mr J. W. House, took out the first motorbus conductor's licence ever issued by the Corporation, on 14th January 1901.

Occasionally the 'bus' ventured as far as Saltaire or even Bingley on a fine weekend, but the electrification of the Manningham Lane tramway in February, 1902, spelt the end of these pioneering peregrinations. In the bright, new Edwardian age the electric tramcar, cheap, efficient and very reliable, was seen as the vehicle of the future, and year by year its steel and copper tentacles reached ever further outwards to suburb and village.

Nevertheless, even Corporation tramways were considered by some to have their limits, and in December 1904, the Elsworth Automobile Company advised the Bradford Corporation Tramways Committee that outlying districts could conveniently be served by petrol-driven motor omnibuses. Not possessing Parliamentary powers to operate such vehicles, the Committee declined the suggestion. Similarly when the Finance and Licensing

Above: Albert House's 6¹/₂ hp Daimler which provided a service along Manningham Lane from 1900 to 1902. The photograph was probably taken outside the Belle Vue Hotel.

[Courtesy Mr J. House

Right: The first motorbus conductor's licence in Bradford issued 14th January 1901, and signed by Frederick Stevens, Town Clerk.

[Courtesy Bradford Industrial Museum

Committee received an application for a privately-operated motorbus service a year later, the Committee loftily replied that it was 'not disposed to look favourably on such a scheme'.

On 13th January 1913, the Daimler Company took the Tramways Committee on a circular safari via Queensbury, Mountain, Thornton, Allerton, Harden and Bingley – an arduous route embodying long, steep ascents and descents over miles of unpaved road, which tested the 40 hp engine and brakes to the limit. An offer from the Hansa Car and General Motor Company to demonstrate its 'patent reversible motor-omnibus' produced no reaction whatever, but having had time to recover from its recent rural ramblings the Committee decided to seek Parliamentary approval for motorbus operation inside and outside the City whenever the next Corporation Bill was promoted.

However, the tramway network had still not reached its peak, and undeveloped territory was being explored by the new railless cars (trolleybuses). The 'European War' which erupted in August, 1914, prevented further development, and no more was heard of motorbuses for a while.

The War deprived Bradford's tramways of manpower and materials, gradually reducing them to desperate straits with half the fleet laid up and the rest grossly overloaded. Even a year after the War ended the tram queues remained

CITY OF BRADFORD.

Motor Car **CONDUCTOR'S LICENCE,**

To be kept by the Conductor, and produced when required, to the Inspector of Hackney Carriages and Omnibuses, or to any Constable.

No. *1.*

This is to Certify, That the Council of the City of Bradford, in the County of York acting for the Mayor, Aldermen, and Citizens of the said City, in execution of the Bradford Waterworks and Improvement Act, 1868, and the Bradford Water and Improvement Act, 1878, DO HEREBY LICENSE

John W House of *4 Victoria Street*

to act as a Conductor of any *Motor Car*

plying for Hire within the City under and subject to the Orders, Rules, Regulations, and Bye-Laws, from time to time in force, and to the Statutes in such case made and provided.

This Licence is to remain in force until the Thirteenth day of January next, and no longer.

Dated the *14* day of *January* in the year 19*01.*

Frederick Stevens,

Town Clerk.

formidable especially during a national railway strike. Nevertheless when charabanc owners offered to supplement the tram service with their ungainly conveyances the Tramways Committee declined 'in the interest of public safety'.

When the 1920 Roads Act empowered local authorities to control the licensing of motorbuses and bus services within their areas, the interpretation of the new legislation varied from place to place. Bradford's Fire Brigade and Licensing Committee's policy was simple and uncomplicated. Proposed services connecting with the tramcar or trolleybus services were approved, and those which sought to compete were rejected in order to protect the ratepayers' immense investment in public transport.

Thus, for instance, Mr Robinson was permitted to begin a service from the Greengates and Thackley tram termini to Yeadon and Calverley respectively, whereas Mr Crabtree's dream of a Wilsden to Bradford service quickly faded, as it would have detracted from the Allerton tramway. New ground was broken, however, when Messrs Blythe and Berwick were allowed to establish a circumferential route entirely within the city, from Lister Park to Bankfoot, which connected with but did not compete with the tramways.

Sadly, the great municipal empire built up at such public expense received its first setback in April 1921, when a miners' strike caused electricity rationing. Faced with a 25% cut the Tramways Committee had to withdraw off-peak services for six weeks and allow up to sixty private buses and charabancs to run at fares 50% above normal rates. Having thus briefly tasted the joys of stage-carriage operation the companies began to look for areas ripe for development, and the Corporation felt it necessary to support the Municipal Tramways Association in its plea for statutory regulation of bus competition.

Not that bus or charabanc travel could, as yet, be considered attractive; tyres were solid and springs unyielding, and beyond the paved limits of the tramways most roads were unmade. In July 1924, a lorry sank up to its axles in the surface of the main Bradford-Wakefield highway at Drighlington.

Since July 1922, Bradford had been urging Keighley Corporation to reinstate its former bus service to Bingley. The service had in fact lapsed in 1913, and for ten years no public service of any kind had ventured over the muddy, potholed highway between Keighley's tram terminus at Stockbridge and Bradford's furthest tramway outpost at Crossflatts. Keighley's dilatory response was to allow the Premier Transport Co to fill the gap on the proviso that the company would withdraw if Keighley decided to resume operation. Needless to say, when Keighley Corporation buses finally reappeared at Crossflatts (and later Bingley) in April 1925, Premier were firmly entrenched.

In September 1923, Bradford prudently decided to seek a Provisional Order from the Ministry of Transport for the operation of motorbuses and trolleybuses on specified routes within the City, but on learning that a full Parliamentary Bill would be needed for the buses, voted to promote a Bus Bill on 14th August 1924.

Neighbouring Halifax Corporation declared their intention of running into Bradford via Shelf and Queensbury until Bradford could participate in a joint service, and Keighley and Bradford expressed enthusiasm for a joint Corporation bus service from Forster Square, Bradford, to Town Hall Square, Keighley. The Bradford Tramways Manager, Mr R. H. Wilkinson, would have preferred a trolleybus service, but acknowledged that 'buses are more popular at present'.

The Keighley press commented approvingly that,

'The Corporation can give a better and more reliable service than the small companies, some of whom run only at peak hours, and it is very important for the satisfaction of the public that the Tramways Department should retain passenger transport.'

The small companies thought otherwise and vowed to oppose Bradford's 'Bus Bill'.

Meanwhile, attracted by the excitement of the new mode of transport, the public beyond the immediate reach of the tramways were happy to disregard the occasional lurid headlines –

'Motor 'bus wrecked at level crossing – brakes fail to act !'
'Bus crashes into Bedroom'
'Workmen's 'Bus Capsizes'
'Motorbus Thrill – fire under driver's seat'
'Motorbus upset down Embankment'
'Bus dashes into Crowd'
'Somersault over Parapet'
'Crash into a Bath-Chair'
'Motor-'Bus turns Turtle'
'Blazing 'Bus Peril'
'Bus suspended over Rail Line' (shades of Pearl White and her silent film predicaments)
'Bus smashed to pieces' (Messrs Briggs Bros' bus on their new Eldwick-Bingley service).

It is common knowledge, of course, that accidents always happen to other people !

The press viewed the rise of the motorbus with interest.

'One of the most surprising features of recent years', they observed, 'has undoubtedly been the enormously increased popularity of the motorbus ... It is rather singular that though the question of the introduction of 'buses to Bradford has been aired for so long, nothing has been done even in the way of a trial.'

Had they known Bradford's tramway management a little better they would have been less surprised. Conceding that from an operational point of view buses were ideal because they were self-contained, Mr Wilkinson stressed nevertheless that in the interests of financial economy trolleybuses would ultimately have to predominate over tramcars as well as buses. Petrol vehicles, small, unreliable and shortlived, were not the answer to urban transport problems.

2 THE WEST RIDING DISPUTE

Local authorities which did not enjoy the privilege of owning a municipal transport undertaking often took a more cavalier attitude towards the licensing of private buses than public transport operators themselves.

Some 25 miles south-east of Bradford the small authorities of Castleford, Normanton and Pontefract were granting licences to any bus operator who applied for one, greatly to the detriment of the Yorkshire (West Riding) Tramways Company's routes in those areas. Despite being one of the towns' most important ratepayers, the Company pleaded in vain for protection and were obliged to withdraw the tram services in November 1925.

Having demanded protection for their own trams against bus competition, the company might have been expected to respect the interests of other tramway operators, but such expectations were ill-founded. Their bus-operating subsidiary, the West Riding Automobile Co Ltd had established a service from Wakefield to Drighlington where connection was made with the Bradford tramways. In August 1924, the company informed the Bradford Licensing Committee that 'they would be glad to know if the Corporation would issue hackney carriage licences to them to allow them to extend their existing ... service along the tramway route to a terminus in Union Street', ie a short distance from the tramcar departure point in Norfolk Street. The Committee decided on 22nd September that they would not be glad to do so.

To their surprise the company challenged the decision and appealed to the Ministry under Section 20 of the Roads Act. At a public inquiry held in Bradford Town Hall the Corporation argued that the twenty-minute Drighlington tramcar frequency was perfectly adequate and that a motorbus service would increase traffic congestion – indeed, the Chief Constable had complained about congestion in the city streets only a month previously.

The company's case was that passengers were inconvenienced by having to change from bus to tram, despite evidence that there was always a tram waiting at the terminus and that on average the number of passengers making the connection was only six per day ! The company's proposed fare over the tramway was 6d, which appeared to offer adequate protection to the trams with their 4d fare, though as the company also intended to offer a 9d return fare, the actual differential was minimal.

Unconvinced, the Minister ruled against the Corporation, who, however, saw no reason to alter their decision. The Minister formally ordered the Corporation to issue a licence to the company: his order was robustly ignored.

In a more conciliatory vein the Minister explained his view that inter-town travellers should not have to change vehicles provided that local services were properly protected. In addition he expressed the opinion that in order to place municipalities on an equal basis to private competitors, his Department should be empowered to issue the necessary authorisation without the need for special Acts of Parliament.

His sympathy for a removal of civic shackles was soon put to the test. The Corporation's new parliamentary Bill contained various proposals for tramway improvements as well as the clause empowering them to operate motorbuses. The tramway clauses were fiercely contested by the Automobile Association, the British Motor Manufacturers' Association, the Association of British Manufacturers and the Yorkshire Division of Motor Manufacturers thus prompting the Corporation's King's Counsel to retort that 'they want us to abolish our tramways and purchase motor omnibuses manufactured by those who have signed the petition'.

The Bill (Bradford Corporation Act 1925 [15 and 16 Geo. V ch. cxxi] August 7th 1925) was passed, but the motorbus powers

Enjoying a peaceful 'layover' at Drighlington terminus, tramcar 248 is more than capable of accommodating the six passengers per day who transfer from West Riding's buses on their journey from Wakefield.

were restricted to the city itself. Thus, despite the Minister's views, the West Riding company buses were to be allowed to enter the City but the Corporation's buses could not leave it, even to travel to Drighlington.

However, when Bradford's Licensing Committee remained obdurate, the Minister re-read the original West Riding enquiry and conceded that,

"It is not free from doubt whether the .... company's letter was a definite application for licences or merely an enquiry". In any case the licensing year had now expired, and it did not seem that further action on his part would serve any useful purpose.

West Riding thought otherwise. Within two days (28th August 1925) they submitted a fresh application which the Committee parried with a request for additional information. The resumption of the duel began to arouse wider interest, and eighteen new applications were received. After due consideration the Committee refused every one.

Following a further public inquiry the Minister upheld the West Riding appeal and prepared to issue an Order enforceable by a writ of mandamus in the High Court, against which there could be no appeal.

Staunchly contemptuous of vengeful threats from distant Whitehall the Committee voted 8-5 on 1st February 1926, to refuse the licence, adding forcefully that the Minister had no judicial power in the matter. The Minister insisted that he had, and ordered that licences for twelve 32-seat buses (HL 1800-1811) and six 20-seaters (HL 2038-2043) be granted by 10th March, this being the first time he had been obliged to use his powers, real or imaginary.

At the ensuing battle in the King's Bench the Attorney General advised that the Corporation should accept the company's assurances, and that if the assurances were not honoured, they would be entitled to refuse future renewal of the licences. Despite the Lord Chief Justice's doubts as to the soundness of this advice the Court ruled on 3rd May 1926, that the Corporation must license the West Riding buses.

At this fateful juncture, seemingly oblivious to the storm now breaking over their employers' heads, the Bradford tramwaymen's union instructed its members to join the colliers and railway workers in the General Strike. Only two evenings after the King's Bench judgement the

Corporation's tramcar and trackless staff obediently ran their vehicles into the depots and left them there for a week.

Scarcely able to believe their good luck the private bus companies were promptly awarded temporary permission from the Licensing Committee for emergency services within the City. Led by Blythe and Berwick they brushed aside the union's appeals not to 'break' the Strike, and a motley horde of charabancs, hastily-converted lorries and the like descended upon Bradford, Shipley and Bingley.

In the Bradford area the Strike was remarkably orderly, with much good humour and mutual assistance. Compelled to walk to their place of work, two portly gentlemen laid bets as to who would arrive first; the prize duly went to him whose protuberant stomach touched the finishing-tape first. In Tyrrel Street fascinated bystanders gathered to behold a hefty lady being pushed up the high steps of a charabanc by no less than five gentlemen whose gallant exertions thus spared her diminutive husband a spell in hospital. And in Bingley the Council's steamroller displayed a sporting invitation to weary foot-sloggers:-

'If you want a lift, please signal !'

After four or five days some of the tramway staff began to report for duty, realising that the Strike was becoming futile, and by 12th May 34 trams were back on the rails. A full service of Corporation vehicles recommenced next day, but the undertaking for which they worked had suffered a serious blow.

The complete and unheralded stoppage of the trams and trolleybuses for reasons which did not directly concern them had angered and alienated many of the public. The assistance provided by the private buses, crude and cramped though they were, had swung public opinion in their favour almost overnight. Many long-accustomed tramcar users now compared the trams unfavourably with the buses and continued to use them wherever they could be found.

On 17th May the legal battle having been irretrievably lost, the Licensing Committee were finally compelled to issue licences for no less than fourteen private bus services. And seven days later the West Riding buses made their triumphant entry into Bradford.

The fourteen new services all reached beyond the Corporation's operating area and provided work for 63 private buses. From a central terminus in Victoria Square they operated over the Manchester Road tramway and the Odsal-Oakenshaw trolleybus route to Cleckheaton, Dewsbury and other parts of the Heavy Woollen District; the Halifax service paralleled the Shelf tramway; Harrogate, Ilkley and Otley buses roared past the Baildon Bridge trams; the Canal Road trolleybuses were overwhelmed by Baildon, Otley, Yeadon and Ilkley buses whilst Clayton, Leeds via Pudsey and Harrogate via Eccleshill buses detracted to a lesser degree from the tramways. More excitingly, a motor-coach service to London was established.

The bus had undoubtedly arrived – and it had come to stay.

Left: Bradford and its neighbours.

3   CAMELS and LIONS

"The people show a sound instinct when they desert the tramway for any other and newer form of conveyance" – J. B. Priestley, "English Journey", 1933

Armed with its restricted motorbus operating powers the Corporation was at last ready to fight back, though the battle was not on equal terms and too much ground had already been lost.

A few weeks after its Bus Bill had received the Royal Assent in 1925 the Tramways Committee had resolved to buy 24 buses at approximately £1,500 each, subject to suitable tenders from suppliers and the granting of municipal borrowing powers. Pending the establishment of a central 'garage' the vehicles were to be housed in a wing of Thornbury tramcar depot.

Two buses had been borrowed from AEC of Southall, Middlesex on 16th November 1925, when the Committee had used them to sample possible routes, and three further buses – presumably lent by other manufacturers – had been inspected on 1st January 1926.

Four initial routes were contemplated:–

(i)   Haworth Road (via Sunbridge Road, Lumb Lane, Oak Lane and Toller Lane) at a 3d fare with five overlapping penny stages.

(ii) Cutler Heights (from Forster Square via Well Street, Leeds Road, Hammerton Street, Bowling Back Lane and Broad Lane).

(iii) Lister Park to Bankfoot (via Manningham Lane, Marlborough Road etc to Grange Road, Park Avenue, Little Horton Lane, Thornton Lane etc and Manchester Road to the foot of Wibsey Bank), fare 4°d with six penny stages.

(iv) Oakenshaw (from Town Hall Street via Nelson Street, Croft Street, Manchester Road and Cleckheaton Road).

The first two were to serve new areas and, by means of circuitous routes, avoid conflict with the tram services; the third would compete with Blythe and Berwick while the fourth would supersede the Odsal-Oakenshaw trolleybus service and provide direct communication with the city centre.

Under the heading of 'Bradford's First Municipal Bus' the press announced the arrival at Thornbury depot on 29th April, 1926 of the first bus from the AEC works at Walthamstow. Interested spectators viewed it as it stood outside the Tramways Offices in Hall Ings prior to being weighed as part of the vehicle licensing procedure. The Tramways Manager announced that it would be tried in service on the Bolton-Bankfoot trolleybus route and that he had notified Blythe and Berwick that as soon as a sufficient number of buses arrived they would join the company's vehicles on the Lister Park-Bankfoot run.

The hurried inauguration of the Bradford Corporation Motorbus Undertaking was briefly but graphically recorded

'Bradford's First Municipal 'Bus' seen outside the Tramways Offices on 29th April 1926, prior to being inspected and exchanging its AEC trade plate for a Bradford registration mark.
[Courtesy *Telegraph & Argus*

13

in the Tramways Department's diary:–

'April 29th, 1926 – First motor bus arrived (A.E.C.). Ran on Bolton-Bankfoot May 1-2-3.

At midnight on May 3rd Strike began.

4th May – 2 buses ran; 5th May 3 and 6th May 4.

13th May – Normal service.'

At 3.30pm on 11th May one of the new buses loaded up 'a detachment of volunteers' and conveyed them to Thornbury for a brief course of tramcar driving to enable them to reopen the Thornbury, Frizinghall and Southfield Lane routes, but their services were not needed for long, as the Strike was ending.

On the Bolton-Bankfoot trolleybus route the unheralded introduction of a motorbus greatly intrigued the regular passengers who, if they had time to spare, spurned the familiar 'trackless' in favour of the novel form of transport, which, not surprisingly, they found to their liking.

Contrasted with the solid-tyred 'tracklesses', some of which were of pre-war vintage, the bus with its pneumatic tyres and well-sprung moquette-upholstered seats provided a distinctly more comfortable ride. True, the journey was laborious and not very rapid; the noise of the engine tended to dominate the proceedings; the gear-changes (a novelty in themselves) were tedious and the petrol fumes malodorous, but on the whole the passengers were well pleased.

The object of their admiration was a small, single-deck petrol omnibus painted in the conventional Corporation livery of Prussian blue and ivory lined in blue, gold and black. The 'Edinburgh' or 'Metropolitan' style body was of the 'forward control' type with the driver seated alongside

the engine, and the small rear platform incorporated an upholstered seat for the conductor. Advance warning of the vehicle's approach was given by a large, melodious footgong later superseded by a bulb horn, and a tramcar-type lifeguard discouraged ardent admirers from throwing themselves under the wheels.

Fleet numbers were not allocated to the buses at first, and for a while they were known by their registration numbers. Then, sensibly, they were assigned the series 301-500 in between the tramcars (1-258) and tracklesses (501-540), although in view of the large dimensions of the fleet numerals used by BCT at that period non-standard numerals were used until 1931.

On the day on which the Corporation employees returned to duty after the Strike (13th May 1926) the four available buses, KW 8601/3/4/5 (later 301/3/4/5), commenced the first scheduled BCT bus service, from Lister Park to Bankfoot, in deliberate and determined competition with Blythe and Berwick whose other buses were poaching the tramways clientele. No love was lost between the Corporation employees who were union members and the company staff who were not. Bus races occurred; unheard-of speeds of 40 mph were achieved along Park Avenue; fists flew and coarse epithets were exchanged.

As soon as the remaining AECs (302/6-10) were available the Haworth Road and Cutler Heights (Broad

Leyland Lion No. 313's optimistic reversed livery reflects the autumn sunshine. The Tramways Committee used this bus for their inspection of the Bierley route.

[BCT/WYPTE/WYAS

Lane) services were opened on 20th July, operating for a time as a through service via Forster Square and John Street. The Odsal-Oakenshaw trolleybus service survived, however, and was extended into the city centre in the following year.

When the bus drivers became accustomed to handling their 'steeds' they pronounced them to be underpowered and barely adequate for Bradford's hills. More seriously, they were slower than their rivals.

It was fortunate, therefore, that for the more steeply-graded Bierley and Fagley routes, opened on 13th October and 3rd November respectively, more businesslike vehicles were available in the form of Leyland PLSC Lions, Nos. 311-317. With their 31-seat Leyland bodies and reliable engines they were the equal of the best of their rivals, and tackled gradients in a dogged, valiant manner. As the manager considered that large expanses of Prussian blue paint could cause the buses to be mistaken for hearses, the Leylands were treated to a reversed livery of ivory with one blue band, black mudguards and blue lining-out. The Committee proudly used the first to arrive, KU 9903 (later 313) to inspect the Bierley route on its opening day.

From their city terminus in Nelson Street ('at t'back o' t' Town Hall' in local parlance) the Bierley buses ascended Wakefield Road as far as Paley Road, passing ancient Bolling Hall on their way to the new but remote Bierley

housing estate. Fagley folk who had previously been obliged to walk half a mile to catch the Undercliffe or Greengates tram now enjoyed a direct service via Pollard Lane, although the Lions, unlike the trams, found the mountainous ascent of Church Bank far beyond their capabilities, and resorted to a lengthy detour from Forster Square via Well Street, Leeds Road, Harris Street, Humboldt Street and East Parade.

Meanwhile a tentative link had been established with Keighley. From 2nd July 1926, cheap through tickets at a return fare of 1/1d were issued on BCT trams and KCT buses which met at Crossflatts. The location of the change-point was not ideal, as the Crossflatts trams ran at a twenty-minutes frequency and enjoyed a leisurely twenty-minutes layover at the terminus; moreover, KCT buses on their return journey from Bingley were often full before reaching Crossflatts. Not unexpectedly a passenger complained of having spent three hours ten minutes on a round trip, and in January 1927 the change-point was removed to Bingley Main Street where the tram service was more frequent.

Not to be outdone, the Premier Transport Co extended their Keighley-Bingley service into Bradford despite possessing no licence; forbidden by Shipley and Bradford to issue tickets in their areas, they were officially unable to pick up passengers between Nab Wood and Bradford unless they already held tickets. Predictably Premier flouted the law by all possible means and finally won a licence in April 1927 after an appeal to the Ministry.

Sensibly refusing to be imprisoned within their own boundaries the Corporation prepared an ambitious new

Bus Bill which was duly endorsed 49-21 by the City Council. Operating powers were to be sought in the local government areas of Calverley, Farsley, Leeds, Hunsworth, Birkenshaw, Spenborough, Batley, Birstall, Dewsbury, Halifax, Hipperholme, Shipley, Keighley, Bingley, Baildon, Hawksworth, Menston, Burley, Ilkley and Guiseley, with moorland routes to Ilkley via Hawksworth and Burley Woodhead, and to Bingley via Baildon and Eldwick. Joint-working powers with other operators were also sought.

Councillor Walter Hodgson, while maintaining his support for private enterprise, significantly added that he had 'long since ceased to regard the passenger transport of large cities as a matter for private concern'.

More robustly Councillor Ellis advocated the London General method of discouraging private competition. "Put one bus behind and one in front !" he said.

Much interest was aroused by the Bill, which was formally endorsed at a public meeting packed with no fewer than 1,500 ratepayers. Questioned about proposals for private hire and the carriage of goods and animals, the Town Clerk replied amid merriment, "I cannot conceive the Corporation asking that horses and cows should be allowed to sit on the seats !" Formidable opposition was voiced by the Bradford Horse and Motor Owners Association, Bradford Chamber of Trade, Bradford Commercial Vehicles Association, the West Riding County Council (who routinely resisted all forms of municipal expansion) and transport operators in Dewsbury, Leeds and Wakefield.

In the Commons Colonel Anthony Gadie, MP for Bradford, conceded that although in theory the Bill empowered BCT to run buses to Worcester Races, in practice a fifteen-mile limit would be acceptable. In vain: the Bill was defeated 203-128 in March 1927, and a similar fate befell Halifax's ambitions for long-distance facilities.

Bradford therefore had to content themselves by closing loopholes within the City which others might seek to fill. The process began with the arrival of further AECs, Nos. 318-324, which sported 30-seat forward-entrance bodies by Northern Counties of Wigan and a reversed livery like the Leyland Lions. In common with the previous AECs (301-310) they were always known as 'the Camels', a nickname which probably owed as much to their sluggish performance as their drivers' memories of wartime exploits with Mesopotamian quadrupeds and Sopwith aeroplanes !

A surburban route from Bankfoot to Horton Bank Top via Odsal Road and Beacon Road opened on 10th January 1927, requiring only two buses. Simultaneously a Duckworth Lane to Little Horton service was launched, linking the Allerton, Thornton, Lidget Green, Queensbury, and Wibsey tramways.

The delightful old-world village of Tong, a full rural mile from the Drighlington tramway, received a service on 28th February 1927, when the first Corporation bus ventured along the winding hedge-flanked lane.

The second delivery of 'Camels' had Northern Counties bodies, and on this photograph taken outside the bodybuilder's Wigan headquarters, No. 318 is seen in an elegant reversed livery.

[Photo: Northern Counties

In March the Tramways Committee devised a tortuous service for the Ripleyville area, from Nelson Street via Ellen Street and St. Stephen's Road to Bankfoot, but even though before the first bus ran on 19th September the schedule was revised to include a more comprehensive route (Hall Lane, Ellen Street, Ripley Terrace and Street, Springmill Street, Baird Street and Bowling Old Lane), little patronage was generated. For most of the day the service was therefore linked with the Bankfoot-Horton Bank Top route.

Further expansion was envisaged with the acceptance of a Leyland tender for twelve 43½ hp PLSC3 Long Lions with rear-entrance 36-seat bodies; these sturdy vehicles arrived as Nos. 325-336 in September/October 1927. Like 311-317 they were in reversed livery.

Although the growing bus fleet was stabled at Thornbury tram depot with an 'overspill' at the nearby English Electric Works, the bus staff considered themselves as a separate entity. The first intake of drivers – all ex-lorry and charabanc drivers – ranked as an 'elite' because they could not be called upon to perform other duties, and exclusively occupied separate tables in the canteen. BCT naturally preferred more versatile staff who could handle trams, tracklesses or buses with equal dexterity, and as soon as possible the normal appointments procedure was applied. Thenceforth employees worked upwards through the ranks of parcels-boy, bus conductor, tram conductor, tram driver, trackless driver, bus driver and, ultimately, inspector.

Being slower and jerkier than the Leylands, the AEC 'Camels' were unpopular with the drivers who regularly reported them for imaginary mis-firing or clutch-slip in the hope of a 'change-over' being permitted, but this practice quickly ceased when a fitter was upgraded to inspector !

Continuing pressure from the motorbus lobby was routinely resisted by the manager, Mr Wilkinson, who pointed out that no less than 442 buses would be needed to replace the 215 trams and 20 tracklesses in daily service. But the private buses were now conveying a quarter of the passengers, and Bradford was said to possess more motorcars per head of population than any other city in England.

On 8th March 1927, the Licensing Committee performed its annual inspection of what the press described as 'half a mile of buses' – 330 motorbuses and one horse-charabanc. The owners condemned the examination as 'a waste of time', but the vigilant Committee pointed out defective brakes and inadequate emergency exits.

The Cutler Heights service was re-routed along Parsonage Road and extended to the junction of Cutler Heights Lane and Fenby Avenue during the year as a protective measure, as longer-distance private buses were now passing through the area on their way to Leeds.

Oswald Tillotson Limited, the Leyland agents, supplied Bradford Corporation with some of its vehicles and also supplied this PLSC Lion to the Calder fleet in Lancashire, not to be confused with the Calder bus service of Bradford Road, Bailiff Bridge.

[Senior Transport Archive; photo Leyland Motors

4 BRIGHOUSE and CALDER

In July 1927 the Corporation resolved once again to seek powers for bus operation outside the City, but conscious of the opposition which this would arouse, not least from the private companies and the County Council as owners of highways outside the county boroughs, took the wise precaution of opening negotiations with their neighbours, including Keighley, who once again expressed a desire for a joint municipal service. Also, for the first time, serious attention was given to the question of Brighouse.

The story of the labyrinthine means by which BCT gained access to Brighouse resembles a murky pond whose uncertain depths have not been thoroughly trawled and probably never will be. Surviving archives of the Corporations of Bradford, Brighouse, Halifax and Huddersfield as well as the fragmentary records of the companies reveal high drama as well as seemingly endless negotiations at town halls – ad hoc midnight bargains and clandestine agreements as well as sober parchments signed by mayors and town clerks.

Until the early 'twenties the only direct means of communication between Bradford and Huddersfield was by railway – the 'Pickle Bridge Branch' via Wyke, Bailiff Bridge and Brighouse (Clifton Road). In 1904 Halifax Corporation had built a Halifax-Brighouse tramway with a branch extension to Bailiff(e) Bridge as an inducement for local people to do their shopping in Halifax. In 1913 Bradford trams had also reached Bailiff Bridge, and Huddersfield trams arrived at Brighouse in 1923 by way of Fixby and Rastrick, but as all three systems had for perfectly sound reasons constructed their tram tracks to different gauges, through travel was impossible.

The first step towards direct communication was apparently made by Huddersfield Corporation who on 6th November 1924 decided to seek Bradford's consent for a bus service between the two towns. Bradford, already locked in dispute with the West Riding and the Ministry and probably not wishing to create a dangerous precedent, waited until July 1925 before giving approval. Various consents had to be sought from Brighouse and the County Council, and a toll had to be paid to Halifax who faced a loss of passengers from their branch tramway, so that it was not until 1st January 1926, that the Huddersfield bus service began to run. For the time being the terminus was at Bailiff Bridge where connection was made with the frequent BCT tram service.

There matters might have rested until BCT obtained powers to operate a joint inter-town bus service. However, on 1st January 1927 Hebble Bus Services (O. & C. Holdsworth of Halifax) and their rivals the Calder Bus Service (Mr E. K. Sykes of Bradford Road, Bailiff Bridge) launched services to Bradford from Brighouse and nearby Hipperholme. Within a few months Calder were summonsed for plying without a licence; officially they were licensed to operate on a pre-paid return ticket basis only, but were detected issuing single tickets to passengers boarding at Slack Road, Buttershaw.

Upon the defeat of their second Bus Bill and as a preliminary to the launching of the third, Bradford enquired whether Halifax would be willing to sell their Brighouse-Bailiff Bridge tramway to enable BCT trams to run into Brighouse town centre, a few yards from the Huddersfield tram terminus. In April 1927 Halifax duly agreed to sell the tramway for £7,500 and to reconstruct it to Bradford's slightly broader gauge.

Had this interesting project reached fruition the whole of the basic service from Brighouse to Bradford and Huddersfield would have been provided by trams, with a jointly-run inter-town bus service operating, presumably, at a protective fare. Following a Ministry inquiry a Huddersfield-Bradford bus service opened on 6th December 1927, operated jointly by Huddersfield (2/3rds) and Hebble (1/3rd).

The tortuous negotiations between the four Corporations and the companies dragged on with the Sheffield manager, Mr A. R. Fearnley, being brought in as arbitrator. In May 1928 Calder offered to sell their business to Bradford for £25,000, but the latter considered the value to be not more than £20,000. At this stage the sale was held to be illegal – at least by the Huddersfield and Halifax town clerks – as the Bradford Bill which would legalise it had not yet been passed, and the Bill could not be passed without the consent of all the interested parties.

After feverish, high-powered behind-the-scenes activities a bargain was struck at £22,500 and an agreement signed in London on 16th July 1928. This successfully eliminated the remaining opposition to Bradford's Bus Bill, to which the Royal Assent was given only eighteen days later.

Unfortunately when Calder passed into Bradford's hands on 1st October the Corporation, despite being owners of the goodwill and the miscellaneous fleet of fourteen buses, had not been able to obtain the necessary licences from the local authorities and were therefore obliged to ask Hebble to operate three of the services on their behalf. Hebble graciously (and no doubt gleefully) consented to do so – at a price. Between December 1928 and the end of March 1929 Hebble received £1,255-11s-9d – about £6-16s-0d per day – from Bradford.

The dilemma was resolved by the outright sale of the Calder fleet to Hebble for a mere £5,000 and an agreement between Bradford and Huddersfield (signed on 26th March 1929) whereby BCT acquired a one-third share of the joint Huddersfield-Bradford service, and Huddersfield and Bradford granted each other consent to operate services to Bailiff Bridge and Brighouse respectively, using either motorbuses or trolleybuses. Bradford also agreed to pay Halifax £7,505-1s-3d to abandon the Bailiff(e) Bridge-Brighouse tramway altogether. Accordingly the trams and the Bradford-owned Calder bus services ran for the last time on 30th March.

Next morning BCT buses at last took up their share of the long route from Bradford (Nelson Street) to Huddersfield via Wyke, Bailiff Bridge, Brighouse, the steep climb up 'Brighouse Hill' to Bradley Bar and the long descent to distant Huddersfield. Bradford's own service to Brighouse (Thornton Square) ie the ex-Hebble ex-Calder working, commenced simultaneously.

The complicated negotiations and disastrous financial transactions had not been widely publicised, and when details filtered through to the Bradford councillors their anger was great. A net payment of £25,000 for full running rights to Brighouse and a third share of the Huddersfield service was a costly venture indeed. Receipts on the BCT trams to Bailiff Bridge fell sharply when the buses began to run, and from 9th November 1932, no tramcars operated beyond Wyke except at peak hours, thus effectively depriving Lower Wyke residents of their cheap tram fares. Their appeals for the Brighouse buses to be diverted via Town Gate fell on deaf ears.

One of the two dual-entrance Bristols, Nos. 337/338, in the characteristic fleet livery of the late 1920s.

[Courtesy J. Copland

Like all motorbuses of the mid-1920s, this rear-entrance Bristol of the 340-351 series was officially restricted to a 12mph speed limit.

[Courtesy J. Copland

5 TITANS TAKE OVER

Significant developments ushered in the New Year 1928, when Blythe and Berwick amalgamated with Premier Transport and Harrogate Road Car to form West Yorkshire Road Car Co based in Harrogate.

Premier had inaugurated a Bradford-Denholme service in competition with BCT's Thornton tramcars, with their practice of maintaining a 'fines fund' for their lawless drivers eloquently illustrated their attitude to Licensing Committees. Later in the year West Yorkshire swallowed up Keighley Brothers who had established a Keighley-Bradford express service, applying for licences as an afterthought. And when Hebble Bus Service acquired Briggs Brothers' Bingley-Harden-Allerton-Bradford and Duckworth Lane-Bingley services, BCT felt themselves being hemmed in by increasingly-powerful combines.

More promising was an agreement with Yorkshire (Woollen District) in May 1928 for joint operation to Dewsbury via Birkenshaw and Cleckheaton, although it was to be several years before operation began, and in a different form.

The longed-for Keighley through-service re-emerged in April when the two Corporations signed a working agreement which was augmented in June to include West Yorkshire. All three operators were to enjoy an equal share of a ten-minute Bradford-Keighley service between 6.30am and 11pm. Joyfully Keighley bought four Leyland Titans (54-57) and licensed six BCT single-deckers for which side-destination boards advertising 'Bradford to Keighley' (with 'Bradford to Fagley' on the reverse) had been prepared. Keighley's Town Clerk was briefed to interview West Yorkshire about the agreement, and local County Councillors were asked to support Bradford's application to run its buses on County roads – which at last they were able to do. The Corporation buses were about to burst their bonds.

The third Bradford Bus Bill, promoted in July 1927, had become an Act on 3rd August 1928 (Bradford Corporation Act, 1928 (18 and 19 Geo. V ch. cxvi)), but not without amendment by the House of Lords. Their Lordships, while conceding the principle of allowing BCT buses to operate outside the City, restricted them to a radius of ten miles from the Town Hall with the exception of Huddersfield (twelve miles), to the disappointment of the Tramways Committee who had requested a 20 miles radius with the specific object of reaching Skipton and Harrogate.

Nevertheless the Act was an important step forward, as

Left: First of the mighty Titans, No. 353 displays its magnificent but sombre livery and business-like bodywork, and was unique in possessing stylish moquette upholstery on the upper deck.
[Courtesy G. Welburn,; photo Leyland Motors

Opposite page: Dressed in the latest 1929 fashions, the ladies of Greengates alight from Titan No. 357 outside the GPO in Forster Square, while an Undercliffe tramcar heads for Church Bank.
[Courtesy J. Copland

it empowered the Corporation to operate buses within the City over all existing tramways and all existing and future trolleybus routes. Outside the City, BCT buses could run on County roads with the consent (not to be unreasonably withheld) of the West Riding County Council. Joint services could be worked with other operators, but no BCT bus could traverse a Halifax tramway (this was a particular reference to Brighouse) without permission from Halifax.

Meanwhile domestic affairs had intervened unexpectedly on 16th April when the Tramways Committee learned that Harrogate Road was to be widened considerably, and that it would be necessary to relocate two sections of the tramway in the near future and renew the remainder within four years at a total cost of £44,427. The Committee decided to abandon the track between Undercliffe and Greengates and operate motorbuses pending the installation of trolleybuses when the Undercliffe trams ceased.

This was the first time that Bradford motorbuses had been selected to replace another form of transport, and large-capacity vehicles were needed as replacements for the trams which carried crush loads of over 70 passengers. Tenders were therefore invited for ten double-deck buses, and, the historic decision having been made, the Committee inspected a Leyland double-deck bus and sampled a journey to Greengates via King's Road and Idle, returning via Harrogate Road, Undercliffe and East Parade.

An avalanche of buses arrived during the year, Nos. 337/8 being Bristol 'B' forward-entrance vehicles and 341-352 identical buses with rear entrances. Numbers 339-340 were Leyland PLSC3 'Long Lions'; not as popular as the earlier Lions because of their fierce 'air-brakes' – presumably hydraulic – (drivers christened them 'rocking horses') they were nevertheless better appreciated than the Bristols which were remembered sixty years later by Mr F. H. Hick as, "The worst buses this City ever had, with heavy steering, shocking gear change on hills, rocking air brakes, the slowest acceleration ever, and unable to keep time on any route."

The successful tenderer for the ten double-deckers was the local Leyland agent Messrs Oswald Tillotson, who offered Leyland 'Titan' 51-seat lowbridge open-staircase models at £1,720-15-0d each. The first of these revolutionary conveyances, No. 353, arrived within three months of the tender and entered service on 29th August 1928 to the fascination of the public, who had never seen a double-deck petrol bus before. Accustomed to the low-height tramcars needed for the Greengates (Harrogate Road) section, they accepted unquestioningly the Leyland patent design of upper-deck four-abreast seating with an offset sunken gangway which protruded into the lower saloon.

Once seated, they travelled in comfort on deeply-upholstered seats – honeycomb-pattern moquette downstairs and brown hide upstairs. When the conductor tugged the bell the driver let in the clutch, and with a tremulous wail and a crackle of blue petrol fumes the bus began its sedate but dogged journey.

Like all its contemporaries it was hand-cranked by means of a starting handle – an operation which required dexterity, as an engine backfire, as fierce as a mule's kick, could and did break the arm of an unwary driver. A backfire of a different kind ignited the carburetter of a Titan on 16th March 1931 in Upper Piccadilly.

Working laboriously through the heavy crash gearbox the driver built up speed; in top gear the bus purred along happily until the thwack of the bell-strap on the ceiling heralded the next stop.

Bristol No. 344, newly returned from Fagley, receives mechanical attention while Titan No. 361, its six companions and their drivers prepare for another day's work. The Lion on the right has been in service on the Bankfoot via Ripleyville route. The tramtrack and trolleybus wires are a reminder that this section of Thornbury Depot was only on loan to the buses.   [BCT

Possibly the new Titan made its debut on the new Greengates (via King's Road and Idle) service which had opened on 27th April as a temporary expedient pending trolleybus replacement of the Idle tramcars. As soon as it had been joined by its fellows, 354-360 (Nos. 361/2 followed later) they triumphantly inaugurated the Greengates (via Undercliffe) service on 12th November 1928 in place of the Greengates trams.

Enthusiasm for the new steeds waned somewhat when passengers realised that, like the Fagley buses but unlike the old Greengates trams, the Titans could not tackle titanic Church Bank and had to circumnavigate East Parade. Even worse, the fare had risen from 2d to 3d because the economic life of a bus was distinctly shorter than that of a tram; a petition of 928 names soon arrived at the Town Hall, and Councillor Amy Sykes protested that if buses could not be run at tram fares they ought not to be forced on Greengates folk. The fares and the buses remained.

Five further Titans (363-7) joined the fleet and, like 353-362 gave great satisfaction; with their smoothly-running six-cylinder 6.8-litre overhead-camshaft engines they were the finest buses on the King's Highway. A steady stream of Leyland products continued to arrive at Thornbury

depot until the summer of 1929. Numbers 368-373 were the final intake of Long Lions and Nos. 374-379, 381-385 the final Titan TD1s, differing from the earlier Titans in having Vickers bodies instead of the identical Leyland product. Number 380 was a novelty – a 'normal control' 26-seater equipped for one-man-operation on the Tong service; a handsome Roe-bodied vehicle. Last to arrive were five Super Lions (386-390) with forward-entrance 35-seat bodies; the most comfortable – almost luxurious – buses purchased so far, they were frequently in demand for the growing private-hire business.

Additional accommodation was urgently needed, as Thornbury depot had become overcrowded. In April 1928 the Tramways Committee opened negotiations with the Gas Committee for the acquisition of a disused gasworks site at Ludlam Street near the city centre, and a tender worth £14,293-17-6d was accepted. The headquarters changed too: in September 1928 the BCT offices were moved from Hall Ings to No. 11 Forster Square, where the administration, canteen and cafe were sited. For the convenience of crews working services based on the Town Hall area, an additional crew canteen was established at Mildred Court (Leeds Road bottom).

Adjacent to Mildred Court was the City terminus of the Leeds Road tramcar services to Thornbury and Stanningley. From 1907 it had also been the departure-point of the unique dual-gauge tram service to Leeds which had been withdrawn in March 1918 because of wartime difficulties, and short-sightedly had never been replaced, with the result that passengers to and from Leeds had to change trams at Stanningley. Rightly suspecting that West Yorkshire Road Car might seek to exploit the situation BCT instituted motorbus trials and without waiting to receive licences from Leeds and Pudsey Corporations began a service from Bradford (Leeds Road bottom) to Leeds (King Street) on 6th December 1928.

As the Leeds service was intended for longer-distance passengers only, the slow, unloved Bristols were used. There was no danger that they might take passengers from the tramcars; indeed, the bus drivers noticed that they were regularly overtaken by the Leeds Corporation trams which Bradfordians usually regarded as even slower than their own ! The Leeds Tramways Committee welcomed the new

facility although they were not yet in a position to participate, but the Leeds Licensing Committee felt obliged to protest against Bradford's action until the formalities were settled on 6th February 1929. Until 1st January 1930, when Leeds buses joined in, LCT paid half the expenses and received half the receipts.

A trial service to the isolated Tyersal area began on 6th December 1928, from a City terminus in Forster Square which it shared with the Cutler Heights buses. Vehicles served the two routes alternately, and low railway bridges in Hammerton Street normally restricted the services to single-deckers. The Haworth Road service (which worked via both Smith Lane and Toller Lane) was extended (by

Above: First of the fine 'Super Lions', No. 386 is seen when new at Thornbury.
[Photo: BCT

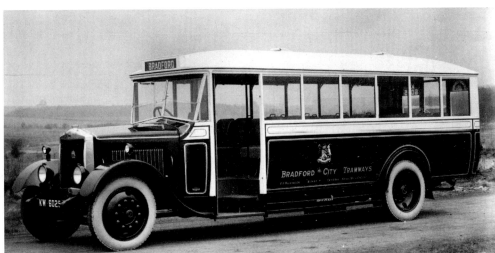

The Tong Village 'one-manner', No. 380, was the only Leyland Lioness owned by BCT   [Photo: C. H. Roe

way of Bay of Biscay !) to the village of Sandy Lane on 18th February 1929; the Huddersfield/Brighouse joint venture (as recorded elsewhere) followed on 31st March, while between 29th May and 18th September 1929, an experimental express service to Thornton (Ashfield Road) was provided at a twenty-minute frequency in an effort to combat West Yorkshire competition with the trams.

These were the last motorbus services to be instituted during the managership of Mr Wilkinson, who despite his own convictions had been compelled during the course of three tumultuous years to acquire a fleet of no less than ninety petrol vehicles. His belief in trolleybuses continued undiminished however; a Bill to enable them to replace tramcars on all routes including the abandoned Greengates section was being piloted through Parliament and, with a few deletions, became law in 1930.

His chairman, Councillor Irvine Smith, observed that although all three forms of urban transport had their merits, statistics did not favour buses. BCT experience showed that the average mileage between intermediate 'dock' overhauls was: motorbuses 910, tramcars 2,100 and the best of the newer trolleybuses 3,700. Also Chesterfield had informed him that when their trams had been superseded by buses pending the installation of trolleybuses, the buses were 'done for' within two years. In Bradford the buses were travelling 50,000 miles a year at a petrol consumption of six miles per gallon, and the Corporation Electricity Department would lose £83,988 per annum if trams and trolleybuses were abolished. The petrol fumes were so objectionable that Bierley Hall Sanatorium had requested alterations to the Bierley terminus.

Meanwhile the proposed joint service to Keighley was still in abeyance, and it was obvious that West Yorkshire

were 'dragging their feet'. In February 1929 they enquired whether Keighley Corporation might wish to sell their transport undertaking, but their intended prey reminded them that an agreement existed and that they (KCT) had already purchased a supply of bus tickets, not to mention buses !

Having received no satisfaction, Keighley initiated further discussions with Bradford and the company, but the talks faltered, and Bradford's application for the renewal of the six bus licences was deferred by Keighley. Bradford therefore resolved on 17th April to request their Keighley colleagues to arrange a meeting of all the interested parties. Three days later KCT accepted an offer of compensation from the company for revenue lost through the delay, insisting nevertheless that they still wanted the joint service.

But the company were tightening their stranglehold. In May they extended their Bradford-Denholme service into Keighley. Then, as anticipated a few months earlier, they applied for a Bradford-Leeds licence. Having forestalled their competitor – but only just – Bradford and Leeds Corporations were able to refuse the licence and were duly upheld by the Ministry.

The refusal enabled the company to play their trump card. 'If we cannot run to Leeds,' they declared, 'Bradford

Bradford in May 1929. A BCT inspector gives directions to the driver of Lion No. 331 which is probably on the shortlived Thornton express service, while trolleybus No. 544 – also on a Leyland chassis – has just returned from Clayton. With its trolley on the overhead reversing triangle tramcar 93 prepares to cross over to the Lidget Green queue barrier; although a few years older than its rivals it outlasted them by many years. The Town Hall (left) and Unitarian Chapel (centre) dominate Town Hall Square, but the New Inn (right) is – despite its name – the oldest building in the area.   [Photo: G. Crowther

cannot run to Keighley'. And with that they finally withdrew from the negotiations in July 1929, munificently awarding Keighley a yearly subsidy of £2,500 for lost revenue. The joint BCT/KCT tickets ceased, only 74 having been sold since 1st April. So, after a quarter of a century, hopes of a joint municipal service were extinguished.

Hostilities between the company and BCT continued nevertheless, and in February 1930 Bradford briefly contemplated supplementing the Baildon Bridge trams with buses in view of the damaging losses.

Meanwhile the railway companies, armed with new bus operating powers obtained in the teeth of almost universal opposition, had approached Corporations and companies alike with schemes of acquisition and co-ordination coupled with threats of dire competition. Agreement was quickly reached with Hebble, West Yorkshire and Yorkshire Woollen; Halifax, Huddersfield, Todmorden and Sheffield Corporations felt it prudent to reach an understanding in the form of a Joint Omnibus Committee (JOC), and Keighley were bullied into surrendering their rights to a new joint company, Keighley-West Yorkshire Services Ltd. Bradford representatives met LMS and LNER delegates in October 1929 but felt secure enough to spurn their advances, as did Leeds after a few weeks flirtation.

Having metaphorically 'skated on thin ice' throughout the year, Bradford's buses encountered the real thing on 29th December when overnight frost transformed King's Road into a 'Cresta Run' and compelled cars, lorries and

buses to perform artistic gyrations. The first city-bound bus from Greengates (via Idle) skated to and fro before felling two gas-lamps and uprooting a tree; less ambitiously the next contented itself with a single lamp-post while the third tobogganed 300 yards before unerringly obliterating a fourth lamp.

A curious contretemps arose on 17th February 1930, when Bradford's Licensing Committee rejected 'certain single-deck buses of the Leeds Corporation Tramways and Railways Joint Omnibus Committee on the Bradford to Leeds service, as they exceeded the Council's regulations as to maximum length.' Promptly the Leeds Watch Committee returned the compliment by refusing to license a BCT 30ft-long bus (their limit being 26ft) and a bus with an enclosed staircase whose rear upper window did not open for emergency purposes. No details of these vehicles are known, but it may be supposed that the single-deckers were experimental six-wheelers and the double-decker a hired Leyland TD1 with enclosed staircase.

Overtures arrived in May 1930 from the relatively friendly Yorkshire Woollen company who renewed earlier proposals for joint services on an equal basis from Dewsbury to Bradford via Oakenshaw/Cleckheaton and Birkenshaw/Batley. The Corporation consented to the arrangement and agreed to pay £2,000 under the terms of the 1928 agreement, but no joint workings materialised for several years.

The Tramways Department combined accounts for the year 1929/1930, published in July, revealed an appalling £30,000 loss which for many City Council members – especially those who opposed the manager and his policies – was the last straw. Wilfully ignoring the financial consequences of the Strike and the ensuing competition, they concentrated their criticisms on the shortcomings of an experimental high-speed tramcar, the costly Brighouse

On a return journey from Huddersfield No. 379 passes beneath the railway bridge which formed the City boundary at Lower Wyke. The tram tracks and wires belong to the Bailiff Bridge trams which were reduced to a part-day service about a year later.　　　　　[Photo: G. Crowther

Lion No. 335, now wearing a more serviceable livery, limps home to Thornbury works after a minor scrape at Sandy Lane.

[Photo: BCT]

venture and certain trolleybus teething troubles for which the manufacturers had admitted full responsibility. Harsh words were spoken in Council, and in September the manager, shipwrecked in a sea of troubles, resigned on health grounds.

In an address to the Institute of Transport earlier in the year he had patiently outlined the 'advantages and limitations of Tramcars, Trolleybuses and Motor Omnibuses' in a way which summarised his overall policy thus –

(1) Tramcars: high capacity, safety, comfort, usefulness in fog, safety in snow, spacious platforms, use of local electricity, easily reversible, but – high cost of permanent way, loading in carriageway, breakdowns delay other trams, noise, need for overhead wires.

(2) Motorbuses: speed and flexibility, but – slow acceleration, gear-changes, foreign petrol, noise, fumes, short life, high depreciation, high operating cost, too many complex parts, fire risk.

(3) Trolleybuses: nearly all the advantages of trams plus relative flexibility, higher speed, silence, home-built, uses home-produced power, increased receipts and low all-in cost, but – lacks the speed of a motorbus on the open road, dependent on electrical supply, needs overhead wires, cannot overtake.

His valedictory message to the industry in October was that within ten years trams would be almost extinct, and that although from an operational viewpoint petrol buses were theoretically ideal and diesel oil engines might be worth investigating, the cheapest form of transport was undoubtedly the trolleybus.

On his departure his predecessor, Mr C. J. Spencer (1898-1918) was invited to investigate the running of the Department. His report criticised overmanning, high maintenance costs, the practice of subsidising concessionary fares for scholars and blind people from other fares instead of the rates, the mushroom growth of the motorbus section and the unreliability of the buses which he attributed to the lack of an experienced automobile engineer.

The effect of the report was dramatic. The workforce, especially at Thornbury works, was reduced by 100; wages were reduced, little-used vehicles scrapped or sold and painting techniques simplified. Significantly the pro-trolleybus policy was endorsed although diesel engine possibilities were considered worth studying. Nevertheless the motorbus network remained intact and the Greengates (via Undercliffe) service was augmented by additional workings into the new Ravenscliffe Avenue estate.

Emphasising that Bradford ratepayers ought to use the facilities which they owned, the Chairman warned,

"If people will insist on ignoring a public service and using a competing service, only one result will follow."

6 THINGS to COME

When the Road Traffic Act 1930 took effect on New Year's Day 1931, local bus licensing powers were swept away and vested in regional bodies of Traffic Commissioners. The Yorkshire Area Traffic Commissioners based in Leeds included among their number Mr Joseph Farndale, formerly Bradford's Chief Constable and champion of his city throughout the West Riding bus battle six years previously. Bradford Corporation's nominee was Councillor John Shee, a former tramways employee.

Designed to regulate motorbus operation and prohibit irregular and unlicensed running, the Act largely fossilised the status quo. Private companies kept their recent gains; municipal shackles remained except that the cumbersome obligation to seek Parliamentary powers was replaced by a system of Applications for Consent duly followed (if successful) by applications for licences. Co-ordination was favoured and too-obvious competition frowned upon; fares, frequencies, service duplications and routes were closely scrutinised and only sanctioned if the Commissioners considered that a need had been proved.

Reactions to the legislation varied widely. Whereas West Riding, Yorkshire Woollen and Hebble usually operated in a law-abiding way, West Yorkshire buses sped, raced and swooped like predatory hawks on passengers waiting at bus stops. Prevented from undertaking private hire with the same freedom as a company or a railway nominee, Bradford Corporation had to conduct its out-of-boundary work by the expedient of nominally hiring buses to Messrs W. C. Forder of Bingley.

The Corporation's first application to the Commissioners related to the replacement of the Idle trams by Greengates (via Idle) trolleybuses and the consequent curtailment of the Greengates (via King's Road and Idle) motorbuses to Five Lane Ends (21st March 1931) and subsequently Swain House Road on 13th April.

In pursuance of further economies the Committee resolved that the unduly lavish and loss-making Tong service should cease forthwith, and that in order to counter West Yorkshire competition on Canal Road the outdated Bolton Woods and Frizinghall trolleybuses should be experimentally replaced by single-deck motorbuses for three months. The last Tong bus ran on 27th September 1931 and the Canal Road services were bus-operated from 25th September to 8th December, achieving an unexpected bonus: West Yorkshire offered to withdraw its Bradford-Clayton buses if BCT would withdraw from Canal Road. Agreement was quickly reached: the Canal Road trolleybuses ceased on 30th April 1932, and the Clayton trolleybuses bade farewell to their competitors.

The only other journeys entirely within the City on which BCT and West Yorkshire competed were on the Lister Park-Bankfoot route. An unusual form of co-ordination was achieved in May 1932: BCT provided three service buses and three duplicates and West Yorkshire two of each for a four-week period, when the ratio was reversed. At first BCT used Long Lions but later Titans, performing nineteen journeys each per day.

The newest Lions (368-373) and the Super Lions (386-390) were usually seen on the Brighouse, Duckworth Lane-Little Horton, Fagley and Wrose routes, the Baby Lions and the oldest Long Lions preferring the quieter Cutler Heights, Tyersal and Bankfoot-Horton Bank Top runs. The wearisome Bristols dragged themselves wherever

'Wearisome' Bristol No. 346 waits thirstily outside the petrol store in the approach road to Thornbury works.   [Photo:BCT

their reluctant drivers could be persuaded to take them, while the mighty Titans presided over the longer journeys – Huddersfield, Leeds and most journeys on the Greengates (via Undercliffe) route.

Titans also provided intensive works services in some parts of the city when the Bradford Exchange – Laisterdyke – Eccleshill – Idle – Windhill railway passenger service ceased in March 1931.

Meanwhile Mr Charles Richard Tattam had been appointed General Manager, and a new era of broader expertise was opening up. With him came the inventive and versatile H. J. Troughton as Rolling Stock Engineer and Norman A. Scurrah, upgraded from Works Superintendent to Car Works Superintendent. Mr T. Stirk, who had been an employee of the Tramways Department since its inception and had progressively risen from tram conductor to Traffic Superintendent (and Acting General Manager when Mr Wilkinson departed) retired a few months later and was succeeded by his deputy, Mr Frank Evans.

The most visible symbol of the new regime and the new decade – the dynamic, fast moving 'thirties – was the drastically simplified fleet livery. Following the reduction of staff at Thornbury works the traditional, handsome craftsmanship of gilding, shading, multi-coloured lining-out and the use of slow-drying oil-based paints had given way to a plainer scheme retaining the standard fleet colours of Prussian blue and ivory. On receiving their first repaint the motorbuses displayed plain gold lining-out, black mudguards and beading, gold-leaf Gill Sans numerals and dark grey roofs – the last-mentioned colour being an overdue acknowledgment that the optimistic ivory roofs of the Titans and the reversed livery of the Lions had never been appropriate for the grimy, smoke-laden atmosphere of workaday Bradford.

On 21st April 1931, the new Ludlam Street motorbus depot was partially opened, becoming fully operational four days later, when the leased accommodation at Phoenix Works and the shared premises at Thornbury depot were vacated. A functional brick and concrete edifice, it featured a sloping floor which in the days of hand-cranked petrol engines assisted drivers to start their buses in greater safety. The special technique of persuading a petrol engine to fire was explained in the Department's instructions:–

'Turn on petrol and close air strangler.

Turn engine over two or three times with switch off.

Retard ignition about halfway and switch on.

Pull sharply on starting handle – if all is in order the engine should start'.

The instruction manual added, slyly, that no instructions were needed for starting a trolleybus !

Reminiscing half a century later the original bus drivers commented,

"It was a good job, but there was lots of discipline in those days, just like in the army."

"We had to look smart, and if we were ever late for work we were sent home !"

"Everyone was friendly, and we never had any strikes."

It was the generally-held view that anyone who had a job with a uniform and superannuation was a lucky man indeed.

The motorbus fleet, already reduced to eighty by the withdrawal of ten 'Camels' and Lions, was kept hard at work, as the 1931 timetable appeared to require 69 buses for scheduled services and an unspecified number for works duties. No further vehicles were on order, however; construction of new tramcars had quietly ceased and the trolleybus fleet was static. The Department needed time to recover from its upheavals.

Anxious to prune unprofitable routes, Mr Tattam proposed in December 1931, that when Bradford's lease of the Bingley tramway expired on 17th May 1932, the outermost section from Bingley to Crossflatts should be replaced by express buses at a 5d minimum fare. As the day neared the press expressed doubts whether 'the change would meet with general agreement.' It did not. At the Traffic Commissioners' hearing the LMS, West Yorkshire, its new ally Keighley Corporation, and the Shipley and Bingley councils were ranged against Bradford. With smug effrontery West Yorkshire complained of Bradford's 'insidious attempt to get buses on the road in competition with ours !' Stung, Bradford asked the Commissioners to refuse West Yorkshire licences for all their services into the City. The case was dismissed however, and the Bingley and Crossflatts trams continued to run until superseded by trolleybuses seven years later.

Thus the only new services in 1932 were extensions of existing services – Swain House Road to Wrose on 7th September and Greengates (via Undercliffe) to Apperley Bridge on 14th March.

Investigations into diesel fuel possibilities bore fruit in July 1932, when the Committee authorised the manager to hire two compression-ignition oil-engine buses for trials, Leyland and AEC being the chosen suppliers.

First to arrive was the AEC, MV 3749, a Regent with an 8.8 litre 49 hp engine and a Weymann 50-seat highbridge body of composite construction. Resembling contemporary purchases by Mansfield and District with its high-domed roof and shallow lower-deck side panels, it was seemingly taller than the later Regents; on sharp corners its tilt was so pronounced that its side guard rail regularly rattled on the granite paving, and its cab bore a stern warning that drivers must not attempt to pass beneath Hammerton Street Bridge. Spacious and roomy with its full-height central-gangway upper deck, it heralded a new standard of motor bus design and passenger comfort when it entered service on 29th October 1932.

In comparison the Leyland TD2 which arrived in December offered little improvement on the previous Titans except for its 46.8 hp 8.6 litre Leyland oil engine and enclosed staircase. The lowbridge composite body was almost as cramped as its predecessors and seated fewer. Registered TF 9821, it began work on 3rd December.

Infinitely more inspiring and futuristic was an AEC 'Q' bus demonstrated to the Committee in October or November 1932, which resulted in a decision on 19th December to order a 'Q' for £1,800. Some members were critical of the revolutionary design which featured an

Displaying the name of the secretary of AEC Ltd as well as that of Mr Tattam, Regent No. 392 was the first oil-engined bus in the Bradford fleet and the fore-runner of a whole generation of AEC Regent products.
[Courtesy M. Hampson

Leyland No. 391 was the only TD2 model bought by Bradford, and no more Leylands were acquired for eighteen years.
[Courtesy G. Welburn; photo Leyland Motors

entrance ahead of the front wheels, a side-mounted 45 hp petrol engine with electric starter, and single rear tyres. Councillor Russell Rose (of Central Garage, Bradford) considered it "Huge, unwieldly and top-heavy"; the strain on its brakes would be 'stupendous', he claimed, and its fluid flywheel 'had not been commercially proved". Alderman Anthony Gadie – not a supporter of the Department – dismissed the 'Q' as a 'Juggernaut' and recalled an earlier 'special vehicle' (the bogie single-deck tramcar of 1926/7) which had been built at 'tremendous cost' without fulfilling its expectations.

Pointing out however that the overall dimensions of the 'Q' were perfectly normal, Councillor George Carter prophesied that, "In a few years this will be the only type of double-deck petrol 'bus in use on account of lower running costs, greater capacity and better platform supervision."

The purchase was approved and the demonstrator (presumably the first of the 'Q's, AHX 63) returned to AEC. Bradford's own purchase – 'Queenie' – sleek, streamlined, spectacular and sparkling in the smart Corporation livery and with a luxurious interior made her debut as No. 393 on 31st August 1933, the TD2 and the Regent having been taken into stock as Nos. 391/2 respectively. An even more handsome 'Q' trolleybus followed shortly afterwards.

Councillor Carter's prophecy was accurate but premature; no more front-entrance double-deckers were ordered for 34 years, and they were diesel-powered.

A new feature introduced with the Regent, No. 392, was the provision of route numbers, which although displayed on the tramcars since 1919, had never been applied to the buses or trolleybuses. The existing bus routes were therefore numbered in a roughly alphabetical form:–

60	Bierley	69	Haworth Road
61	Bankfoot (via Ripleyville)	70	Sandy Lane
62	Bankfoot-Horton Bank Top	71	Leeds
63	Brighouse	72	Lister Park-Bankfoot
64	Huddersfield	73	Little Horton-Duckworth Lane
65	Cutler Heights and Tyersal	74	Tong
66	Fagley	75	Swain House Road
67	Greengates (via Undercliffe)	76	Wrose
68	Ravenscliffe Avenue		

The relative unimportance of route numbers was demonstrated when Leeds Corporation buses displayed '72' on the joint Leeds service and Huddersfield Corporation and Hebble Motors showed '38' and '12' respectively on the Bradford-Huddersfield workings. All were co-ordinated eventually.

The tremendous snowfall of late February 1933 brought the city to a halt for several days and induced the Department to buy thirty sets of chains for bus tyres. A Gardner oil engine was hired in June from W. H. Goddard of Leeds and

fitted to Titan 355 before being bought for £300.

The acquisition of Nos. 391-3 permitted a modest expansion: the Drighlington tramway closed on 8th August 1933 and sufficient buses were mustered as replacements, though at a higher fare to protect the trams which continued to run to Tong Cemetery. The new service (77) was very popular, as the long-suffering trams on their worn-out tracks had provided a rough ride. Initially the buses turned at Drighlington crossroads but from November reversed into a gateway leased from Drighlington Cooperative Society for £10 per annum. The Tong bus service re-started on the same day, but the 'one-manner', 380, did not return, having been disposed of to the Tramways Parcels Department.

Only one new bus entered service in 1934, but it was a very fine specimen. The first Daimler in the fleet, it incorporated a 36.5 hp Gardner 5LW engine and a 56-seat all-metal Weymann body not dissimilar to that of No. 392 but slightly more rounded and less angular, with five bays, deeper side panels and a flatter roof dome, thereby reducing the overall height. Its destination display set a new standard for future deliveries with a route name at front and rear and a route number above the front destination. For the first time tubular framed seats were fitted, with fawn moquette upholstery; the rear platform was almost level with the pavement edge, and the entire vehicle, No. 394, was comfortable, quiet, unobtrusive and wholly civilised.

The tramway replacement programme was now gathering speed. Although trolleybuses were to predominate, motorbuses were to be used wherever routes were lightly-loaded or excessively tortuous. In April 1934 plans were prepared for a City to Little Horton (via Heaton)

Right: Number 394, seen here in Rooley Lane in 1933, was the first of many fine Daimlers operated in Bradford.

[Photo: BCT

Below: Tramcar 128 has just entered Forster Square from Church Bank and will shortly depart for Heaton. New AEC Regent No. 396 waits at the Haworth Road loading point in this February 1935 view, and is one of the 25 buses bought to replace the Heaton, Undercliffe, Shelf and Birkenshaw trams.

[Courtesy M. Hampson; photo AEC

bus service superseding not only the Heaton trams but also the Duckworth Lane-Little Horton buses. The Bankfoot via Ripleyville service, curtailed since January 1932 because of poor patronage was reinstated as part of a Horton Bank Top via Ripleyville service with most journeys beginning at Bankfoot; it was extended to Cooper Lane on 23rd August.

In October the condition of the Shelf permanent way was declared to be so bad that the passengers were deserting to Hebble, and simultaneously new negotiations were opened with Yorkshire Woollen for the previously-agreed joint Bradford-Dewsbury bus service. Then in January 1935 licences were sought for the replacement of the Undercliffe tramcars by a part-day bus service, the original aim of constructing a Greengates (via Undercliffe) trolleybus route having been abandoned.

For these proposed services twenty-five new buses were sought. An AEC tender for compression-ignition (diesel oil) buses with Weymann bodies was accepted subject to a patriotic proviso by the City Council that five of the chassis should receive English Electric bodies as the English Electric traction works in Bradford were a major employer; the bodies themselves were to be built at Preston.

The rapidly-expanding network also needed a new design of bus-stop sign, easily affixed and clearly visible. The original signs, adaptations of the 1904 tram-stop design, were quaint and cumbersome. About 1929 a more adaptable flat plaque in dark blue enamel proclaiming in white letters the legend, 'BCT Buses Stop Here on Request' had been introduced, but in 1934 a plain orange /gamboge plaque bearing the simple text, 'Bus Stop (BCT)' was devised for use by motorbuses and trolleybuses alike. Following Ministry objections the orange was superseded by white (motorbuses only) in 1936, displaying the new initials 'BCPT ' – Bradford Corporation Passenger Transport, the new name of the former Tramways Department.

The plans laid in 1934 were fulfilled a year later when no fewer than four tramways were converted to motorbus operation. Shelf buses (Nelson Street-Bottomley's Arms, 82) commenced on 20th February 1935, and Heaton (79), Little Horton via Heaton (80) and Undercliffe (81) began simultaneously on 8th April. Undercliffe was a part-time facility only (Forster Square GPO to Northcote Road via Harris Street and East Parade); passengers used the Greengates buses at other times and the latter now ran through to Haworth Road and Sandy Lane as a useful cross-city service.

Heaton (79) was a full-time short-working of Little Horton (80) which also superseded the old Duckworth Lane-Little Horton (73) workings. After 6.22pm (Sundays excepted) the city terminus was outside the Alhambra Theatre, as Heatonians were thought to be assiduous theatre-goers. City-bound buses ran via Forster Square, Well Street, Vicar Lane, Croft Street and lower Manchester Road, while the outward journey was via Godwin Street, John Street and North Parade. Unfortunately the intended beneficiaries disliked both the new arrangements and the increased fare (2°d), and in May the city terminus reverted to Forster Square with a saving of one bus. At Heaton terminus (Leylands Lane bottom) the steep camber of the road caused the buses to tilt alarmingly when they turned, and a new terminus was arranged at Leylands Lane (Garden Lane).

When the Birkenshaw trams ceased on 29th October 1935, they were replaced next day by a joint BCT/Yorkshire Woollen bus service from Bradford (Nelson Street) to Dewsbury. Extras to Birkenshaw were provided solely by BCT, but the fare to that point was raised to 4d. An indication of the scale of passenger losses from the trams to the company buses was provided by the new allocations – six Woollen District buses to one BCT – although Woollen District's Bradford-East Bierley-Hunsworth-Cleckheaton and Bradford-Birstall services were also theoretically joint. A protective fare was imposed as far as Tong Cemetery, and BCT buses displayed no route number until 1938 when (in conformity with YWD) they showed the newly-vacant number 4.

For these new facilities the AEC Regents ordered in 1934 had been delivered. Numbers 395-7 and 399/400 launched the Shelf service while of the remainder all but 419 were available for the April conversions. Like No. 392 they were powered by sturdy AEC 8.8 litre 6-cylinder 'Heavy Six' oil engines and bore 51-seat Weymann (395-414) or English Electric (415-9) all-metal bodies. Smart, serviceable and extremely reliable, they also replaced the

Seen here towards the end of its days, AEC No 419 displays the angular, upright lines of its 1935 English Electric body as it stands at the Drighlington loading-point at the rear of Bradford Town Hall. The large queue is probably waiting for the Bierley bus.
[Courtesy A. A. Townsin; photo R. A. Mills

Below: AEC's photographer took this view of Regent No. 395 outside the Barrack Tavern but he was unlikely to have had the opportunity to sample Bentley's Yorkshire Beer which was available inside. The Weymann bodywork is more neatly finished than the contemporary English Electric example seen above.
[Photo BCPT/WYPTE/WYAS

Bradford in 1935. Specially posed for a new timetable frontispiece tramcar 193 is flanked by new AEC Regent No. 401 and even newer AEC/EE trolleybus No. 624. [Photo: BCT

last of the original AEC 'Camels' as well as three Bristols. For a week or two they were allotted exclusively to the new routes but were subsequently interspersed with Titans and single-deckers which were older than some of the displaced trams.

Fortunately better things were in store. Impressed by the quiet, silk-smooth behaviour of Daimler 394 but finding its 5-cylinder engine slightly underpowered, BCT ordered a 6-cylinder version for £1,822 which arrived as No. 420 in December. By this time the Department was profitable again, and Mr Tattam aimed to keep it so; with an eye to weight reduction and fuel economy he limited the seating of the new bus to 52.

Agreement was reached in September 1935 that if BCT would abandon its operating rights on the Baildon Bridge tramway (long since overwhelmed by company buses) West Yorkshire would relinquish its share of the Lister Park-Bankfoot service. This was a hard bargain, as Bradford would no longer have a direct service to Shipley town centre; unfortunately negotiations for a joint bus service to Baildon fell through and the trams performed their last journeys on 4th February 1936.

Oil engines having thoroughly proved themselves to be much more economical and reliable than petrol machines – and much safer too, as the compression-ignition starter mechanism rendered obsolete the hazards of hand-cranking – nineteen 1800 rpm Gardner 6LW engines were ordered for Titans whose petrol engines were reaching the end of

their lives. At £532 per bus the solid, indestructible Gardner units were not cheap, but the resulting economies and improved performance soon outweighed the outlay – though the drivers, continually shaken by the heavy throb and vibration, looked forward longingly to the end of each shift.

The beneficiaries of the conversion were Titans 355, 358-360/2-5, 374-9 and 381-5, which thenceforth were able to bound up many steep gradients in confident top gear. Number 353 received an AEC 7.7 litre unit in 1937 for a mere £250 but proved a sluggish performer. This left Titans 354/6/7, 361/6/7) the single-deckers and 'Queenie' (393) as the only petrol-driven buses.

With the influx of modern double-deckers the low-capacity single-deckers were dwindling fast; the petrol-powered Titans as well as No. 353 were now confined to works services, and even 'Queenie' had fallen from grace, her unusual weight distribution and single rear tyres having proved a hindrance in icy weather; moreover, her side-mounted engine tended to overheat and her open front-entrance was considered dangerous for passengers who might leap aboard while the bus was moving.

Danger of a different kind was posed by newly-installed Belisha beacon crossings which enterprising Bradfordians insisted on using as unofficial bus stops.

It might have been supposed that the bus fleet, in no way route-bound and operating from a single depot, would have been completely interchangeable apart from the limitations imposed by Hammerton Street bridge. Certain buses, however, appeared to envy the ordered existence of the trams which, housed at five scattered depots, were content to plough a predestined furrow. The prototype AEC 392 served the Lister Park route so constantly that its unique rear number blind could not be persuaded to display

any number other than 72, and the original Daimler, 394, although more amenable, particularly enjoyed a rural run to Tong. Daimler 420 and its later cousin 449 conceived such an attachment to Haworth Road that their appearance on another route was a 'nine-day wonder'.

No further expansion of the motorbus empire was contemplated for several years, and the accent was therefore on replacement of single-deckers by modern double-deckers. Tenders were invited in November 1935, materialising in the following year as ten AEC 7.7 litre 'Small Sixes' – Nos. 421-5 with Weymann and 426-430 with English Electric bodies, Nos. 431-443 as Weymann-bodied Daimlers identical with No. 420 apart from seating capacity (54), and Nos. 444/5 as elegant AEC Regal/Weymann petrol-engined semi-coaches available for private hire, committee visits or public service. All shared two distinctive features – a large gold-leaf 'Bradford' fleetname on the side panels and 'envelope'-type rainshields designed to deflect rainwater from partly-open windows.

The Daimlers proved to be the most popular with their low-loading platforms, quiet, smooth motion and the pleasant, tenor warble of their Gardner engines; the AECs were prone to slight vibration, higher noise levels and a penetrating stench of fuel-oil.

The two handsome semi-coaches with their saloon heaters, moquette-faced lining panels, concealed lighting and folding entrance doors were

A wet day in Leeds. Advertising the merits of Fennings' Fever Cure, No. 430, one of the English Electric-bodied AEC 'Small Sixes', prepares to return to its home city.
[BCPT/WYPTE/WYAS

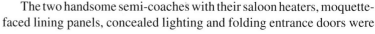
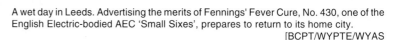

Above: Departure time – a raincoat-clad Bradfordian sprints to catch Daimler No. 432 as it prepares to leave Infirmary Street, Leeds, in September 1936.

[Photo: G. H. F. Atkins

Right: In this early postwar (1946) view of Market Street the Midland Bank is still advertising Defence Bonds while the new, but as yet unoccupied, building on the right looks forward to better, brighter days. AEC Regal semi-coach No. 445, already ten years old, still bears the pristine livery of its youth, unsullied by wartime camouflage.

[Photo: the late J. A. Pitts

eagerly sought after; when not in use they were housed at Thornbury and carefully sheeted over. At the same time one of the comfortable 'Super Lions', No. 387, was overhauled, repainted and re-upholstered for occasional use as a 'second reserve' coach.

A fire at the Corporation Electricity Works on 24th February 1936 plunged the city into darkness and halted all trams and trolleybuses except in Shipley and Bingley. Mr Tattam, a Shipley resident, was not aware of the breakdown until notified by telephone; hurrying to his office he was started to find his astute engineer, Mr Troughton, already at his desk and calmly making alternative arrangements, as a result of which, buses borrowed from Leeds, West Riding and Yorkshire Woollen provided a skeleton service until normal supplies were restored a day or two later. It was noticeable that West Yorkshire claimed to have no buses to spare, but one

wonders how many duplicates (or triplicates !) they provided on their own services into Bradford during the emergency !

The last of the Bristols, probably retained while the Titans were receiving Gardner engines, were discarded in September, 1936. Curiously, however, a West Yorkshire Bristol single-decker was borrowed for a few days and used on the Heaton (79) route.

The year 1936 proved to be a watershed in many ways. National unemployment stood at 2,225,000 and in the stagnant Bradford textile trade the workers sometimes 'played' (were laid off) or 'laiked' as often as they worked. But in March Nazi troops seized the demilitarised zone of the Rhineland while Herr Hitler was piously affirming that he had 'no further territorial ambitions in Europe'. Not surprisingly the most popular song of the year, regularly played in Bradford dance-halls such as Barracloughs' and Gledhills', was entitled, 'It's a Sin to tell a Lie !'

On a happier note the Coronation of King George VI and Queen Elizabeth in May 1937 was joyfully celebrated in Bradford. The Corporation distributed commemorative books, new pennies and toffee in patriotic wrappings to every schoolchild; flags flew, trees were planted and the old 'one-manner', No. 380, was reconstructed in the form of an illuminated crown to tour the city at night.

Being now in undisputed possession of the Clayton route the Corporation felt free to attend to the low railway bridge at Pasture Lane which had hitherto prevented the use of double-deck trolleybuses. From 16th April 1937, to mid-November, trolleybus duties beyond Pasture Lane (Scholemoor Avenue) were performed by motorbuses operating via Bradford Road, with a protective fare to deter short-distance riders. The drivers were spare men or tram and trolleybus drivers holding bus driving licences and whose normal duties were covered by conductors holding tram and trolleybus licences.

Agreement was reached with Yorkshire Woollen in June for a joint shortworking to Birstall via Birkenshaw Bottoms (4).

Now happily restored to its normal profitable ways, the Transport Committee was looking forward to reducing its capital debt from 1944 onwards, thus prompting Councillor Flanagan to prophesy,

"We shall be using aeroplanes by then !"

('They' were indeed, but not for purposes of passenger transport.)

Awakened at last to the threat of Nazi domination, the nation was hastily re-arming, and in September 1938 the Chairman and Manager were instructed 'to take all necessary steps in relation to Air Raid Precaution services'. They took their duties seriously; the last of the Leyland single-deckers were quietly converted into grey-painted 'ARP' ambulances, stretcher carriers and mortuary vans and stored out of sight in the now redundant Bowling tramcar depot and the deepest recesses of Thornbury sheds.

The final slaughter of the single-deckers was made possible by a tender from Transport Vehicles (Daimler) Ltd for twenty double-deckers accepted in March 1938 at a cost of £41,960. As previously the Committee divided the body contracts between English Electric and Weymann, and Mr Tattam continued to look for weight reductions. (He saved 2cwt 1qr by reducing the capacity of the fuel tank from 40 to 35 gallons, using alloy gear cases instead of steel, fitting new types of shock absorbers and placing the batteries under the seats.) There were cost savings too: a seating reduction from 54 to 52 saved £5 per bus and a dozen minor adjustments a further £3-8s-6d, but Weymann had to pay back £5 per body when the floor sagged around the flywheel casing.

One or two new features were introduced into the specifications: Geecen speedometers incorporating a warning light operative at 29 mph, rubber mudguards, and experimental RP automatic lubrication on the last chassis of the delivery.

In these days of ever-brighter street-lighting it is worth recalling that in 1938 it was not customary to use headlamps except where no street lamps existed. For the twenty Daimlers separate switches for each headlamp were specified; the nearside lamp was permanently focussed on the kerb at 25ft, and the offside lamp could be switched off altogether in case of fog.

The Weymanns (456-465) arrived first, in September 1938. Attractive in an ultra-modern, smoothly-streamlined style, they differed from previous deliveries in having the route number box alongside the destination box instead of above it, and, experimentally, the destination and number blinds were illuminated by blue-tinted bulbs.

Number 455, the first of the English Electric-bodied buses, arrived in December 1938, followed a month later by Nos. 446-454. Striking, with their swept-back frontal appearance and one-piece upper rear window, they incorporated the conventional destination layout.

All twenty Daimlers boasted royal blue interior handrails and 'Pronto' bell-strips on the cantrails, as well as the usual Daimler low (13in) platform height. Lower saloon seats were upholstered in Listers' 'Wypdri' moquette with Listers' wool repp seat backs; upper deck seating was Connolly-hide upholstered, with ICI rexine for seat backs and side panels. The admiring public considered them to be the height of modernity, which they certainly were.

Apart from the indomitable but obsolescent Titans the fleet now comprised modern, handsome vehicles far superior to the company vehicles, and the latest purchases represented the best of contemporary taste – the passenger transport equivalent of the practical elegance of a Supermarine Spitfire, an Austin 8 motor car or a Blackpool railcoach.

During the previous year the fleet livery of Prussian blue and ivory had been undergoing subtle changes, firstly to blue-black and pale cream in July 1937 and secondly to a more pleasing blue-black akin to Belfast's 'Princess Blue', again with pale cream.

A fine example of late 1930s taste – the smoothly-streamlined English Electric body of Daimler No. 447 is complemented by its smart, serviceable livery. [BCPT/WYPTE WYAS

The new Daimlers were the first to display the latest hues, Mr Tattam having notified the manufacturers on 8th July that he was 'contemplating making a change in the shade of blue which has been our standard in the past'.

In addition to the ten bodies supplied for the Daimlers, Weymann had also built an identical body for an AEC Regent which, bearing the fleet number 466 and the Middlesex registration JML 409, was completed in October 1938, and placed in service on 10th November. It was hired to allow BCPT to evaluate a new and completely re-designed 8.8 litre direct-injection engine classified as type A182. In service the engine proved to be quieter than the earlier A165 engines fitted to 395-419 although not without a persistent buzzing vibration, but BCPT were sufficiently impressed to propose a return to AEC for future bus purchases. In the event, A182 engines proved to be shortlived but formed the basis of the 9.6 litre unit used in the later Regent III and RT types. Number 466 was ultimately bought by BCPT in April 1940.

The Leeds (71) route was extended on 7th December 1938, to the new Leeds Central Bus Station, and in the following May a Sunday morning bus service between the two cities was provided for the first time, as the withdrawal of the Leeds-Pudsey tram service had broken the long-standing passenger connection at Stanningley.

An entertaining disagreement arose early in 1939 when the Committee decided to institute a service to Moore Avenue (Poplar Grove) via Great Horton Road, Laisteridge Lane, Canterbury Avenue and St. Enoch's Road to supplement the Wibsey trams which travelled by way of Morley Street, Laisteridge Lane, Park Avenue and Little Horton Lane. The City Council decreed that the buses should serve St. Luke's Hospital in the lower part of Little Horton Lane, hitherto bypassed by BCPT services. Perversely the Committee insisted on routing the new service via Great Horton Road, but when the first bus left

Tyrrel Street on 22nd March it followed the tram route as far as Canterbury Avenue. Officially listed as 'Moore Avenue via Canterbury Avenue', the service took the number 61 from the old Bankfoot via Ripleyville workings which now shared the number 62 with the Bankfoot-Horton Bank Top service.

The same disagreements flared up again in June when the Committee decided to replace the Wibsey trams by eighteen motorbuses costing £39,000. The decision itself was surprising, as the Wibsey route, steep and requiring an intensive service, was ideal for trolleybuses, and some tentative preparations had in fact been made. Possibly the Department did not wish to operate trolleybuses in Morley Street and Easby Road while the Queensbury trams were still running, and no public comment arose.

However, Wibsey was destined to see neither motorbuses nor trolleybuses. The storm clouds which had been gathering over Europe finally burst on Friday, 1st September 1939, when German armies smashed their way into Poland. In Bradford plans which had been maturing for a year swung smoothly into action: before midday large numbers of schoolchildren had been conveyed to the railway stations by Corporation transport for evacuation to safer areas fifteen or twenty miles away, and a total blackout was imposed. War was declared on Sunday, 3rd September.

Hurriedly meeting on Monday the Transport Committee delegated to the Chairman and his deputy powers to "deal with matters of urgency during the continuance of the present national crisis".

Return of the exile – tramcars returned to Undercliffe terminus a few days after the outbreak of war in September 1939 when bus services were curtailed to conserve fuel. Ravenscliffe Avenue-bound Daimler No. 438 squeezes past tram 226 while AEC No. 428 pauses on its way to Haworth Road via Smith Lane.

[Courtesy J. H. Cheetham; photo F. Hartley

There were plenty. Petrol and oil supplies were immediately restricted, and the motorbus services suffered accordingly. On 10th September the Undercliffe (66, previously 81) and Tong (74) buses ceased altogether and the Undercliffe tramcars returned to work next day, but Tong residents had to walk. All the disused bus stop signs remained in place: how many hopeful passengers waited in vain for a bus which never came ? The Leeds (71) buses reverted to their old terminus in Infirmary Street, Leeds, with the saving of one vehicle.

Depot skylights had already been coated with black paint; bus headlamps, front destinations and interior lights were masked and route numbers and rear destinations unlighted. Bus platform edges, mudguards and pavement kerbs were whitened to assist pedestrians, and only in the main thoroughfares was a glimmer of street lighting permitted, in case of air attacks. Last buses now ran at about 9pm, and Sunday morning buses were few.

Tram and trolleybus services, not being dependent on imported fuel, continued unchanged, and (in the ponderous phrasing of the Department), 'The projected suspension of tram services was curtailed' – in other words, the trams were reprieved. With the virtual disappearance of private cars, the pressure on public transport became intense.

Weymann-bodied AEC Regent No. 402 climbs Heights Lane en route to Greengates in this wartime view. Note the liberal use of white paint on lamp-posts, pavements and walls, and disused gas street lamps in addition to the bus.   [Photo: G. Crowther

7 TOILS and TRIBULATIONS

Now working at full stretch the Transport Department strove to ensure that all its vehicles were still maintained to pre-war standards. Fears of mass air raids fortunately were not fulfilled, and although sirens sounded and bombs fell, the transport services were never disrupted, and the 'shadow' fleet of ambulances was little used.

From August 1940 to February 1943 anti-blast netting was glued to bus windows, but the only damage it sustained was at the hands of passengers anxious to check their whereabouts. No motorbus was damaged by enemy action.

The non-standard 'Q' bus, No. 393, ended its career with a spectacular calamity. On a late-night depot run from Drighlington its driver attempted a high-speed 'racing change' as the bus hurtled down Wakefield Road; off flew the cylinder heads and that was that.

Looking forward to the days when air raid sirens, searchlights and night alarms would be no more, the Department sampled the London Passenger Transport Board's new RT19 which was touring the country under the auspices of AEC. Painted emerald green and white and moquette-upholstered on both decks it was much sought after during its month's holiday in Bradford in September 1940.

Even more optimistically the Committee accepted an AEC tender, now inflated to £45,980, for the twenty (originally eighteen) buses sought a year earlier. The buses would have replaced trams on the Wibsey and Stanningley routes, but in fact it was to be six years before AEC were able to fulfil the contract.

Only three days after receipt of the abortive tender London Transport issued an urgent appeal for buses to replace vehicles damaged or destroyed in air raids. Eight BCPT Gardner-engined Leyland Titans were despatched immediately; on arrival they worked from the Plumstead depot with occasional visits to other garages. In December Nos. 358/9, 362/4 and 374/6/7 left London for Sheffield where a similar crisis had arisen, but 365 lingered in the capital until August 1941. On their return home they bore on their side panels a tiny, proud plaque emblazoned, 'London, 1940-1', kindly presented by the capital city in its darkest hour.

A present help in time of trouble: Gardner-engined Leyland Titan No. 365 with masked headlamps is seen on London Transport route 53 during its period of service in the capital. Sales of Wimsol at 6d. a bottle were unaffected by wartime shortages.

In addition twelve more buses were loaned to Sheffield and four to Hull, several bomb-damaged Hull Corporation buses being repaired by BCPT at Thornbury at the same time as Bradford school kitchens were cooking meals and despatching them to Hull where many families were unable to cook a meal.

When the worn condition of the Cleckheaton Road trolleybus overhead equipment was reported in July 1940, the cost and scarcity of new cadmium-copper wire outweighed the need to conserve fuel, and Oakenshaw (85) motorbuses replaced the obsolete single-deck trolleybuses on 1st August 1940.

Bus conductresses made their first appearance on the Haworth Road-Greengates service on 31st March 1941 replacing men who had been 'called up' for war service. Their popularity was such that many were soon known by name, and their brisk, businesslike efficiency earned them lasting respect.

Faced with a threat of German invasion following the Dunkirk evacuation the Government directed that all place-names and signs which might assist enemy intruders should be obliterated. Remote from threatened areas BCPT disregarded the order, and fleetnames and destination displays remained undisturbed. But when the Ministry of War Transport (MOWT) recommended that buses serving munitions and aircraft factories should be camouflaged to escape detection from the air, the Transport Department decided to paint the motorbus fleet in a flat khaki-grey. Accordingly EE-bodied Regent 418 was the last bus to emerge from Thornbury Works in dark blue and cream on 15th April 1942; EE-bodied Regent 428 appeared ten days later in the drab camouflage, only the gold-leaf fleet numerals and name remaining as reminders of more colourful days. One or two vehicles such as 375 and 452 escaped for a while by dint of a thorough re-varnishing, but within little over two years the cheerless process was complete. Only the two prized semi-coaches, 444/445, were allowed to retain their original elegance.

The munitions and aircraft factories in the Bradford area such as GEC in Sharpe's factory at Bingley Road and Avro at Yeadon were served by BCPT and West Yorkshire, the latter fleet being supplemented by vehicles borrowed from East Kent and York-West Yorkshire. The remaining BCPT petrol-engined Titans, 354/6, 357, 361, 366/367, were used exclusively on these duties, the high-pitched whine of their engines and leisurely acceleration providing a sedate contrast to the resolute roar of their Gardner-engined brothers.

Drastic bus service reductions were foreshadowed in May 1942 as vital fuel oil supplies dwindled, but the deteriorating state of the Stanningley tramway obliged the Ministry to sanction its early closure. Mr Tattam's long-standing hopes for forty new buses were brushed aside, and he was ordered to 'patch up' the Wibsey tram track for a few more years. For the Stanningley route BCPT were allowed to hire four buses from Leeds and six from London. Buses on the new service (90) which opened on 20th October 1942 followed the tram route and turned at Stanningley Bottom via Varley Street and Richardshaw Lane beneath a low railway arch which in blackout conditions accounted for many a crumpled roof dome.

The four Leeds buses, 40/41, 43, 46, all elderly Roe-bodied AECs, were used in general service, unlike the even more venerable LPTB ST Regents which were allotted to the Stanningley route where they received an unusually warm welcome.

'There is one feature of Bradford life which gladdens the hearts of the evacuees from London', commented the press, 'and that is a glimpse of one of the red buses which run between Bradford and Stanningley still bearing the name 'London Transport'. During the first few days of the arrival of the evacuees it was interesting to watch for the gasp of astonishment when they saw one of these 'buses. Indeed, some of the London youngsters wander down to Hall Ings to get a sight of one, just as some Bradfordians exiled in London often wander to King's Cross or St. Pancras to watch a Bradford train depart.'

Three of the buses boasted a large, square platform with an excellent straight staircase, but the three 'Tillings' had a much smaller platform with an open staircase, and all – to the disgust of the drivers –lacked cab doors. In addition ST 879 had evidently suffered blast damage, as every alternate window was boarded up. Their petrol engines having been considerably de-rated, they found the gentle ascent of Leeds Road a severe trial when well-laden and in the teeth of a contrary gale. Once – only once – ST 966 strayed on to the Little Horton via Heaton (80) route where the stiff gradient of Squire Lane defeated it utterly. The passengers dismounted and walked.

For Bradford schoolboys an even more pleasing event was the unexpected resurrection of Leyland Super Lion 388, withdrawn four years previously with all its fellows. The author was surprised to see it rounding Cheapside corner one November afternoon in 1942, in well-varnished pre-war livery and bound for Heaton. The half-hour wait for its return soon passed, and the ensuing journey, enlivened by the tremulous warble of the petrol engine, the slow gear-change and the slap of the bell-strap on the stripwood ceiling revived half-forgotten memories. Although the old bus did not remain in service long, it provided much pleasure during a dreary period of wartime life.

Restrictions multiplied. From 1st November 1942, last buses were at 9pm; Sunday morning services were rare, and stopping-places were reduced in number. The engineering staff were dismayed to receive Ministry orders for the conversion of 10% of the fleet – ie nine buses – to producer gas by July 1943. Successful trials were carried out with an AEC 'Small Six' which, towing an anthracite-burning trailer – a stove on two wheels – managed to operate at half the normal fuel oil consumption. Like the London STs, the producer-gas buses had to be limited to the fairly level Stanningley run, where, distinctly short of breath, they had to halt at least once per journey for the conductor to revive the glowing embers. Nevertheless the eight (not nine) buses actually equipped ran 208,405 miles using 133 tons of anthracite and saving 9,600 gallons of precious oil.

The Department was therefore relieved when the

The loan of six London transport buses enable Bradford to close the Stanningley tramway in 1942. LPTB Regent No. ST851 collects passengers in Hall Ings while Thornbury-bound tramcar 89 waits patiently at the end of the track.

[Photo: the late N. N. Forbes

Khaki-clad AEC 'Small Six' No. 421 turns its back on its anthracite-powered gas producer trailer when photographed in Gain Lane, Thornbury. [BCPT/WYPTE/WYAS

Ministry sanctioned the purchase of nine new buses of which six, Nos. 468-473, arrived one by one in the Spring of 1943 with chassis and engines not dissimilar to that of No. 394, ie Daimler/Gardner 5LW. The bodies were built by Massey to the recently-introduced austerity ('utility') specifications with single-skin steel panelling, although cheerfully upholstered in red hide. Quiet, comfortable and reasonably pleasant to behold, they assisted on the Stanningley run where the tinkling, musical ring of their engines became a familiar feature. Let loose on hillier routes they tended to 'boil over', however.

Wholly unwelcome acquisitions were three Guy Arabs, No. 467 and Nos. 474/5 whose slow, grating crash gear changes, reversed gear positions and steeply-inclined pedals made driving hard work and timekeeping erratic. Passengers could not decide which version they disliked more – 474/5 with their stark, highbridge Weymann bodies and unyielding wooden slatted seats or 467 with comfortable upholstery but cramped lowbridge body. Dull and sonorous, they were relegated to driver-training uses as soon as the vehicle shortage eased.

Next came the first of the 'utility' Daimler CWAs, 476-9, with AEC 7.7 engines, Duple bodies and wooden seats; spartan but lively with their pre-selector gears, they were infinitely superior to the Guys. Northern Counties-bodied CWAs 480/1 were unhandsome but very sound, while 482/3 and later 484-6 were replicas of 476-9.

A notable feature of the desperate wartime conditions was the practice of starting buses in second gear in the

Above: Fine feathers don't make fine birds. The colourful post-war South Sea blue and primrose livery of Guy No. 467 cannot disguise its lowbridge discomfort as Undercliffe passengers clamber on board outside the partly-completed Ritz Buildings, Leeds Road. [Photo: M. Peck

Two of the petrol-engined Titans – 354 and 367 – spent a happy retirement with Sabena, the Belgian airline. [Courtesy J. H. Cheetham

Austerity and spartan simplicity is the keynote of Duple-bodied Daimler CWA No. 476 – the seats are slatted wood, the livery khaki and the destination display (which unlike the headlamps and interior lights has not yet been masked) has been reduced to an absolute minimum. The gilt fleetname and the coat of arms indicate that Bradford does not fear spies or 'fifth columnists'.

[BCPT/WYPTE/WYAS

interests of fuel economy. The strain on the transmissions must have been considerable, but timekeeping was not affected as the roads were virtually devoid of traffic other than the trams and trolleybuses which in any case had superior acceleration and hill-climbing powers.

When the all-welded English Electric bodies of Regents 415-8 and 428-30 deteriorated beyond repair the Ministries of Supply and War Transport authorised their replacement by shapely East Lancashire composite bodies incorporating the original seats.

In the Spring of 1944 extensive tram track repairs were being carried out as a matter of urgency between Odsal and Low Moor, but the work was barely completed before the Department took fright at the infinitely worse state of the track from Low Moor to Wyke terminus, and as soon as sufficient buses could be mustered they took over the Wyke route and its peak-hour extension to Bailiff Bridge as services 86/87 on 12th June 1944, with a minimum fare to protect the Odsal tramcar passengers.

Two months later the last of the London 'evacuees' returned South.

'Passengers on the Stanningley route will not again travel by the familiar red London buses', the press announced. 'The remaining three loaned to Bradford by the London Passenger Transport Board were taken back to London today. They left Thornbury depot driven by three Corporation drivers at 8am

and were given a cheery send-off.'

With the heartwarming success of Allied landings in Normandy on D-Day, 6th June 1944, came a welcome realisation that the end of hostilities was approaching and that post-war planning could begin. Initially the plans were little more than tentative statements, as vehicles, fuel and manpower would not be readily available until industry reverted to peacetime production, but at least drawing-boards could be dusted down and a sketchplan produced to show possible patronage for trolleybuses to Wibsey, Moore Avenue and Queensbury.

Blackout restrictions were relaxed somewhat – although

Above right: Desperate situations require desperate remedies. When the Wibsey permanent way was condemned as unfit for further use, BCPT had to accept fifteen lowbridge wooden-seated Duple-bodied Daimlers in place of the trams. Photographed outside Britannia House, Leeds Road bottom, after the end of hostilities, No. 487 still retained its wartime khaki camouflage.
[Photo: the late J. A. Pitts

The unloved lowbridge Guy Utility was taken out to be 'shot' one damp morning, and the photographer duly recorded this by then decidedly down-at-heel specimen. Note the single opening window on each deck which was part of the wartime specification.
[Photo: BCPT/WYPTE/WYAS

Above: When the Wibsey trams were withdrawn in January 1945 they were replaced not by new 'Utilities' but by more civilised buses – the ten-year old Regents. Seen in Tyrrel Street in June 1948, No. 395 was advertising Woods' music shop which is still popular 47 years later! Note the typical BCPT sign – 'Motor Bus for Little Horton via Canterbury Avenue'. [Photo: Roy Marshall

Below: Not all 'utility' buses were uncomfortable or unpopular. Massey-bodied Daimler No. 471, seen at Odsal in 1951, was quiet, comfortably-upholstered and not unhandsome.

[Photo: M. Peck

briefly reimposed when a V1 pilotless weapon streaked across Bradford skies one sunrise – and the NFS (National Fire Service) commander at Bowling depot, Mr Jack Downs, presided over a farewell party before handing back the premises to BCPT who needed accommodation for fifteen more Daimler CWAs which arrived in early January 1945.

The old-world comfort of the departed London buses was not reproduced in the new delivery whose lowbridge Duple bodies and Daimler chassis were afflicted with austerity-specification solid engine-mountings. The pitiless thudding of the pistons was distinctly felt by the upstairs passengers crouched beneath the low roof and crammed four abreast on the slippery wooden benches with the end passengers braced with one foot in the sunken gangway to stem a human avalanche whenever the bus lurched around a left-hand bend. Downstairs passengers found the underside of the same gangway to be, literally, a headache. Not for nothing were 487-501 dubbed 'Pigtroughs' or 'Flat Harriets', and all were characterised by shrill, screeching brakes.

Tactfully, BCPT did not inflict these little-loved vehicles on the Wibsey route when, after five years delay, buses superseded the comfortably-upholstered trams on 8th January 1945. In compliance with the decision of June 1939, the new service (84) covered the full length of Little Horton Lane, except that for a few weeks the outward-bound buses (mostly pre-war Regents 395-419) travelled via Morley Street and Wilton Street to include a bus stop outside the Alhambra Theatre. Extras ran to St. Enoch's Road Top (83), and such was the scarcity of materials that a few of the old tram-stop signs were retained temporarily.

Ironically, the Wibsey buses had to observe the 9pm curfew for several months, unlike the trams which had operated until 10pm throughout the war. Fuel remained in short supply; sickness and absenteeism were at record levels, and reports that a Wrose bus had carried 21 standing passengers (including a few on the platform) raised no eyebrows whatever.

A transport strike in Leeds posed problems for the joint through service, No. 72.* At first the BCPT buses continued to penetrate 'hostile territory' by means of unorthodox diversions, but when violence threatened, the service was curtailed at Stanningley until the dispute ended.

Three of the petrol-engined Titans 354, 361 and 367, were loaned to Middlesbrough Corporation in February/March 1945; 361 faltered and was exchanged for 366, being espied in the North Yorkshire outpost by a surprised Bradfordian. When the trio returned home on 31st August they were immediately delicensed; the last of the petrol-powered double-deckers, they never ran in Bradford again, although 354/367 enjoyed a brief but happy retirement with Sabena the Belgian airline.

As Chairman of the Municipal Passenger Transport Association (MPTA) in 1944-5 Mr Tattam called for the introduction of larger vehicles, 30ft long and 8ft wide, in place of the standard 26ft x 7ft 6in dimensions, but the Ministry remained obdurate despite having previously allowed BCPT to operate ten 8ft trolleybuses originally intended for Johannesburg. The extra width was conceded in 1946, but 30ft vehicles on two axles were not permitted for another decade.

*BCPT buses had originally displayed route No. 71 and (for some reason) LCT buses No. 72. The difference was unimportant, as no one paid much attention to route numbers. When the anomaly was rectified in 1942 BCPT re-numbered its Lister Park-Bankfoot service from 72 to 71, as it would have been more difficult for Leeds to alter their one-piece destination blinds.

Although all the Utility buses were supposedly built to the same specification the initiated could soon tell them apart. This Northern Counties example shows subtle differences from its Massey-bodied compatriot at the foot of the facing page. Both were built in Wigan, though at this time the two companies were not connected.
[Photo: BCPT/WYPTE/WYAS

8   PERPLEXING PATHS

The gradual reappearance of men who had served in the Armed Forces posed new and interesting challenges. Whilst many of the staff were glad to put war behind them and resume normal life, others, such as 'The Mad Major' brought with them some of the carefree disregard for protocol which had proved so invaluable at the battlefront.

'Ginger', reputedly an ex-tank driver, treated his 'Pigtroughs' like Shermans as he stormed round the curves and corners of the Heaton route (79/80); pavement edges felt the kiss of his tyres as the hard-driven vehicles canted at unusual angles; elderly ladies stepped back sharply but schoolboys thought it marvellous.

'Grumpy' was consistent in his unspoken surliness as he collected fares and hawked timetables upstairs and downstairs, whilst a small, unnamed but fiendish conductor resembling a Changi gaoler determinedly harassed fare-evaders – real or imaginary – well past the point of rudeness. But Joyce with her bright, efficient charm achieved lasting popularity as did quiet George who was never seen without his uniform cap or smartly-knotted tie.

"Hold tight, please !"

"Fares, please !"

"Have you all got tickets, please !" – and (until, on union insistence, the number of standing passengers was reduced to a mere eight) –

"Pass right down the bus, please !"–

these were the time-hallowed cries of generations of conductors.

Less welcome were the occasional ticket-inspectors on their unheralded rounds which rarely failed to arouse guilty feelings amongst even the most law-abiding passengers who, on hearing the polite but sinister challenge, "Tickets, please !" could be seen feverishly searching pockets or even the floor for the ticket they had so thoughtlessly discarded or frayed into artistic patterns of illegibility. Awful was the fate of those who, slyly or carelessly, had overridden their fare-stage or lost a ticket beyond recall; with burning cheeks they felt the unspoken reproach of the other passengers.

The trappings of austerity were slowly beginning to fade away. The next delivery of Duple/Daimler CWAs, 502-511, boasted lightly-upholstered brown leather seats backed with an orange-brown patterned uncut moquette. Their rear roof domes were tastefully curved instead of being formed from angular segments, and, encouragingly,

Huddled together for warmth in the depths of winter, tramcar 70 advises passengers that Aspro will cure their headaches and that Lanry will bleach whites whiter, while Brush-bodied Daimler CWA 517 insists that 'Wimsol is made to be maid'. Trolleybus No. 717 is posed with its colleagues for a timetable frontispiece in 1947.   [BCPT

46

Not long to go – Titan No 358, photographed outside the Stanningley waiting-room in Hall Ings in October 1946, was allowed to retire six months later.

[Photo: the late J. A. Pitts

they arrived in a grey undercoat as a hint that they were to join the trams and trolleybuses in a peacetime livery. The first three incorporated blackout masks inside and out, but these were removed without being used.

Last of the legion of Daimler CWAs, Nos. 512-517 entered service on the first day of 1946 painted in the colourful livery of South Sea blue and primrose, dark grey roof, 'chrome yellow' lining-out and black beading and mudguards, which had been adopted by the tramcars and trolleybuses in 1942. Their shapely Brush bodies equipped with route number boxes foreshadowed a gradual return to better standards.

The new colours were also applied to buses receiving a full overhaul in Thornbury Works. Daimler COGs 432/435 were the first to receive this very welcome treatment, but it soon became evident that buses due for early withdrawal would not escape from the drab khaki-grey even if repainted. Wartime colours therefore did not vanish finally until the autumn of 1950. Several of the old Titans were allowed to retire, but others battled on and were occasionally called upon to tow younger buses away from the scenes of breakdowns.

The first of the post-war motorbuses, AEC Regent III No. 527 was a very popular vehicle. The scene is Wibsey terminus (Acre Lane) which retained gas lighting until the advent of trolleybuses in 1955.

[Courtesy J. H. Cheetham; photo the late R. F. Mack

Left: Not all wartime bodies were spartan. When the original English Electric bodies of 1935/36 AECs became unserviceable in 1944 they were replaced by shapely East Lancashire products. Number 428 was photographed in August 1948 at the Dewsbury loading point in Nelson Street, adjoining a humble cafe whose window always displayed a magnificent fruit cake (regrettably never sampled by the author). The site is now occupied by the Bradford Transport Interchange.
[Photo: R. Marshall

Left: A comfortless end to a working day – employees of Crofts, Thornbury, board Guy Arab No. 474, circa 1948.
[Photo: M. Peck

Below: Rugged but reliable: Northern Counties-bodied Daimler CWA No. 480 rests in Nelson Street outside the offices of Frank Christelow, wool merchant, circa 1952.   [Photo: M. Peck

An unorthodox breakdown recovery procedure was witnessed one hectic peak-hour in busy Town Hall Street where a fully-laden Wyke 'Pigtrough' refused to start. Attached by a chain to an equally laden Odsal tramcar, it was towed away out of sight. The ultimate fate of vehicle and passengers was not recorded.

Addressing the National Joint Council of the Road Passenger Transport Industry at its Silver Jubilee luncheon, Mr Ernest Bevin, Minister of Labour, chose to attack what he termed the 'parochialism' of public transport. From Bradford, Alderman Walter Hodgson refuted the slur and pointed out the successful joint-working arrangements with neighbouring operators, though he endorsed the Minister's suggestion of 'regional transport systems throughout the country to sweep away vested interests'. Alderman Hodgson evidently did not realise that the Minister was intent on nationalisation and expropriation, and Mr Bevin appeared equally unaware that the municipalities were 'parochial' only because the 1930 Road Traffic Act and similar legislation forbade them to be otherwise.

When the public operators learned that nationalisation had become part of the post-war parliamentary programme, the Association of Municipal Corporations formed a committee to investigate the threat, and Councillor B. W. Berry, successor to Alderman Hodgson as Bradford's transport chairman, was appointed to sit on it.

Other election promises were in the air also. Some candidates in the 1945 municipal elections had undertaken to restore the Tong (74) and Ripleyville (62) services suspended since 1939, and having been duly elected they attempted to honour their pledge. While agreeing in principle the Transport Committee lay low, pleading lack of vehicles and fuel.

An even more longstanding pledge was fulfilled when AEC offered to execute the order for twenty buses placed in 1939. The Committee gladly agreed in July 1946, even though the price had exactly doubled in six years.

More than a year elapsed before the first of the order – motorbus 527 – arrived in September 1947 in the last days of a long, glorious hot summer season. The sleek, handsomely-painted Northern Coachbuilders body was comfortably mounted on a well-sprung AEC Regent Mark III chassis; peacetime standards had returned and the passengers were very appreciative, although the platform step-height was somewhat higher than normal. The remainder of the order – Nos. 524-6 and 528-543 – arrived by March 1948, just in time to encounter the longest and bitterest winter since 1940.

Hard-packed with partially-ploughed, inadequately-gritted snow and ice, the roads resembled corrugated-iron sheets over which the popular new buses bounced from one frozen rut to the next, their composite bodies creaking and cracking disturbingly. Nevertheless, despite atrocious conditions the staff battled on. Attempting to halt at the foot of steep Victor Road a fully-laden 'Pigtrough' slid bodily into Lister Park whence its shaken driver retrieved it with difficulty. Other buses became stranded on the hills and had to be dug out.

Smoother paths lay in store, however. When Summer returned the Corporation Highways Department began a programme of surfacing the countless miles of granite-setted roads with a 'carpet' of Trinidad Lake asphalt. Wakefield Road, Little Horton Lane, Cheapside, Manningham Lane, Canal Road and Lumb Lane were among the first beneficiaries of this welcome transformation, but other major thoroughfares and the city centre itself had to wait until the tram tracks became redundant.

An unusual accident occurred on 6th November 1946, when Daimler 442 collided in thick fog with a gas lamp near the Toll Bar in Toller Lane; escaping gas ignited a blaze which engulfed the bus and reduced it to a skeleton.

Plans for an enclosed bus station were revealed as part of a proposed redevelopment of the city centre, though its precise location was debatable.

But which form of transport should be used in the new Bradford ? The correspondence columns of the local press seethed with conflicting views.

Motorbuses were the way forward, declared H. Wigglesworth; large organisations such as London Transport, Ribble, East Kent and Midland Red could not all be wrong, and though modern buses emitted noise and fumes, these were not excessive, and the latest London buses operated 'as silently as any trolleybus, the fumes disadvantage having completely disappeared.'

Modern tramcars with their large overload capacity were strongly advocated by many who stressed the durability of the existing fleet which had battled undaunted through snow, fog and blackout.

More trolleybuses, urged others, including Councillor Addy who in the firm belief that 'the health of the people must come first' considered that 'electric traction must be the rule within densely populated areas'. In order to eliminate duplication of services the Department should banish motorbuses to the outer area to act as feeders to trolleybus circular routes such as City-Odsal-Rooley Avenue-Rooley Lane-Dudley Hill-City.

The official verdict on this lively discussion was pronounced in September 1947, by the Chairman (Councillor Berry), who, announcing the imminent replacement of the Bowling Old Lane tramcars, forecast the complete abandonment of the tramways by the end of 1949, thus saving an annual outlay of £35,000 on track repairs.

"It is not our policy, however", he added, "to substitute motorbuses for trams on all routes – it would take 90 buses to do that (replacing 80 trams) – but if opportunity offered some routes will be converted to trolleybus running. Because of shortages of overhead and other equipment it is simpler at present to use motorbuses. If it becomes possible later to equip these routes for trolleybuses, the motorbuses will be useful in replacing worn-out vehicles on other routes."

Implementation of this policy began when in place of the Bowling Old Lane trams a Union Street to West Bowling (88) bus service opened on 14th December 1947, traversing part of the Ripleyville route whose restoration had been promised two years previously. Vehicles used initially were the upholstered khaki-clad 'utilities' 502-511. Reactions varied sharply. 'Happy Housewife', an ex-conductress, welcomed the return of a Ripleyville service after eight years of 'Shanks pony', but the West Bowling Protest Group bewailed the loss of the connection with the Manchester Road shopping area and presented a 2,000-name petition to the Chairman. However, as the buses were carrying 5,000 more passengers per week and earning 10% more revenue than the trams with their shorter route, the Chairman reaffirmed his decision, adding, "As far as we are concerned, that is the end of the story." And so it was.

The undertaking was continuing to expand. In the year ended 31st March 1948, 155,064,870 passengers had been carried and 11,500,000 miles travelled, an increase of 3,218,047 and 400,000 respectively, although loan charges and delays in obtaining a fares increase had caused an accumulated deficit of £50,000 which would have to be met from the rates.

Faced with increasing difficulty in obtaining new vehicles, the Manager was authorised to order 40 motorbuses for delivery in late 1949 and to purchase other buses when opportunity arose, in order to maintain services, avoid obsolescence and complete the abandonment of tramways. Unable to obtain delivery of the eight trolleybuses ordered for the Undercliffe service, he decided to restore the pre-1939 motorbus service 'until such time as the route is converted to trolleybus operation.' The AEC 'Small Sixes' (421-430) which had temporarily replaced the Undercliffe tramcars during major track renewals at the 'Cock and Bottle' junction in 1944 replaced them permanently on 18th July 1948, prudently avoiding Church Bank, however.

Ten elegant Daimlers (544-553) which arrived simultaneously were much admired by the passengers. Their stylish Brush bodies displayed a larger than normal area of primrose paint; the well-radiused windows were larger also, and the mahogany interior facings, brown leathercloth panel linings and chrome lampholders gave a luxurious finish. Number 546 was proudly despatched to Denmark to participate in a 'British Week' in Copenhagen from 18th-25th September. The largest, costliest and most ambitious exhibition of British goods and services ever staged outside the United Kingdom, it embodied displays by 1,000 British firms including 300 Yorkshire textile companies. Driven by a relay of BCPT drivers – Ernest Hayhurst, Harry Coleman and George Taylor and conducted by Harry Gobby, No. 546 attracted much attention with its un-Continental appearance and lively

Flying the Flag for Britain: Daimler CVD6 No. 546 seen in Dick Lane on its return from Copenhagen.

[BCPT/WYPTE/WYAS

The squat silhouette and curious configurations of Crossley coachwork were emphasised by their livery details. Preparing for yet another journey to West Bowling, the driver and conductor view the photographer – Roy Marshall – with interest and curiosity.

Above: Now recovered from its wartime gloom, lowbridge Daimler No. 487 guards the approaches to Thornbury Works in the early summer of 1949 as newly-delivered Leyland PD2s are put into store in the 'Tin Shed' (the 1915 'railless' shed) from which the last of the old Titans (whose roofs are visible to the left of No. 487) have been evicted.   [Photo: the late R. F. Mack

Below: Against an exotic background of poplars in the park at Leyland, Lancashire, PD2 No. 554 prepares to join its new owners in Bradford in 1949.
[Courtesy G. Welburn; photo Leyland Motors

performance, and ever afterwards wore a 'GB' plate on its rear panels.

A new feature introduced with Nos. 544-553 was the provision of an extra conductor's bell-push at the front of the upper deck above the centre pillar. However, uncertainty reigned as to whether the conductor could see the rear platform clearly enough, and the bells were removed in 1951.

So intent was the Manager on maintaining and modernising the services that he accepted a batch of six Crossley DD42s in September 1948. Numbered 518-523 they had been due for delivery a year earlier, but the long delay had allowed Crossley to take advantage of new regulations permitting increased width. The first 8ft wide motorbuses in the BCPT fleet, they were broad, squat, tastelessly-designed but solidly-built. Their stiff steering and slow crash gearboxes doomed them to perpetual service on the fairly level West Bowling (88) route. Drivers said that the Crossleys 'sat down in the road' at every gear-change, and only rarely did they escape to prove how unsuitable they were for Bradford's hills. Unwisely allotted to the Wrose route one peak-hour, Crossley 522 dragged its cumbersome way up the relentless gradient of King's Road in second gear while nimble AECs and Daimlers soared serenely past.

More variety was introduced into the fleet with an order for twenty all-Leyland PD2s (554-573). Their all-metal bodies resembled an 8ft-wide version of pre-war designs, and the bodybuilder's refusal to provide the normal yellow lining-out imparted a greenish hue to the blue paintwork. On arrival in Bradford the first few were stored in the 'Tin Shed' outside Thornbury Works, where they fleetingly

The conductor of Bradford Moor tramcar 225 shouts encouragement to his colleague on the platform of AEC No. 428 as it struggles to the summit of Church Bank on its slow ascent to Undercliffe. Although in fine condition No. 225 was compulsorily retired in May 1950, only 19 years old, whereas 14-yearold No. 428 was worn out when withdrawn only three months later.   [Photo: the late J. A. Pitts

The Brush-bodied Daimlers were regularly used on the Leeds route for a year or two and No. 551 is seen in the familiar setting of Infirmary Street, Leeds on what was clearly a warm day. The setting of the indicator blind leaves something to be desired.

[G. H. F. Atkins

encountered their twenty-years-old ancestors, the last of the 'Titans' stored there since final withdrawal a year earlier, still in wartime khaki. Like the Crossleys, the PD2s had synchromesh gearboxes which were not appreciated by drivers accustomed to smooth, effortless pre-selector gear changes. Sturdy if unexciting, with a deep, throaty roar rising to a resolute whine, they gave sterling service.

Meanwhile, the whole future of the Transport Undertaking had been in question, as the Transport Act, 1947, empowered HM Government to nationalise all public transport. The railways and canals had become State property on 1st January 1948, but the fate of road transport was less clear.

A Board of five members – which would nowadays be termed a 'quango' – Sir Cyril Hurcomb, Lord Ashfield, Sir William Wood, Lord Rusholme and Mr John Benstead – had been appointed to acquire, by agreement or otherwise, all municipal and company operators. Whereas companies would receive market value for their assets, the municipalities stood to lose heavily, as they were obliged to repay capital debts by means of a sinking fund. If nationalisation were to occur immediately, Bradford might receive up to a

tenth of actual value, but if it were delayed a few years and the debt was eliminated, no compensation would be due.

Whilst emphasising that the Transport Committee had "done its job thoroughly well – no outside body could do it better", Alderman Leach argued that even if large cities were allowed to keep their transport they would have to forego jurisdiction over inter-town services and fares. He concluded that the days of municipal transport were numbered.

Although companies large and small – including West Yorkshire Road Car – queued up for nationalisation, the municipalities did not, and it was not until October 1949 that the British Transport Commission prepared a scheme for the North East (Durham and Northumberland). Bradford Transport Committee stated that if the worst happened and transport was transferred to Area Boards, membership should consist of councillors. They heartily endorsed the Association of Municipal Corporations' view that,

'Local control of local passenger transport is essential to the development of the locality and the proper implementation of the social services by the local authority, and wherever possible ownership and control should go together.'

Away in the North East, Northumberland County Council at first accepted the proposal, but on learning the actual details they instructed their Chairman, Lord Ridley – prophetic name ! – to reject the scheme as 'restrictive, vague, neither necessary nor desirable; harsh and impracticable'. Similarly, on the casting vote of their Lord Mayor, Newcastle City Council voted not to hand over their undertaking. The matter was not pressed further, and the municipalities turned their attention to everyday affairs again.

A perennial and thoroughly unpleasant feature of city life was the fog which occasionally descended over the Bradford basin like a thick, dirty blanket as droplets of moisture and the smoke from thousands of industrial and commercial chimneys coalesced into an impenetrable grey mass. When night fell, conductors often walked in front of their buses bearing a torch, and many passengers waited in vain for transport which did not arrive, leaving them to feel and fumble their way home through the grimy gloom. In December 1948 the Committee expressed its appreciation of

'. . . the splendid way in which the Staff of the Department especially the drivers, conductors and inspectors maintained services on the Corporation's bus and tram routes during the recent prolonged period of dense fog.' Not until the creation of 'smokeless zones' many years later did the nuisance disappear.

As supplies and staff were more freely available now, small service improvements could be allowed; the Fagley route was extended to Falsgrave Avenue (81a) at peak hours; on the Undercliffe route extras ran to Peel Park (66) and Tyersal/Cutler Heights (65) buses were re-routed via Parsonage Road.

A more dramatic re-routing attracted much criticism. In May 1949, the Undercliffe and Peel Park buses were at last allowed to make the steep ascent of Church Bank which had previously been the sole preserve of tramcars; the journey time and vehicle mileage thus saved were used at the outer end of the route, where the terminus was removed from Northcote Road to the 'Prince of Wales'.

Had the new Leylands or Regent IIIs been used on the diversion, all might have been well, but the retention of the 1935 AEC 'Small Sixes' aroused derision as they were not designed for such an arduous haul. Stop-watches were produced; it was discovered that on the climb from Forster Square to 'Cock and Bottle' the Bradford Moor trams took 75 seconds and the unfortunate buses 105. In order to avoid dangerous hold-ups in the Bank the policeman on point duty in the Square usually delayed the tram until the bus was out of sight, but even then the tram always caught up.

'The bus I rode in', wrote Charles Leonard, 'set off with a terrible row, and very slowly rounded the corner into Church Bank. It shook so much going up the Bank that a gentleman stood up to grasp two handrails firmly to stop the terrific vibrations. By this time the bus stank like a poke of devils !'

The problem was 'solved' by the removal of the tramcars. Semi-utility buses of the 502-511 Daimler CWA series took over the Bradford Moor service on 24th June 1949, pending the introduction of trolleybuses a few months later. Number 502 was one of the first vehicles noted. Occasionally they were joined by a 'Flat Harriet' (487-501) or more popularly a Daimler/Brush of the 512-517 series which were the only buses able to display the temporary route number 89. This time the only complaints were about the lack of accommodation for prams and bicycles.

By this time the remaining tram drivers (age permitting) were being instructed in the more complex art of manipulating motorbuses, and two driver-training schools were in regular session.

The forty AEC Regent IIIs ordered in 1947 were at last ready for delivery, and as the bus fleet numbers had so outgrown their original series (301-500) that they were rapidly gaining on the trolleybuses (597-751), all tramcars numbered under 50 were re-numbered to make way for their successors, Nos. 1-40.

During the morning and afternoon of 5th November 1949, all tramcars were removed from Horton Bank Top Depot and replaced by gleaming new AECs Nos. 1-18 which commenced service next morning on the Queensbury (73) route and its two short-workings to Horton Bank Top and White Horse (74). Previously the highest tram route in the country, it posed a challenge to any motor bus, especially the Hebbles which struggled over the hills to Halifax, and Guy Arab 474 which had been used to train the Queensbury tram drivers. The AECs took it in their stride. Their deep-sprung, luxurious suspension easily absorbed the inequalities of granite setts and potholes as their smooth, powerful 9.6 litre engines bore the supremely handsome buses up Horton Bank, past wintry Littlemoor and Scarlet Heights to their lofty terminus in the shadow of the famous Black Dyke Mills. Joined by Nos. 19/20 a few days later when demand outstripped supply, these superb vehicles were to give twenty years faithful service to the people of Horton and Queensbury.

Leyland 53, one of the second batch of PD2s, was a 'regular' on the Odsal route, at whose loading point outside the west entrance to the Town Hall it was photographed on 8th April 1951 by Roy Marshall.

Equally fortunate were the Thornbury passengers when, on 5th March 1950, Nos. 31-40 commenced duties on new service 89 in place of the trams. Stabled at Thornbury depot, they were joined there in May by 'utility' Daimlers 468-473 and 476-9 for the Stanningley service (later replaced by new AECs 21-30 from Ludlam Street when Stanningley passengers complained of 'second-class treatment') and the six buses needed for the Leeds service.

It had been expected that Thornbury would be served by trolleybuses, as overhead wires existed over the route for access to Thornbury depot and works, but the economic situation had changed. In a speech to the Chellow Dene Veterans (January 1950) the Chairman (Councillor Berry) revealed that although trolleybuses were "clearly the best vehicles for a hilly city", they now cost nearly half as much again to run as a motorbus, for which reason motorbuses might become the principal form of transport.

Thus, when the last of the valiant tramcars bade farewell to the Odsal route on 6th May 1950, they were replaced not by trolleybuses or the hoped-for second series of Leyland PD2s (41-65) which did not arrive until autumn, but by a scraped-together miscellaneous collection of 'utilities', pre-war AECs and Daimlers (some still khaki-clad) and new AECs 21-30 (until transferred to Stanningley), housed at Bankfoot depot which had previously seen no buses except the few needed for Bankfoot-Horton Bank Top (62) and old Daimlers (462/4 etc) awaiting scrap.

Tramcars were still encountered by BCPT buses in the neighbouring city of Leeds, and on Ministry insistence modern 8ft-wide buses were excluded from the joint through service (72) for fear of being squeezed. Municipal pride naturally insisted that only the best buses should present themselves before neighbours' critical scrutiny, and as the latest 7ft 6in vehicles (544-553) were no longer new, six Daimler CVD6s (574-579) were placed in service in January 1950. Their handsome Barnard bodies bore a close resemblance to those supplied by the now-defunct Northern Coachbuilders concern (AECs 524-543) having in fact been created by the former NCB designer. Used exclusively on the Leeds route until Ministry regulations were relaxed, the 'Barnards' were the last new 7ft 6in buses bought by Bradford.

Modern ticket machines in the form of 133 'Ultimate' units were hired from the Bell Punch Co in January 1950, followed by another 220 plus 100 TIMs for routes burdened with fares of 6d or more.

Trolleybuses having by this time established themselves on a new Bradford Moor-Crossflatts through service with a central loading point on the south side of Forster Square, the Heaton and Little Horton (79/80) motorbuses were removed on St. George's Day 1950, from their accustomed stand in front of the offices of Messrs T. I. Clough, solicitors, to the dismal backwater of Commercial Street. An unwise move ! Emulating St. George in his dragon-slaying pursuits the residents of Heaton arose in wrath to slay the Transport Department. 'Bureaucratic stupidity' and 'Official ineptitude' were among the epithets printed by the startled press. Overnight the loading barrier sign mysteriously vanished from Commercial Street and reappeared in Forster Square. The residents' amusement was not shared by BCPT, who promptly returned the sign to its official location.

But Heaven was on the side of Heaton. A great fire arose and consumed much of Commercial Street and the north side of the Square on June 8th. Next morning only the Haworth Road/Sandy Lane (69/70) and Heaton/Little Horton buses were using the Square – and the latter were once again loading outside Clough's ! The Undercliffe, Greengates, Ravenscliffe Avenue, Apperley Bridge and Fagley buses (66-68, 78, 81) were banished to the Ritz in Broadway/Leeds Road while the trolleybuses were dispersed far and wide.

The effect of the fire was far-reaching and, sadly, permanent. When the Square eventually re-opened to traffic, only the trolleybuses and the Fagley, Heaton/Little Horton and Haworth Road/Sandy Lane buses returned. The lively throngs and patient queues which had populated the Square for generations were not seen there again, and the Corporation's decision to leave the burnt-out site vacant (apart from a single-storey brick-built row of shops) until total redevelopment of the area many years later, destroyed the dignity of the Square, thus facilitating its obliteration in 1959-1963.

On 13th August 1950 the Leeds (72) service which had commenced at the Ritz Cinema since its removal about 1943 from the original Leeds tramcar starting point in Leeds Road (Mildred Court) was moved to Hall Ings, adjacent to the other Leeds Road services to Thornbury (89) and Stanningley (90), although protective fares on service 72 discouraged short-distance passengers.

With the arrival of the second batch of Leyland PD2s (41-65) with stylish 'Farringdon' type bodies, many pre-war buses of all types were allowed to retire. Bankfoot depot became a Leyland preserve; Bowling housed Daimlers and pre-war vehicles; Horton Bank Top saw nothing but AECs 1-20; the small Thornbury contingent comprised new AECs and the 'Barnards', while Ludlam Street accommodated everything else.

The construction of Corporation housing estates, suspended during the war, had recommenced, and between Wibsey and Horton Bank Top a large

AEC Regent III No. 15 was photographed at the Reevy Road West terminus of the new Buttershaw (74A) route only a few months after returning to service following a front axle breakage which caused it to overturn when leaving Horton Bank Top depot in 1950.
[Photo: Author

Daimler 483 squeezes through the grim portals of Hammerton Street Bridge on a return journey from Cutler Heights in 1952.
[Courtesy J. H. Cheetham; photo J. Copland

development taking its name from nearby Buttershaw was now being occupied. On 5th December 1950, its first service (74A) was begun as an extension of the Horton Bank Top (74) workings, operating via Speeton Avenue, Beacon Road and Gracey Lane to a point halfway along Reevy Road West pending the completion of the carriageway. A twenty-minute service with a leisurely twenty minutes layover sufficed initially.

Another housing estate having been built between Pasture Lane and Bradford Road, the Committee decided in November 1950 to supplement the Clayton trolleybuses with a motorbus service along the old B&B route – Shearbridge Road, Woodhead Road, Spencer Road and Clayton Road. As the service would have undermined trolleybus finances it was adjourned while the actual demand was assessed, but on 29th January 1951, the Committee agreed to begin the service as soon as vehicles, staff and licences were available. At the same time tenders for thirty (later increased to forty) new buses were invited as replacements for the twenty-eight remaining pre-war double-deckers and the Guys. But only eight days later the Corporation appointed Mr C. T. Humpidge as General Manager in succession to Mr Tattam who had retired.

Although manager of the all-bus Rochdale Corporation undertaking since 1942, Mr Humpidge was equally experienced in electric traction and favoured the retention and expansion of Bradford's trolleybus network. The Clayton project was therefore not pursued, and the new manager took advantage of a surplus of trolleybuses to persuade the Committee to approve the conversion of the Thornbury (89) route from motorbuses to trolleybuses. AEC Regent III No. 39 was therefore the last Thornbury bus on 1st March 1952, when all fifteen 'Flat Harriets' (487-501) were delicensed and sold.

The carriageway beneath the Hammerton Street bridges having recently been lowered by 6in the Tyersal/Cutler Heights (65) route was now accessible to all types of bus; previously only the 'utilities' – high as well as low-bridge – had been able to venture there in safety, and journeys were more comfortable now, as the 'utility' Duple/Daimlers had received upholstered seats from scrapped pre-war buses.

In March 1952 the title of the undertaking was changed to Bradford City Transport.

9   THE ELECTRIC ERA

By 1952 the economy both national and local was booming; rising costs were affecting the working expenses of the Transport Department, and economies were increasingly sought.

Attention was turned to the livery. Commencing with buses 30, 539 and 550 the neat yellow lining-out was omitted in the Autumn of 1950, Daimler 503 being the last to receive any when its lower deck was repainted a few months later. In June 1951 'Barnard' 578 emerged from the paintshop with no primrose bands beneath the lower-deck windows, and all subsequent repaints omitted the upper-deck primrose bands also – Weymann-bodied 1-40 had never borne any.

From April 1952 the rain shields (drip rails) above the upper deck windows ceased to be painted primrose; No. 485 was therefore the first bus with an all-grey roof. Then, following the example of trolleybuses bought from the Nottinghamshire and Derbyshire Traction Company, BCT began to paint roofs South Sea Blue instead of grey, Crossley 520 being the 'guineapig', though AEC 9, uniquely, was treated to an incongruous 'Notts and Derby'

blue roof which contrasted strangely with the paler South Sea hues of the side panels.

Departmental signs also received attention. Signs at the central loading points indicating that (for instance) 'BCT Motorbuses for Wrose (76) start here' were now blue on white, and from July 1951 bus-stop plates, previously black on white, received similar treatment.

However, the worsening financial position could no longer be retrieved by the paintbrush. An estimated loss of £100,000 was announced in March 1952, the causes being increased wages, excessive electricity charges and a Traffic Commissioners' insistence that BCT be content with a 1½d minimum fare in place of a 2d minimum sought by the Department. Nevertheless ½d stages were abolished during the year.

The simplified livery introduced in 1951 was applied to 'Barnard' Daimler 579 when it received its first repaint in February 1952. Woods' music shop was still as popular as ever !

[Courtesy J. H. Cheetham; photo J. Copland

Old friends prepare for retirement: English Electric-bodied Daimler 452, new in January 1939, had finally shed its remaining advertisements when seen in Tyrrel Street on 16th August 1952, only three months before being withdrawn from service.
[Photo: J. Copland

In its last weeks of service, 1938-vintage Weymann-bodied Daimler 460 halts at the Admiral Nelson Inn, Manchester Road, on a return journey from Wyke (Town Gate) on 4th October 1952.
[Photo: J. Copland

"We are hoping that we have come to a point where we cannot charge any more for fares", Councillor Arthur Downey (Transport Committee Chairman) announced hopefully, "but how we are to overcome these difficulties by other economies I don't know at the moment." Sadly the Chairman's hopes were not to be fulfilled, as the long-standing fares stability of the 1932-1945 era had gone, never to return.

However, help was about to arrive from an unexpected direction. Within three weeks of the Chairman's announcement electricity charges for the trolleybuses were reduced by £30,000 at the very moment that Budget increases of £27,775 on diesel fuel were imposed. Mr Humpidge was therefore able to persuade the Committee that for economy reasons trolleybuses would have to be used wherever practicable, commencing with the Wibsey (84) route. The great Bradford Trolleybus Renaissance had begun.

For the pre-war Daimler and AEC motorbuses retirement was fast approaching. Most were still smart – fully-lined No. 452 in particular – but all were weary after

hard years of unremitting toil, especially the 1935 8.8 litre Regents (395-419) which with replacement engines had borne the brunt of the arduous Wibsey route since it opened.

Their replacements, AEC Regent IIIs 66-105, began to arrive in September 1952 and took up service between November and the following September. Built to the latest 27ft x 8ft dimensions they were Mr Humpidge's 'pride and joy'; indeed, they were his principal motorbus purchases. Their spacious East Lancashire bodies incorporated destination displays at front and side assisted by twin-track number displays at front and rear, their Birmingham-style bonnets concealing the radiator instantly earned for them the title of 'Tin Fronts'.

The interior decor as always incorporated polished woodwork and cream-painted ceilings, but stanchions and grabrails were stainless steel in place of the traditional blue or black Doverite, and blue upholstery and lining panels superseded brown materials. Possibly the total of 59 seats was achieved at the expense of structural solidity, and the sliding ventilator windows rattled infuriatingly.

Wintry conditions prevailed when 'Tin Front' Regent III No. 71 was photographed at Apperley Bridge on 1st February 1954.
[Photo: J. Copland

East Lancashire-bodied Regent III 66 emerges from the viaduct at Stanningley in 1954.
[Courtesy J. H. Cheetham; photo: the late R. F. Mack

A pleasing feature – publicly criticised by a ratepayer signing himself, 'You Spendthrifts !' – was the provision of enamelled badges bearing the city arms. Costing £2-4s-6d each and supplied by Messrs Fattorini, identical badges were affixed to the bonnet or front panel of every new motorbus and every new trolleybus body until 1974.

An experimental service opened on 10th May 1953, from Lister Park to Undercliffe (50) via Queen's Road, Lister Avenue and Northcote Road, connecting the Lister Park-Bankfoot motorbus route (49, previously 72) with the Bolton-Bankfoot trolleybus route. A demand having been

established, a City Circle (50) service operated by Leyland PD2s was commenced on 25th July 1954; it replaced the experimental service and was superimposed on service 49 and the trolleybus workings which continued at reduced frequencies. Buses were diverted from the Lister Avenue/ Northcote Road routing to Bolton Road and Dudley Hill Road.

Another Corporation housing development having been laid out between Eccleshill and Idle, some Greengates journeys labelled 'Thorpe Edge, 65', were diverted into the estate via Orchard Grove as far as Hawthorn Drive from 23rd November 1953.

Joyous celebrations marked the Coronation of Queen Elizabeth II on 20th June 1953, when Weymann/AECs 21 and 30 were adorned in a special powder-blue and off-white livery with coloured bulbs inside; other service buses displayed a plaque emblazoned with the Royal arms, and the ever-resourceful Thornbury works staff constructed a small replica of Sir Francis Drake's galleon, 'Golden Hind', complete with cannons and wave effects, to be mounted on the chassis of old No. 380 in place of the illuminated crown used at the local 1937 Coronation celebrations.

A major shortcoming of public transport in Bradford was the lack of communication between the twin hubs of the city centre, Forster Square and Town Hall Square. Market Street had always been deemed too narrow and congested for public transport, and no bus or

Top left: The driver and conductress of Brush Daimler 550 scan the pages of the *Telegraph and Argus* at Thorpe Edge terminus on 5th April 1957.
[Photo: J. Copland

Centre left: The old Tong Village 'one-manner', Leyland 380, was converted into a display vehicle for the 1937 Coronation, and is seen in Broadway advertising National Savings on 8th March 1952, while cinema-goers at the Ritz are enjoying a performance by Humphrey Bogart and Katherine Hepburn in *The African Queen*.
[Photo: J. Copland

Bottom left: The display vehicle was refurbished with a replica of Drake's *Golden Hind*, a symbol of the New Elizabethan Age which the Coronation of Queen Elizabeth II in 1953 was to usher in. Seen outside the Town Hall in 1955 Sir Francis Drake is advertising not doubloons but National Savings.
[Photo: J. Copland

trolleybus had ever been allowed in Broadway, a new, wide thoroughfare opened twenty years earlier.

Mr Humpidge therefore aroused much interest – and actual applause – when he informed the Committee of his ambition for cross-city links between Moore Avenue, Fagley and Wrose as well as the relocation of some of the central area termini, particularly those in Tyrrel Street.

Urged by Councillor Jack Leonards (an officer of the Transport and General Workers Union) the City Council referred the matter back for further discussion, to the anger of the Chairman who threatened resignation, as the West Yorkshire Road Car Co had already stolen a march on BCT by diverting some of its buses along Broadway – with the approval of the Corporation's Watch Committee !

Following a heated debate in which the Manager revealed that since 1938 the number of passengers in crowded Tyrrel Street had soared from 256,000 to 344,000 per week, the Council voted 45-9 in favour of his proposals. In an apparently irrelevant rearguard action Councillor Leonards blamed the Government for having restricted municipal transport in 1933-5 (did he mean the 1930 Road Traffic Act ?) and the Watch Committee for having always opposed the use of Broadway.

The Moore Avenue buses (now displaying the route number 75 and re-routed via Great Horton Road and Broadway) were duly linked with Wrose (76) and Fagley (81) on 7th June 1953, and the Queensbury/Buttershaw/ Moore Avenue (73-75) loading points were transferred from Tyrrel Street to the rear of the Town Hall.

Bradford was changing in many ways. In May 1954 the garish hues of sodium-vapour street lights began to supersede the gentler glow of gas and tungsten, and on 4th July the last traces of food rationing were swept away after fifteen years duration. On the Exchange Station to Leeds railway the steam trains were replaced by diesel units capable of accomplishing the journey in 16° minutes. The effect on the joint bus service (72) was immediate, as the BCT buses took 25 minutes and their Leeds counterparts 35 minutes for the same distance, and bus frequencies had to be reduced as passengers deserted to the 'diesels'. Throughout the whole area evening services were also

Upper: Repeated layers of tar and chippings underneath Greengates railway bridge eventually caused damage to a bus roof, and in October 1953 the road surface was hurriedly lowered to enable Daimlers 484 and 514 and AEC 24 to pass safely.　　　　[Photo: J. Copland

Lower: Snow shovels and sledges at wintry Littlemoor as AEC 2 struggles across the city boundary on its ascent to Queensbury in February 1953.　　　　[Photo: J. Copland

being reduced as television steadily destroyed cinemas.

A summer revival of the wartime 'See Your City' tours proved immensely popular. Fleets of buses, all full, conveyed local holidaymakers around Allerton, Sandy Lane, Heaton, King's Road, Thorpe Edge, Undercliffe, Odsal, Buttershaw, Littlemoor, Clayton, Spencer Road and back to the Town Hall. It was evident that few passengers had any idea of their whereabouts and the drivers even less ! The fare was 2/-.

An attempt by the West Yorkshire Road Car Co to extend its Shipley-Wrose service into Bradford in competition with the BCT City-Wrose (76) service and the Manningham Lane trolleybuses was firmly repelled; instead, the Traffic Commissioners sanctioned a new BCT

service to Wrose (74) from Nelson Street via John Street, Manningham Lane, King's Road and Five Lane Ends, which began on 24th November 1954, at a 5d fare. The Queensbury/Buttershaw route numbers had been altered from 73/74 to 53/54 in June.

Meanwhile, the electrification of the Wibsey (84) service had been progressing slowly, and trolleybuses took over the Little Horton short-workings on 8th November. Decorated with a few desultory flags AEC 541 made the last ascent to Wibsey on 23rd April 1955, only to be briefly recalled two mornings later when YEB power supplies proved insufficient.

At Whitsuntide 1955, beautiful weather assisted by a rail strike filled local parks to bursting point, and public transport was in heavy demand.

The Drighlington (77) buses, on the other hand, faced ever-decreasing demand, being reduced to a peak-hour-only service on 9th October 1955, when journeys were extended to Adwalton (Oakwell Road). Passengers used the West Riding Wakefield service at other times – thirty years after the company had begun competition on the route.

Increasing complexity of services led to a greater emphasis on route numbers, and from March 1955 rear destination displays were gradually superseded by numeral blinds.

A few weeks later sharp-eyed observers detected that destination blinds now included the name 'Halifax'. The mystery was solved in June when the manager was authorised to negotiate with Halifax for a joint through service via Queensbury in order to eliminate the absurd situation whereby the Bradford to Queensbury (53) and Halifax to Queensbury (59) buses shared a common terminus outside the Granby Inn, but only the Hebble (17) buses were allowed to run through. In December the negotiations were widened to include the Ovenden and Illingworth areas also. Regrettably Halifax terminated the talks, stating themselves satisfied with the status quo, and thirty years were to elapse before a Bradford-Thornton-Ovenden-Illingworth-Halifax service was launched.

The development of new Corporation estates at Woodside and Delf Hill between the Halifax and Woodside Roads led to the institution of a Woodside (83) service via Abb Scott Lane to Fenwick Drive on 9th July 1956 and a diversion of the Brighouse (63) buses via Woodside Road on 31st December. Minor adjustments were made to other estate services at Bierley and Buttershaw, and when a further estate was laid out at Holme Wood the Cutler Heights service was discontinued and replaced by a Holme Wood via Fenby Avenue (51) service.

The increasing volume of private cars was beginning to congest the main highways, and the Corporation obtained powers to lay out 'No Waiting' zones near bus stops. However, the brief Anglo-Egyptian conflict and the closure of the Suez Canal obliged the Traffic Commissioners to require a 10% saving on fuel oil; the increased price of that commodity would cost BCT £57,000 in a full year. As an emergency measure off-peak bus services were reduced to achieve a reduction of 6,000 miles per week; extra trolleybus journeys were instituted on 1st January 1957, and the 3d fare was abolished on motor- and trolleybus routes alike. Restrictions on private motoring brought increased patronage to BCT who had lost 17,000,000 passengers every year since the abolition of petrol rationing.

Unfortunately, the ending of the emergency did not solve the Department's difficulty in recruiting an adequate number of staff. Now fully recovered from wartime shortages, commerce and industry were thriving to such a degree that unsocial jobs were being shunned in favour of more attractive forms of work. Textiles and transport suffered most. Shift work, split turns and night duties were particularly unpopular, and the BCT driving school was kept busy. It became apparent that an underlying trend had developed among new recruits, who progressed through the various stages of trolleybus and motorbus conducting and driving until they became fully-proficient motorbus drivers, at which point they left to become better-paid heavy goods vehicle drivers.

As the local press patiently explained,

'Services have had to be cut because there is a shortage of staff. In this era of full employment and a five-day working week bus duties are less attractive than they used to be. If, therefore, full employment continues, as everyone hopes and prays it will, the vacancies will never be filled unless the job is made more attractive – and the only way of doing so is to increase the pay. But if the pay were increased the fares would go up, and there would be more protests. The trouble is that we expect too much. We want the bus brought to our doorsteps. In spite of the staff shortage the Bradford service is a good one – you do not need to travel far (outside Bradford) to realise how good it is.'

Tiring eventually of these incessant shortages the Department, in common with textile employers, began to forage far and wide for staff likely to remain in their employ.

The outcome was a trickle of immigrants, who were universally termed 'Indians' until it was realised that most originated from the new state of Pakistan.

Many and varied were the dilemmas faced by the newcomers as they grappled with the complexities of a new life and an unknown geography.

"Bankfoot, please !" said the author one day, tendering a shilling.

"Oh, yes, sir, and where is that ?"

"It's where we're going !"

"Oh indeed, and how much is it ?"

"I don't know – you're supposed to know the fares !"

And the author had to borrow the conductor's fare table and show him how to calculate fares, for which he received profuse thanks !

On another occasion a passenger boarded a Manchester Road bus, paid his fare, and was treated to a fascinating dialogue.

"We go to Self" (Shelf), declared the driver. "No, no, we go to Oakenaw !" (Oakenshaw) protested the conductor. Fortunately the passenger

The pleasant village of Norwood Green, a mile from the Huddersfield Road near Wyke Station, received its first Corporation bus on 8th February 1954. A peak-hour service only, it did not receive a route number until 1962, and Leyland 57, seen at the terminus on 6th August 1956, is displaying the untruthful indicator, 'Duplicate Bus'.
[Courtesy J. H. Cheetham; photo J. Copland

alighted before the 'point of no return' was reached, and often wondered how the issue was resolved – the toss of a coin or a majority vote by the passengers ?

The search for economies continued. As the long, continuous descents of Bradford's hills caused heavy and expensive wear on brake-linings, trials were made in 1954 with an Ashanco exhaust brake (manufactured by T. Ash & Co). Worthwhile savings having been achieved, similar brakes were progressively fitted to most AECs and Leylands, beginning in 1957. Buses so equipped were identifiable by a deep booming sound as the brake was applied, followed by a puff of black smoke when it was released. Simultaneously the seating accommodation was increased where practicable; some of the 'utilities' were re-seated from 56 to 57 (as also 524-543); the Crossleys from 56 to 58, AECs 1-40, Daimlers 544-553 and the Leylands from 56-59, and AECs 66-105 from 59 to 61. The only batch not to be adapted was the 'Barnards', in which body movement was by now discernible. Some rehabilitation of the 'utilities' was undertaken in an endeavour to prolong their lives; No. 484 was rebuilt with 'Kelbus' half-drop stainless-steel framed radius-cornered windows, and several received rear number blinds (and front number blinds where these did not already exist).

Flashing trafficators were now in vogue following experiments with trolleybuses in 1952; AEC No. 105 was fitted with Lucas units and PMG motors in 1954. Wilmott Breedon and Salendine Plastics units with Simms and ECO motors were also tried before a decision was made to adopt Frankmann units for existing buses and CAV units for new vehicles, using Ericson motors in each case.

Buses on the White Horse service were re-routed along the lower part of Great Horton Road, rejoining their original route at Grange Road, the new section having been the sole preserve of Hebble for three decades. When major sewer excavations closed lower Leeds Road from April to August 1957, Stanningley (90) buses terminated in George Street whilst the Tyersal (52) and Leeds (72) buses continued to load in Hall Ings, travelling outwards via Well Street and returning via Vicar Lane and Bridge Street.

The Duckworth Lane to Little Horton (73) shuttle service, discontinued in 1945 when the Little Horton via Heaton (80) service resumed full-time working after wartime curtailments, was briefly revived on weekend afternoons in 1957-8 until the fuel situation eased, but curiously the route was extended to Bankfoot on 17th November 1957, presumably cancelling out the savings ! On the following day the Brighouse (63) and Wrose (74) routes were linked as a cross-city service, and on 19th May 1958, Bowling-based AEC 526 opened a new service (59) from Union Street to Holme Wood via Wakefield Road, Lower Lane, Fenby Avenue and Holme Wood Road to Broadstone Way.

In June 1957 a strike of Yorkshire Woollen staff obliged BCT to confine vehicles to its own operating area; buses therefore reversed at Birkenshaw (Halfway House) and waited there for a full length of time it would have taken them to travel to Dewsbury and back.

Reversing into South Street, Little Horton, on the last day of the Little Horton via Heaton (80) service (16th November 1957) AEC 95 pauses alongside two members of the new Asian community who are reading a startling advertisement for 'Reynolds' News'.

[Photo: Author

Although Mr Humpidge's progressive modernisation programme for the trolleybuses was yielding beneficial results, no new motorbuses had been bought for four years, and the 'utilities' were looking distinctly dated. The manager, therefore, drew up a four-year capital expenditure schedule for the purchase of 69 buses at a total cost of £379,500, but the cautious Finance and General Purposes Committee ordered him to reduce capital outlay by increasing fares by 1d. Mr Humpidge therefore had to content himself with inviting tenders for only fifteen buses in the first year instead of 27 as he would have preferred.

Surprise journeys into the unknown were experienced by a few unobservant passengers when the Heaton (79/80) and Fagley (81) services exchanged loading-points in Forster Square in May 1957. Several Heatonians were startled to find themselves being transported up Church Bank, and grievous were the complaints of two Fagley ladies when the unsympathetic Heaton conductor informed them – too late – that his bus did not stop to set passengers down before Lister Park Gates !

Retirement now arrived for the two 21-years old AEC Regal semi-coaches, 444/5. Since February 1948 they had boasted AEC oil engines, but following a lively staff outing which left 445 overturned in a ditch, governors had been fitted to restrict top speed to the then legal maximum of 30 mph, with the result that an unsuspecting party who hired 445 for a trip to Grimsby and Cleethorpes via Keadby Bridge found their journey time unexpectedly lengthy ! Number 444 was the last bus to retain a rear destination name display (which 445 lost when it capsized), and so well-cherished had they been throughout their lifetime that they had only twice needed a repaint, about 1946

and 1953, omitting the 1938-style ultramarine blue and, of course, the wartime khaki.

Their replacements, also by AEC, were Roe-bodied Reliances intended as Nos. 106/7 but renumbered 301/2 in a separate series on arrival in March 1958. Both assumed a different livery with each repaint: originally almost wholly cream with a minimum of blue, they reappeared in May 1962 with blue below the waistrail and primrose above, and finally in 1964 their roofs turned blue also. Although in regular demand for private hire they took a liking to the Bankfoot-Buttershaw (62) route which had been extended from Horton Bank Top in 1957.

When HM Government instituted an MOT test for cars more than ten years old, BCT's Bankfoot depot was equipped and licensed as a testing centre. Operational on 12th September 1960, its staff inspected 376 vehicles in the first six months.

The next bus deliveries created considerable surprise. Despite having bought numerous second-hand trolleybuses BCT had never entered the used motorbus market, but the availability of ex-London Transport AEC 'RT' buses recently overhauled with a five-year Certificate of Fitness provided an economical way of eliminating the obsolete 'utilities'. 'RT' HLX 235 was acquired in February 1958,

Upper right: With the saloon door closed to exclude intruders, AEC Regal 445 has been parked outside the Rates Office at the rear of the Town Hall.
[Courtesy J. H. Cheetham; photo the late R. F. Mack

Right: The successors to Regals 444/445 were Roe-bodied AEC Reliances 301/2. Photographed in its original livery on 17th June 1958, No. 302 is standing at the Cooper Lane terminus of the Bankfoot-Buttershaw (62) route.
[Courtesy J. H. Cheetham; photo J. Copland

Above: When first placed in service in Bradford, the ex-London RTs' such as No. 408 (seen here in Ravenscliffe Avenue) appeared drab in comparison with conventional BCT buses.

[Courtesy J. H. Cheetham; photo J. Copland]

Below: The red, cream and brown livery of AEC Bridgemaster 76 MME attracts attention as it reverses at Haworth Road terminus on 8th May 1958.

[Photo: Author]

and after having been repainted and fitted with Bradford destination equipment was found to have cost a total of £1,825 compared with £6,000 for a new bus. Further 'RTs' followed in April/May, and by August all were in mainly peaktime service as Nos. 401-425, based on Ludlam Street. The repainting consisted of a one-coat overpaint in Bradford colours but in London Transport style, ie one narrow primrose band and the rest blue. Not all destination displays were rebuilt to BCT standards: several RTs entered service with very small route name apertures (for which special blinds had to be manufactured) and the incongruous London roof-mounted route-number box. Like long-forgotten RT19 of 1940 fame they were lively performers, and the news that the 'utilities' had been taken in part exchange evoked few regrets for the passing of an era.

Also withdrawn were the staid Crossleys, 518-523, their ten-year reign on the West Bowling (88) route ended at last, although 518 survived as a driver-training bus. Their demise enabled Bowling Depot to be filled entirely with AEC Regent IIIs, albeit with three body styles – Northern Coachbuilders, Weymann and East Lancashire.

A foretaste of future trends was provided by trials with an AEC Bridgemaster, 76 MME, from 5th-15th May 1958. Chassisless and fitted with a low-height rear-entrance Park Royal 72-seat body; it was the first double-decker built to the newly-authorised 30ft length to operate for BCT, and the air-suspension on its rear axle absorbed the tendency to roll when cornering. Its synchromesh gearbox was considered a backward step, however, and the bus was allowed to go on its travels, eventually being purchased by Barton Transport in whose red, brown and cream livery it

Forward entrances and jack-knife doors were a novelty when AEC Regent V No. 111 halted to allow two young passengers to alight at Buttershaw Mills, Halifax Road, on 22nd August 1959.
[Photo: J. Copland

was painted.

The fifteen buses whose purchase was authorised in 1957 began to enter service in early May 1959, as Nos. 106-120, and were the first 30ft forward-entrance AEC Regent V double-deckers owned by the Corporation although not the first to be seen in Bradford, as Hebble, uncharacteristically, had 'stolen a march' on BCT. Improved passenger comfort was ensured not only by G. D. Peters electro-pneumatic folding entrance doors but also by Clayton Dewandre saloon heaters – a welcome protection against Pennine winters. The provision of Smith's cab heaters was not a novelty, as similar heaters had been installed in the existing fleet at the insistence of frozen drivers who no longer shared the desire of their tramcar predecessors for 'plenty of fresh air' !

They were allocated to Bankfoot depot whose drivers, so long accustomed to the strenuous gear-changes of the 1949-50 Leylands, found the light AEC two-pedal monocontrol gears difficult to manipulate smoothly at first. Equally wary were the passengers who thought the totally-enclosed Orion lightweight bodies were claustrophobic and ill-ventilated, and having always been able to 'leg' on or off the traditional open rear platforms at will, they resented the entrance steps and the slow loading and unloading, which also lengthened journey times. Little did they imagine that 106-120 would eventually become the most popular of all Bradford's Regent Vs !

When AEC 526 reached Holme Wood on the first day of the service via Fenby Avenue (19th May 1958) only one passenger alighted, and the only visible building was a distant farmhouse.

[Photo: Author

Enthusiasm for football, rugby and speedway activities continued unabated, to the pleasure of BCT staff for whom it provided valuable overtime earnings. A Hull v Workington fixture at Odsal in 1958 required no less than 46 'specials', whilst a St. Helens v Leeds match at the same venue in May 1959 involved the use of ten Daimlers (544/6/8/9, 550/2/3, 574/6/7), fourteen 'RTs' (401/2/6/8/9, 411/4/5/8/9, 421/2/3/5), seven MCW/AECs (25, 30/1/3/4/8/9), four East Lancs AECs (75/6, 84, 98), two Leylands (47/573) and a single-decker (302) as well as six Leeds City Transport buses (211, 305, 378, 406, 606, 651) – a total of 44 vehicles.

This was the swansong of the fine Daimler CVD6s – Brush-bodied 546-553 and 'Barnards' 574-9 which retired soon afterwards; for the first time since 1934 there were no Daimlers in the fleet, a situation much regretted by connoisseurs of good-quality transport. Most saw further service elsewhere.

Passenger facilities were adjusted from time to time to meet changing demands. Tickets issued on the Dewsbury (4) route were now interchangeable on BCT, Yorkshire Woollen and Sheffield Joint Omnibus Committee buses; the Holme Wood (59) service was allowed an all-day half-hourly frequency from 12th April 1959, whilst on the same day its sister service (51) was re-routed into Holme Wood via Tyersal Lane and Broadstone Way to Lymington Drive, thus depriving Cutler Heights Lane of a facility (admittedly little-used) enjoyed since 1926.

Simultaneously a Holme Wood trolleybus 'spur' was being constructed along Knowles Lane, and plans also existed for a Bierley trolleybus route (via Dudley Hill) as

an extension of the City-Bierley Church workings instituted during the Suez crisis; the West Bowling (88) buses would then have been extended to Bierley Church via Parkside Road and Bowling Hall Road. However, frequencies were low and the Bierley Estate roads so narrow that for years they were restricted to 7ft 6in-wide buses only, so trolleybuses never superseded the Bierley buses.

Journeys up Manchester Road were adjusted in June 1959 so that Woodside (83) enjoyed as many buses as Shelf (82) while Odsal (84) was reduced to part-time service only and Bailiff Bridge (87) was almost extinct. Oakenshaw (85) was extended across the city boundary to Oakenshaw Church on 15th November, but frequencies on Bankfoot via Heaton (80) were reduced, the Heaton (79) and Duckworth Lane to Little Horton (previously 73) – Fagley (81) had been re-numbered 73 in May – short-workings being discontinued.

As from November 1960, buses ran to Thorpe Edge (65) and Ravenscliffe Avenue (68) alternately.

The continuing success of the Bradford-Leeds diesel train service impelled Mr Humpidge to suggest to Leeds Corporation that they should combine their separate services to Stanningley (BCT 90, LCT 14) to form a much-improved inter-city service with an additional single-deck limited-stop facility. Leeds, however, managed to misinterpret this approach as a request for the cessation of the existing

At their first repaint the 'RTs' received the standard BCT livery and, in some cases, rebuilt destination displays. Number 422 has just turned from Forster Square into Broadway on 29th June 1961.
[Courtesy J. H. Cheetham; photo J. Copland

through service (72) and chose instead to link their own Stanningley service as a cross-town route to their eastern suburbs.

Until the retirement of Mr Tattam in 1951 motorbuses had generally received a full overhaul and repaint every three years with an intermediate 'dock'-overhaul and 'touch-up-and-varnish', which ensured that the fleet remained smart and presentable. Mr Humpidge had replaced this with a 50,000 mile overhaul and repaint only, thus reducing costs and diminishing the smartness, especially when mechanical bus-washers superseded hand-cleaning. Standards varied according to environment; Horton Bank Top depot, far removed from city smoke, took pride in immaculate presentation, whereas Bowling and Ludlam Street employees who had to store many vehicles in the depot yard, struggled vainly against industrial grime, and the lower decks of hand-washed buses housed at Bankfoot were noticeably cleaner than the upper parts.

Closer attention was therefore given in 1960 to the appearance of the fleet. The 'RTs' (401-425), spectacularly dull and unattractive in their mostly-blue livery, reappeared much more pleasingly in standard BCT livery at their first repaint. New yellow fleet numbers replaced the unsatisfactory gold paint numerals which, in turn, had superseded the expensive gold-leaf figures in 1953/4; the new numerals were applied to all vehicles including the 'RTs', East Lancs buses (66-105) and Regent Vs (106-120) which, because of lack of a flat surface, had always

displayed a microscopic fleet numeral. The badly-chipped and flaked interior woodwork polish of the East Lancs bodies was overpainted cream (which in the author's view caused them to resemble seaside fish and chip parlours), and all ceilings were now painted white instead of pale cream as hitherto.

An unusual increase in patronage was reported in June 1960, 2,000,000 more passengers having been carried than in the previous year, but this merely aggravated the chronic staff shortage (250) and the difficulty of maintaining schedules. A long-smouldering grievance against their Indian and Pakistani workmates was therefore voiced by a deputation of twenty platform staff who alleged:

(i)   they were risking passengers' lives by working excessive overtime

(ii) they started queuing at 3am for overtime – one man had reputedly slept overnight on seats in the messroom to ensure first place;

(iii) a conductor was known to have worked 150 hours in one week;

(iv) although the net wage for a normal week was about £10, one employee had been able to buy two harvesting machines, send them to Pakistan and then save a further £1,000 before returning to his homeland;

(v)   some conductors habitually worked two consecutive shifts without meal breaks, thus becoming so fatigued that they did not trouble to collect fares or stand on the platform.

By contrast, they said, the West Indians were steady and reliable employees who worked regular hours. However, saving money was not a crime, retorted a spokesman for the

AEC Regent V No. 125 was newly in service when it was loaned to Rochdale Corporation in May 1961.
[Courtesy J. H. Cheetham; photo R. S. Kenney, Surfleet Transport Photographs

Pakistani staff who considered that his countrymen "made better drivers and conductors than, say the Irish !"

On the general score of fare collection the public unquestionably had reason for complaint, as particular conductors of all origins tended to ignore the upper deck altogether, with disastrous results for BCT revenues.

In defence the TGWU officials stressed that if there were any substance in the allegations there were also proper procedures for investigating them, and the manager added that although there were no rules for conductors, drivers could not exceed five hours in any shift. It transpired, however, that there was an age limit of 37 for new conductors on account of the strenuous nature of the job, an admission which accorded strangely with the rigours of wartime conductors' work – blackout, buses crowded to the limit, and old-style Bell Punch ticket machines with hand-held ticket racks. Fortunately a national reduction of the working week to 42 hours began to ease the recruitment problem.

By this time redevelopment of the city centre, long threatened, was gaining momentum. From the Transport Department offices in Forster Square it was now possible to see Exchange Station across a vast wasteland; familiar buildings were disappearing wholesale, to be replaced by new vistas and glass-and-concrete structures.

Other vistas were opening too. In the deep recesses of Thornbury works there lurked a fugitive tramcar, formerly Sunderland Corporation No. 100, which had been stored there for several years through the good offices of Mr Humpidge pending its removal to a permanent home. When the owners were given three months notice in

November 1960 to remove it, mild surprise was registered but no alarm bells rang. Not even the most observant realised that Mr Humpidge was 'clearing his desk' in preparation for leaving Bradford. The 'Apostle of the Trolleybus' was set to depart.

Some weeks earlier when Mr R. C. Moore had announced his retirement as General Manager of Sheffield Transport and Joint Omnibus Committee, Mr Humpidge had been shortlisted as a possible successor, but the prestigious post was awarded to Mr J. G. Timpson, manager at Plymouth in December. Unfortunately, being in need of recuperation after surgery, Mr Timpson had to decline the appointment, and as a formality Mr Humpidge was invited to re-apply. His appointment and consequent resignation from Bradford was announced on January 1961 and took effect on 2nd May.

His achievements had been impressive. Despite progressive modernisation and remorselessly rising costs (wages had doubled in ten years while passenger numbers had fallen by 30,000,000), the capital debt of £690,000 which he had inherited in 1951 was due to be eliminated in June – and indeed it was. His chairman, Alderman Herbert Clayton, could now proudly announce that, "From now on the Department will finance its renewals and replacements out of current revenue, with a consequent saving on interest charges". He could have added, ". . . provided that present policies continue".

But would they ? The financial prowess of his successor, Mr John C. Wake, had impressed the all-party sub-committee which appointed him in March. A trained engineer with experience of the Anglo American Oil Co and the transport departments of Middlesbrough, Burton-on-Trent and St. Helens, he had left the last-named undertaking debt-free with a reserve fund of £153,000 and one of the most modern fleets in England. However, he had also presided over the demise of the St. Helens trolleybus fleet, some of whose sadly-neglected survivors had, ironically, found refuge in Bradford.

Before he took up office the Committee placed orders for ten additional Regent Vs (and more bodies for reconditioned trolleybus chassis) all of which were to be bought out of revenue, and five similar Regents (121-125) entered service in May at Bowling depot. Number 125 was immediately loaned to Rochdale Transport Department for one week's evaluation, whilst monocontrol Regent V No. 111 was loaned to Grimsby/Cleethorpes.

The author has always believed that it is unsafe to compare one transport undertaking with another. The compact and well-integrated St. Helens network was totally unlike the largely self-contained and highly-diverse Bradford operating area, separated as it was from most of its neighbours by challenging terrain and subjected to covert competition from the National Bus Company. Mr Wake quickly discovered the truth of this belief. At St. Helens he had (he claimed) imposed "only one real fares increase in ten years", but on the day after his arrival in Bradford he had to apply to increase all 2d and 3d fares. In response to protests that dearer fares repel and cheaper fares attract passengers, he provided the classic reply:–

"Cheap fares do not necessarily mean more revenue in the long run. If you cannot make an undertaking pay on its existing fare level, and you reduce the fares, you have to gain many more passengers to bring the revenue back to its previous level, let alone increase it. This just doesn't work." Or, as his successor expressed it more succinctly a decade later, "If you halve the fares you must double the passengers just to stand still !"

The increase was granted, and the minimum adult fare was now 3d.

10 PERVERSE and FOOLISH ?

A meeting of the Yorkshire Transport Society at Bradford Technical College on 16th January 1962 was used by Mr Wake as an opportunity for publicising his views. While admitting the virtues of trolleybuses he made five critical points:–

(1) Admittedly, in times of emergency, oil became scarce, but he had known times when coal was scarce;

(2) In a civil emergency buses might be needed to evacuate the population, which trolleybuses could not do;

(3) Although trolleybuses paid better profits than motorbuses on their existing routes, if the roles were reversed, the motorbuses would make a larger profit and the trolleybuses a larger loss;

(4) In an expanding city motorbuses were more suitable;

(5) All over the country other towns were concentrating on motorbuses – surely they could not all be wrong.

Critics were quick to seize on these controversial comments. The fabled 'three minute warning' for a nuclear attack having been quoted as one of the possible 'civil emergencies', they pointed out that even the newest Regent Vs would barely reach the top of Cheapside by the time that the bomb fell, let alone find time to transport the 298,000 residents to distant parts beyond the reach of 'fall-out'. Similarly they observed that as the city had ceased expanding, point (4) did not arise, but even if it did, why were trolleybus extensions so easy in 1960 and not in 1962 ? And clearly point (3) could neither be proved nor disproved without colossal expenditure which would cancel out theoretical savings.

Unimpressed by any of these arguments the City Treasurer, (Mr John Ruscoe) bluntly retorted to the author, "You and Humpidge and Wake – you're all alike !

A wintry greeting for AEC 73 as it performs the first trip to Thornaby Drive on 4th March 1962. [Photo: Author

You've all got axes to grind ! There's Humpidge trying to prove that trolleybuses pay and pushing them for all he's worth, and now here's Wake trying to prove they don't pay, and pushing his buses. Myself, I prefer to ride on a trolleybus, but I don't care if the Transport Department operates pedal cycles as long as it gets on its feet !"

He continued, "You can make these figures prove anything if you try. I don't say these fellows are dishonest, but they've got bees in their bonnet. I'm simply after the truth – I know it sounds bigheaded, but it's true. These transport men always stall when you try to get to the bottom of things."

Faced with such a divergence of professional advice, what chance had mere councillors of reaching a rational decision ?

In the meanwhile a petition had been received for an extension of the Clayton trolleybus service into the Corporation housing estate. The petitioners were informed that a trolleybus extension would be 'difficult' and that they were to have motorbuses instead. And when the service (Clayton 36) commenced to Thornaby Drive via Bradford Road, observers noted that other trolleybus place-names (Pasture Lane, Lidget Green and Chapel Lane) now appeared on motorbus destination blinds. Mr Wake explained this by a shortage of trolleybuses, but as he had just scrapped twelve recently-acquired trolleybus chassis, it seemed that the shortage would continue. Questioned by the author, the Chairman (Alderman H. Clayton) denied that the Clayton decision was intended as 'the thin end of the wedge', but conceded that it could be !

The buses themselves seemed reluctant to be drawn into the controversy. Selected as the first bus to Thornaby Drive on 4th March 1962, AEC No. 80 diplomatically failed to start and relinquished the duty in favour of AEC No. 73.

Contemplating the long-term future of public transport, the experts disagreed once again. Traffic congestion would become so appalling, predicted Mr Wake, that motorists would not bother to use their cars at all – they would merely take them out and polish them. Equally pessimistically, the Traffic Superintendent (Mr Leonard Lisle Christie) recommended that the only way of dealing with the private car challenge was to concentrate on the trunk routes and abandon the rest. More perceptive than his professional colleagues, Inspector Boothroyd of Bradford City Police Traffic Division forecast that new parking regulations might force cars so far out of the city centre that BCT would be able to run bus services from the car parks to the places of work.

Pending a decision on long-term policy everyday activities continued as usual. Interior decor underwent a transformation when the trimmers' shop began to reupholster entirely in blue in vehicles both old and new, and in June 1962, the customary rounded fleet numerals were superseded by a new, distinctive square type with rounded corners.

Mr Christie, the Traffic Superintendent, retired happily on 31st October, his vision of an all-motorbus Bradford in sight at last. His lively successor, Mr David R. Smith from Leicester, had wide experience not only with Nottingham and Bolton Corporations but also with West Yorkshire Road Car.

Local rail services were slowly dying now. Passenger services to Queensbury, Clayton, Thornton and beyond were already but a memory; the Worth Valley line had closed and when the last train called at Drighlington station in December 1961, seven passengers passed through the station turnstile instead of the usual none ! Buses and cars had long since lured patronage away.

In the world of commerce and public service certain standards of personal appearance were traditionally required of employees, and anything of an unkempt or exotic nature was considered unacceptable. Thus when a trainee bus conductor reported for duty with a beard, he was asked to shave it off, but did not do so. Summoned by the Traffic Superintendent, he stated that his religious beliefs required him to be bearded, but could not explain why his brother who accompanied him and shared his religion was clean-shaven. Despite being given time to reconsider, he refused to comply and was dismissed. Most of the public agreed that standards must be upheld – but not all. A Fagley resident protested that if the Chairman had to wait fifteen minutes for a bus on a damp, cold evening, "he would not object if a chimpanzee took his fare !"

The trolleybus versus motorbus controversy finally burst upon the City on 4th June 1962, when the Committee debated ways of maintaining services through Forster Square during its impending redevelopment. Advised by the Manager that the necessary alterations to the trolleybus overhead equipment would cost up to £17,000, the Committee decided that it was 'not worth while spending this money, and that in planning fleet requirements they would convert the two routes (Bradford Moor-Crossflatts and Eccleshill-St. Enochs Road) to motor buses'. The Chairman, now Councillor H. A. Sissling, added reassuringly that "modern vehicles such as those operated by Bradford Corporation do not emit diesel fumes". Complete flexibility was the only way forward, he explained. Motorbuses could overtake at will; trolleybuses could not.

In the local press the correspondence columns seethed with indignation and accusation; the author counted 51 letters defending trolleybuses and ten supporting motorbuses. Flexibility was a mixed blessing, it was claimed. Whenever two buses approached a queue, one would stop while the other passed by, but if (as frequently happened) the first bus could not accommodate all the queue, some would be left behind.

Far more serious were the financial implications. In order to avoid spending £17,000 on alterations to overhead wires, the Department would have to purchase 30 new buses (£176,894) and make 1,000 traction poles redundant (£5,100). Did this constitute sound economics, and could the buses be paid for out of revenue, as promised earlier ? The Department's net profit for the year ended 31st March 1962 was £714 ! And what about noise and hill-climbing abilities ? Was it true that a motorbus had only half the lifespan of a trolleybus ?

None of these questions was answered satisfactorily,

The Bradford Moor trolleybus wires hang forlornly as Regent V A133 storms past the 'Coach and Horses' on its first journey on 18th November 1962.

[Photo: Author

The new Forster Square towers above the cordoned-off remains of the old as Regent V No. A132 halts outside the Transport Offices before making its way to Eccleshill on 18th November 1962.

[Photo: Author

and on 24th July 1962, the motorbus proposal was approved 36-32 by the full Council. Nineteen days earlier Mr Wake had been appointed General Manager at Nottingham. He did not wait to measure the success of his recommendations.

The arrival of the ten Regent Vs originally ordered in March 1961 for motorbus replacement enabled the first stage of the trolleybus conversion programme to take place. On 18th November 1962, they took over the City to Bradford Moor (30) and the cross-city Eccleshill to St. Enoch's Road (33/44) services, although the peak-hour journeys from City on routes 33/44 continued to be worked by trolleybuses.

Like the newest trolleybuses the Regent Vs had fluorescent lighting, non-slip simulated cork floor covering and three small entrance steps, but there the resemblance ended. Modern monocontrol and pre-selector gearboxes being considered by the new management to cause fractionally higher fuel consumption than manual

synchromesh types, the latter were fitted to the new vehicles which, in St. Helens fashion, bore an 'A' prefix before the fleet number to denote the year of purchase. Whilst admittedly the older Regent Vs (106-125) were by no means quiet vehicles, the boom of their engines was perfectly acceptable, but A133 on its maiden voyage from Bradford Moor was audible fully half a mile away, and the harsh snarling bellow of A132 as it stormed up The Bank from Eccleshill terminus appalled all who heard it. The news that 30 similar vehicles were already on order and that 30 more were to be bought every year was received with dismay.

On a private visit from Sheffield Mr Humpidge confided deep disappointment at recent events, as the Department had plunged back into the debt from which he had extricated it. Ten years of work and planning had been wiped out, he said; Bradford Moor, short, steep and populous, had been the ideal trolleybus route.

AEC sent their photographer to Bradford many times over the years but the big order for the Regent Vs was naturally one they were keen to publicise. The new paint glistens as the office workers and shoppers climb on board and the crews wait for departure time.

11

O BRAVE NEW WORLD

– that has such buses in it !

("The driving is like the driving of Jehu the son of Nimshi, for he driveth furiously."
2 Kings ch. 9v20)

"What filthy, noisy, rough monsters we have now !' complained a discontented Hanson schoolboy shortly after the Bradford Moor changeover, "I have waited half an hour many times for a bus home, with hours of homework ahead of me."

"Horrible, uncomfortable, smelly diesel buses !", wrote "Black and Blue Housewife", who admitted that if the Bradford Moor trolleybuses were restored she would "miss the wartime-like camaraderie which exists at present – when the bus sets off or stops, if you are standing up you are flung the length of the bus."

Other tributes poured in.

"When the time comes to get off, the relief is tremendous – the jerking gets so bad that I can hardly keep my feet when I get to the door."

"It's like sailing across the Atlantic on a dinghy over six-feet rollers."

"They'll be lucky to last ten years" observed a fourteen-year-old, one of whose contemporaries added, "When you hit a bump you really know about it !" (he admitted, however, that he enjoyed the sensation).

In the circumstances, the registration letters YAK borne by the new Regent Vs seemed peculiarly appropriate.

More fuel to the flames was added by the arrival of further Regents Nos. 136 to 165 five months later. They differed from A126 to A135 only in reverting to tungsten interior lighting and having no letter prefix to the fleet number; this feature did not survive Mr Wake's departure, and, indeed, the only feature imported from West Lancashire which gained universal approval was the excellent St. Helens-style destination layout with helpful 'via' blinds and large route numbers; immediately adopted as standard, the layout was applied to all future vehicles and, retrospectively, to the earlier Regent Vs, (106-135). A large, useful luggage rack was provided behind the staircase, and with their more shapely roof domes and deeper band of primrose between decks they were more handsome than the earlier deliveries.

During the 1963 reconstruction of Forster Square the Bradford Moor departure point was outside Kesslers' wool warehouse in Commercial Street, where AEC Regent V No. 142 with St. Helens-type destination layout was seen on 6th April. [Photo: Author

Vain were the repeated official reassurances that when the newness of the clutches, brakes and springs wore off, the buses would "settle down"; passengers knew a painful bruise when they saw one. Letters flew and embrocation sales boomed, especially when the Regent Vs began to roam far and wide.

When a Haworth Road resident protested that his district had to endure buses "only fit for the scrapyard" (he cited 'RT' No. 410 whose windows allegedly refused to close), and yearned for "the many new buses which appear to have been assigned solely to the Bradford Moor route", a long-suffering passenger volunteered to release his "first-rate new bus" if he could have his trolleybus back, whilst a Heaton passenger who had endured the Regent Vs for weeks added, "I have never travelled on buses like them. Let the Haworth Road people have them, and give us back our old ones. Let them have travel sickness and learn how to board and alight without an accident."

These sentiments were echoed by "All Shook Up" and "Disgusted with Bradford" ("... a curse to older folk cramped with rheumatism ... flung all over the place..."), while a rueful driver of ten years experience complained that, "Now some of my best friends won't speak to me !"

A graphic account of a lively ride on No. A126 on service 80 from Great Horton to Lister Park was provided by a lorry driver curious to sample one of the notorious 'YAKs'.

"On receiving the starting signal," he wrote, "he tore down Arctic Parade, engaging top gear within 100 yards (through the box from second). His speed was such on the bend that he was braking on and off to hold her back. Violent braking at the last moment at most stops throughout. At Four Lane Ends the lights held him – and he held the bus on the clutch ! On the amber light – off. A bus-length over the crossing on green. Stop at Squire Lane bottom, up the hill with the driver trying to coax it up in too high a gear, repeatedly dropping back into lower, then changing up when the governor cut the engine revs. Bus held at the top again on the clutch."

Had John Gilpin known of these remarkable rodeos he would never have written of his much less stirring ride from Edmonton to Ware !

Even more notoriety accrued for the AECs when the driver of Tyersal-bound A133 apparently suffered a blackout. The bus fled up Bowling Back Lane and across Sticker Lane, mounting the pavement and rocketing 150 yards over two boulder-strewn demolition sites before coming to rest on a 10ft high mound. It was probably the unusual angle (about 50°) at which the bus halted that alerted the passengers to a realisation that this was something more than a normal Regent V ride.

As late as 1971 a St. Enoch's Road resident threatened to report BCT to the Traffic Commissioners if these buses continued to afflict his area, and whenever misguided enthusiasts later requested the Transport Committee to sell them one, the author's response was invariably,

"Why stop at one ? Offer them as many as they will take !"

12 BINGLEY and CROSSFLATTS

In preparation for the next stage of the trolleybus conversion programme BCT applied for a licence to operate buses on the seven-mile route to Crossflatts (24) and its shortworkings to Bingley (26), Saltaire (25) and Frizinghall (27), and to restore the cross-city service to Bradford Moor (30).

The old enemy stirred. In due course West Yorkshire Road Car inspectors were observed surreptitiously checking the number of passengers carried by the trolleybuses, and BCT 'checkers' kept an equally vigilant eye on the company's buses. This time, however, the battle was to be fought on more equal terms, as the Traffic Superintendent (Mr Smith) had formerly worked for the company, and the new General Manager, Mr Edward Deakin from Chesterfield, was a shrewd and skilful negotiator despite being a courteous gentleman.

While the plans were being drawn up, control of the City Council reverted to the party which had governed it from 1945 to 1960. The incoming chairman, Councillor Laurie Dunne, himself a former trolleybus driver, favoured electric traction, as did his Committee. Discussions with the author revealed shared preferences for radical action, ie,

(i)   Retention of trolleybuses as far as Saltaire;
(ii)   A 'first-stop-Saltaire' motorbus service to Bingley and Crossflatts;
(iii)   Restoration of the Bradford Moor trolleybus service (the installations were still virtually intact);
(iv)   New trolleybus services to the Clayton and Allerton housing estates using material reclaimed from Bingley.

Although electricity charges were due to rise by 33%, the chairman considered efficiency more important than cost. But what could be done with the sixty Regent Vs on order ? The author suggested that part of the order could replace the 'RTs', the 1949 Leylands and defective vehicles from the 1-65 series, with the balance of the order being taken in the form of BUT trolleybuses (which of course were built by AEC). However, internal differences behind closed doors at the Town Hall stifled the plan at birth, and the conversion programme continued on its way.

A new form of timetable, more comprehensive than any since 1947, listed individual journeys and enabled passengers to deduce at a glance whether buses returning from Haworth Road and Sandy Lane would voyage via Smith Lane or Toller Lane, thus solving a thirty-year enigma ! Regrettably, lethargic drivers failed to make full use of the new destination layouts which enabled them to exhibit all the possible route permutations.

The remorseless onward march of city centre redevelopment had now moved to the area around the Town Hall, and at midday on 17th March 1963, a six-lane extension of Hall Ings was opened to traffic, replacing Union Street. The Wakefield Road services – Holme Wood

Where there's a space there's a bus . . . the not-yet opened northern carriageway of new Hall Ings was used as a parking place by Regent Vs Nos. 216 (left) and 158 on 17th May 1964. In the centre trolleybus 589 is about to depart for Tong Cemetery while in the remains of Union Street (site of the future Norfolk Gardens Hotel) a West Riding 'Wulfrunian' and a West Bowling Regent V await departure time.
[Photo: Author

(59), Bierley (60), West Bowling (88), Adwalton (77) and Tong (now 20) as well as the trolleybuses (17-19) were immediately transferred to the new thoroughfare.

For several years minor route changes were made as neighbouring Nelson, Norfolk and Town Hall Streets underwent alterations. Many of the changes were shortlived – none more so than the ill-advised removal of the Holme Wood (59) loading point to a location outside the 'Telegraph and Argus' buildings, whence harassed queues were promptly driven away by gleeful starlings.

A glimpse of motorbus luxury was provided early in 1963 by West Riding's 'Wulfrunians' on the Wakefield-Bradford service. With air suspension and entrance ahead of the front wheel, their riding qualities were immensely superior to anything that Bradford's latest purchases could offer.

Mr Kenneth Griffiths, Rolling Stock Engineer since 1958, left on receiving appointment as manager at Ashton, and was succeeded by Mr Alan Gurley from Aberdeen Corporation.

A request from Queensbury and Shelf UDC for a service into their Hungerhill estate was not considered worth pursuing, but Bradford's own large new estate at Allerton was undoubtedly in need of additional facilities. On 2nd June 1963 Regent V No. 164 began a new service (Allerton 35) up Allerton Road and along Saffron Drive to a terminus at Bell Dean Road. A year later it was merged into a new two-way circular service: Holme Wood-City-Thornton Road-Bell Dean Road (59), returning to City via Saffron Drive and Sunbridge Road and thence to West Bowling. A logical renumbering was carried out in 1966:–

Holme Wood-Allerton 5, Allerton-West Bowling 15 and City-Allerton (trolleybus) 16.

Holme Wood was fast becoming a rendezvous for many services. On 6th October 1963, the Bankfoot (via Heaton) 80 and Holme Wood (51) services were combined as a cross-city service (80) with buses routed via Leeds Road, Laisterdyke and Broad Lane, leaving Bowling Back Lane and Parsonage Road as the exclusive preserve of the Tyersal (52) buses.

The remaining trolleybus journeys to St. Enoch's Road Top (44) and Eccleshill (33) were taken over by motorbuses on 25th August 1963 and 1st November 1964 respectively.

Redevelopment of the city centre (1959-1973) was frequently punctuated by dangerous incidents resulting from carelessness, suspected arson or a secret desire to eliminate listed buildings which had outlived their original function. Scaffolding erected around condemned warehouses collapsed into the streets; tottering walls tottered prematurely; unexplained blazes gutted old wool stores and coping-stones inexplicably tumbled from rooftops.

Probably the most disruptive of all these calamities occurred on 18th May 1963 when a fire in old property in Union Street closed parts of Bridge Street, Hall Ings, Nelson Street and Norfolk Street from 2pm to 4.30pm. The Wakefield Road trolleybuses were temporarily replaced by motorbuses which, together with the Holme Wood (59),

Not quite ready . . . Regent V 164 lacked a proper destination display when it set out for Allerton (Saffron Drive) from Sunbridge Road on 2nd June 1963.   [Photo: Author

Bierley, West Bowling, Adwalton, Brighouse, Huddersfield, Dewsbury and Wakefield buses were diverted along streets still remaining open. Then, before the fire hoses had been removed from Town Hall Square a large coping stone plunged into nearby Victoria Square, dislodging a length of trolley wire but failing to interrupt services. For the Fire, Police and Transport Departments it was indeed an eventful afternoon.

As autumn approached the Traffic Commissioners granted licences for the Crossflatts-Bradford Moor buses, and Regent Vs 166-173 were therefore despatched by the makers. Identical to Nos. 136-165 except for an air-intake vent in the front dome, they were the first BCT buses to carry reversed registration marks (2166-2173 KW). The long-lived series of Bradford marks which had begun at the turn of the century with AK1, progressing through KU, KW and KY and variations thereof, had drawn to a close with YKY 999, recommencing with 1 KW in preference to 1 AK or 1 KU, presumably to avoid confusion with trade plates such as 164 KU used on BCT's AEC Matador recovery vehicle.

Hard on the heels of 166-173 came identical vehicles 174-195 which during the afternoon and evening of 31st October 1963 took possession of Saltaire depot, several of them somewhat tactlessly displaying the letters 'OIL' on their three-track number blind. Next morning they sallied forth to take up their new duties on the Crossflatts/Bingley/Saltaire to Bradford Moor service, the pre-1962 cross-city journeys having been restored. The first bus to venture forth was No. 191.

Six of the 'RTs' and two dozen trolleybuses were now redundant, though RT No. 423 together with AECs 30/32

and 40 and single-deckers 301/2 were soon seen on the Frizinghall (27) peak-hour shortworkings, as modern 30ft buses were unable to turn at the constricted Ashfield Avenue terminus.

Sensibly though tardily determined to recapture the passengers lost to West Yorkshire, the Corporation had reduced the number of bus stops between Saltaire and Crossflatts, and therefore felt able to invite the public to "Look at these timings! 26 minutes from Crossflatts to Forster Square!" (trolleybus 842 had in fact achieved the same timings with effortless ease a few days before the changeover).

Next, in preparation for the closure of Saltaire railway station Messrs Salts (Saltaire) Ltd, owners of Sir Titus Salt's world famous wool textile mill, asked BCT to divert an occasional bus down Victoria Road to their stately portals. Following a trial run with a Regent V on 19th June 1964, a peak-hour service was opened on 5th October with the aid of Nos. 144 and 171. Initially labelled 'Saltaire, 23' but later 'Shipley Glen', the buses worked through to Bradford Moor.

Consideration was also given to a service to Shipley Moorhead, either as a diversion of the Saltaire (25) workings or an extension of the Saltaire via Thackley (40) route when the trolleybuses were eventually superseded. Although the name was inserted on destination blinds, the proposal was not carried out.

Regent V No. 191 was the first arrival at Crossflatts when buses replaced trolleybuses on 1st November 1963.   [Photo: Author

The final intake of the seemingly endless cavalcade of Regent Vs began to reach Thornbury works in February 1964. Numbered 196-225, they dispensed with the exhaust brakes which had become a feature of the fleet, and the spartan interiors of their lightweight Orion bodies were improved by a welcome return to moquette upholstery in the lower saloon. Seat backs were a powder-blue formica which matched the plastic window-pans.

On 1st March the City Circle service finally absorbed and replaced the original Lister Park-Bankfoot bus service and the historic Bolton-Bankfoot trolleybus service operated since 1911. Clockwise journeys were now numbered 49 and anticlockwise 50, and the new facility which intersected every radial road in Bradford was understandably less punctual than its predecessors. On the same day the Undercliffe (66) and Canterbury Avenue (61) services were combined as a cross-city journey (61) via Great Horton Road. As a means of eliminating an awkward three-point turn in Parkside Road the West Bowling (15) route was extended to Springwood Gardens on 20th May.

In a display of co-operation BCT and Hebble installed a new design of bus-stop sign on all routes traversed by both operators except Queensbury and Shelf where the stops did not coincide. The BCT half of the sign was blue and the Hebble portion red, with white lettering.

Co-operation with Leeds was also in the air; for a Test Match at Headingley BCT and LCT ran a joint through service using each other's licences. Also at BCT's request, Leeds agreed to re-extend service 72 to Leeds Central Bus Station, but before the extension actually took place on 31st October 1965, buses departing from the traditional Infirmary Street terminus were diverted from congested Wellington Street into East Parade and the Headrow in April. Peak hour limited-stop buses between the two cities now displayed the route number 72L.

The rapid expansion of the motorbus routes necessitated alterations to the destination displays of the older vehicles so that they could operate on all routes, and the destination apertures (name and numeral) of AECs 1-40 and the Leylands were made smaller to accommodate more names; AECs 66-105 were similarly treated, though their twin-track number displays naturally needed no adjustment.

Below: A new combined BCT/Hebble bus stop sign in Allerton Road in 1964. [Courtesy J. H. Cheetham; photo J. Copland

Foot: During a decade of incessant change bus stops were continually on the move. In this November 1964 view the Leeds Corporation bus and Tyersal-bound Regent V No. 155 are standing in the newly-created Petergate with Forster Square in the distance. [Photo: Author

Above: AEC/Park Royal Renown low-height bus 7552 MX at Crossflatts on 18th April 1964. Despite its BCT-style livery it did not find favour in Bradford.

[Photo: Author

Below: Forerunner of a new generation of Daimlers, demonstrator 565 CRW painted in Edinburgh colours waits in Nelson Street while its driver decides whether to go to Birkenshaw or Huddersfield. Single-decker No. 302 passes one of Bradford's multitude of wool warehouses, while at the rear of the Town Hall a crane takes part in yet another excavation.

[Photo: Author

Thoughts now turned to vehicle specifications, as further buses would be needed as replacements for the ageing 'RTs' and the trolleybuses, and clearly something better than Regent Vs was called for. Various demonstrators were therefore borrowed for trials. First to arrive was an AEC Bridgemaster, 7552 MX, which traversed several routes during its visit in April 1964. Despite boasting air suspension on its rear axle it was considered little better than the Regent Vs, and after eleven days it was passed on to Hebble, who thoughtlessly used it on their Halifax-Bradford services where its pale blue and primrose livery (a hopeful hint to Bradford by AEC ?) caused confusion among the bus queues.

Three months later there appeared a vastly-superior product – 565 CRW, the first Daimler Fleetline seen in Bradford. With its handsome Edinburgh-style maroon and ivory Alexander body and quiet, civilised performance it created a first-class impression before migrating to Huddersfield. Within a few days the Fleetline was followed by a stylish Alexander-bodied Leyland Atlantean Mark II, SGD 669, whose bright Glasgow livery of orange, green and cream created a stir as it toured the city.

A series of Friday-only strikes of bus company employees in February 1965 had only a slight effect on BCT services; the Dewsbury (4) buses reverted to the Birkenshaw terminus when Yorkshire Woollen staff struck, but

a strike of Hebble crews on the joint Huddersfield workings was barely noticed, as Bradford and Huddersfield buses ran as usual.

Winter ice and snow caused many mishaps, the most serious occurring on 20th March 1965 when at the height of a blizzard Leyland 568 left the road and overturned into a snow-filled field near Norwood Green. Three passengers were slightly hurt but the bus was written off. Carelessness not climate claimed Leyland 50 when it attempted to squeeze under the ultra-low Mill Lane bridge outside Ludlam Street depot; schoolchildren on board were taken to hospital but released the same day, whereas the largely-wrecked upper deck was not repaired for months.

Cheap off-peak fares for pensioners were authorised for

the first time in April 1965. Half-fare travel was made available between 9.30am and 3.30pm every day except Saturday to pensioners in possession of a valid pass costing 1/- per annum, and as the cost of the scheme (£37,250) was provided from the Bradford rates, the concession was not available outside the city boundary.

The morning of 14th March 1965 ushered in the most extensive service alterations ever carried out in the city. Three new cross-city bus links were established:–

Stanningley (90) to Buttershaw (54) as new route 9
Newlands (91) to Buttershaw (55) as new route 10
Wrose-Manchester Road-Wibsey as new route 34
continuing to Fagley via Moore Avenue as new route 14
(superseding services 73/75/76 and 84)

Opposite page:

Upper: On a misty March day in 1965 Regent III No. 33 ascends Morley Street on its long climb to Queensbury. This panorama showing the domed Alhambra Theatre, the stately buildings in Victoria Square and the shadowy silhouette of the Town Hall (now City Hall) tower, was familiar to generations of Bradfordians, while the lamp standards were relics of the tramway era.   [Photo: Author

Foot: Colourful SGD 669, an Atlantean demonstrator in Glasgow livery, comes to rest outside Argus Chambers on its return from Leeds on 16th August 1964. On the left 'Tut's Tomb' – the former Thornbury/Stanningley waiting room – has been bulldozed for an extension of Bank Street to Hall Ings.   [Photo: Author

This page:

Below: The lower portion of Great Horton Road housed the Alexandra Hotel, Wallace Arnold's tour offices and – sixty-nine years earlier – Mr J. E. Tuke's pioneering Yorkshire Motor Car Co. Glimpsed on 13th March 1965, AEC No. 4 is journeying from Moore Avenue to Wrose.   [Photo: Author

Two services were extended:–
Canterbury Avenue to St. Enoch's Road Top (61)
Eccleshill (ex 33) to St. Enoch's Road (ex 44) extended to Horton Bank Top as service 43 and to Buttershaw as 44.

In addition Queensbury (53), Hollingwood Lane (58) and White Horse (57) were renumbered 11/12/13 respectively.

Other route numbers were re-grouped at a later date so that most of the Wakefield Road services were numbered 16-22 and the Haworth Road-Greengates workings 28/9, 32/33. The time-hallowed destination 'City' was superseded by the more logical 'City Centre'.

Mr Gurley, the Rolling Stock Engineer, moved to Yorkshire Traction in May 1965 and was replaced by Mr Bernard B. Browne who had been Engineer to Wallasey Corporation Transport.

In the same month the various trials with new types of bus bore ample fruit when tenders for no fewer than sixty vehicles were accepted. Staff and passengers were delighted to learn that the newcomers were to be a distinct improvement on recent acquisitions, ie

15 Daimler/Gardner forward entrance chassis
15 Leyland PD3A/2 forward entrance chassis
15 Daimler Fleetline rear-engine chassis
15 Leyland Atlantean rear-engine chassis.

The forward-entrance chassis, part of an order cancelled by Leeds, were to receive East Lancashire bodies whilst Metro-Cammell-Weymann (MCW) were to build the Fleetline and Atlantean bodies. The total value of the contracts was £438,540.

Before their arrival an attempt was made to improve the Regent Vs. Two AEC AV691 engines with monocontrol transmission were bought in July 1966, when No. 225 was

converted by AEC at their Nottingham depot and 224 at Thornbury works. Although their performance was undoubtedly improved, the cost of similarly converting Nos. 126-223 was prohibitive, and no further adaptations were attempted, although No. 167 was fitted with an experimental device in the fuel injection system as a means of reducing the aggressive shuddering to which the Regent Vs were particularly prone.

It seemed to be an accepted fact of life in the transport industry that whenever other operators sought to hire buses they were rarely allocated the best vehicles; thus, when Ministry of Transport inspectors condemned numerous Oldham Corporation buses as mechanically defective, Bradford lent Regent Vs 207/209 for a short period. Then, feeling that the bruised morale of the Regents might benefit from a cosmetic face-lift, BCT experimented with livery variations. Numbers 112, 143 and 144 emerged from Thornbury paintshop in April 1966 with a vast expanse of primrose extending from the bottom waistrail to the bottom of the upper deck windows; only the roof and lower deck panels were painted blue, which in the case of 144 was the deeper (Notts and Derby style) shade normally reserved for interiors. Public reactions varied:–

"Dazzling" – "A modern image" – "A touch of brightness" and, inevitably, "Would it matter if they were painted the proverbial sky-blue pink with yellow dots so long as we can travel in them comfortably, quickly and on time ?" Fortunately the Department believed that it did matter. When the gloss and newness wore off, the buses developed an insipid appearance, and the conventional tasteful livery of well-balanced blue and primrose separated by black beading was happily reinstated, providing a colourful contrast to the cheerful red and cream of Huddersfield, Halifax's unusual orange, off-white and apple green, the discreet two-tone green of Leeds and the assorted reds, maroons and greens of the companies.

Pending the arrival of the new stock, a dozen of the 1-40 series Regents IIIs (including 20/35, delicensed for two years) were thoroughly overhauled, their chassis steam cleaned (some at the Bowling chassis-cleaning plant and others by Halifax) and recertified in preference to newer East-Lancs Regents IIIs whose bodies had not stood the test of time.

Help was at hand, however, as the new forward-entrance Daimlers, 226-240, were received from East Lancashire's Neepsend works in the autumn of 1966. The first new Daimlers since 1950, they achieved instant

Unsure whether its experimental livery is inspiring or insipid, Regent V No. 143 poses for comment outside Saltaire Mill, terminus of the Shipley Glen route, on 30th March 1966.

[Courtesy J. H. Cheetham; photo J. Copland

popularity. Wholly comfortable, with smooth acceleration and handsome appearance, they sported mellow fluorescent lighting and a highly-attractive interior decor adopted as standard for all future orders – blue/grey tartan moquette upholstery downstairs and blue leather upstairs, mid-blue/grey weave-pattern formica seat backs and lining panels, and easily-cleaned white Darvic ceilings. They were divided between Saltaire and Ludlam Street depots and were quickly followed by the Leyland PD3A/2s, 241-255, virtually identical to the Daimlers apart from the St. Helens-type bonnet. The Leylands were housed at Bowling depot. Several of the new vehicles were equipped with external illuminated advertisement panels which achieved popularity for a few years.

Hard on their heels came Nos. 256 and 271, forerunners of a new generation of front-entrance rear-engine buses on which Bradford's livery took on an entirely new aspect. Number 256 was an Atlantean and 271 a Fleetline, distinguished from each other by their makers' emblems on the front panels and the rear engine shrouds borne by 256 and its companions, 257-270, but not by 271-285. All bore extremely well-designed MCW bodies with the latest 'wrap-round' front upper-deck windows and low platform entrances.

"They are very comfortable to ride in", observed Mr Deakin with justifiable pride, "People have told crews and inspectors, and if they had not liked them we would have heard about it. Bradford people are not slow to say when they don't like something !"

The Fleetlines joined their fellow Daimler CVG6s at Saltaire depot but rarely ventured up to Eldwick on account of the awkward reverse at the terminus; the Atlanteans took up service on the Allerton-Holme Wood and associated services.

Equivalent numbers of pre-1959 vehicles were scrapped or sold, and 30ft-long buses were at last permitted to operate on the Frizinghall (27) short-working, this time reversing into Ashfield Avenue before fighting their way back into Bradford Road through the hordes of traffic which were becoming an increasingly serious problem on Bradford's highways.

Warmly welcomed by Bradford passengers, East Lancs. bodied Daimler CVG6/30 No. 233 is passing Bradford Moor Park on 20th September 1966.　　　　　　　　　[Courtesy J. H. Cheetham; photo J. Copland

Built for Bradford's hills, this Leyland PD3A/2 climbs to the summit of Highgate, Heaton on its way to Bankfoot on 4th February 1967.   [Photo: Author

13 ELDWICK & DICK HUDSON'S

Meanwhile 'the Opposition' had over-reached themselves at last.

In February, 1962, Keighley Corporation as joint owners of Keighley-West Yorkshire had been so irritated by proposed service cuts on every route except that to Bradford (which, together with the equally lucrative Bradford-Baildon route, was reputed to subsidise all the rest) that they had resurrected their long-defunct Transport Committee to monitor the company's activities. The proposed cuts were abandoned.

Next, determined not to lose any passengers to BCT when motorbuses superseded the Bradford-Crossflatts trolleybuses, West Yorkshire had in December 1962, sought to extend their Eldwick-Bingley service into Bradford and to increase their Keighley-Bradford frequency from ten minutes to seven minutes.

To their surprise BCT promptly sought licences for a rival service to Eldwick, (the author urged the manager to seek licences not only for Eldwick but also for East Morton, Cottingley, Saltaire Mills, Shipley Fields and (in conjunction with Hebble) a Bradford-Bingley-Harden-Wilsden-Bradford circular) stressing nevertheless that

they would accept a WY limited-stop peak hours Eldwick service or, alternatively, an amalgamation of Hebble's Bradford-Wilsden-Bingley service with the existing W. Y. Bingley-Eldwick service, thus avoiding hostile competition. Judiciously the Traffic Commissioners authorised West Yorkshire to operate a peak-hour only Eldwick-Bradford service for a trial six-months period with a minimum fare to protect BCT.

Shortly afterwards West Yorkshire applied for an overall fares increase. Once again wrath and indignation erupted at Keighley, who pointed out the gross discrepancy between the Bradford-Crossflatts fare (11d for 7 miles) and the Crossflatts-Keighley fare (10d for 3 miles), caused by the company's monopoly in the Keighley area. Bingley UDC voted to support Bradford's services and to seek assistance from the West Riding Urban Districts Association. The Eldwick-Bingley fares increase was dropped.

O happy day ! Regent V No. 178 arrives in Station Square, Bingley on its inaugural journey to Eldwick on 6th March 1966.

[Photo: Author

Next, West Yorkshire opposed Bradford's application for buses to supersede the Crossflatts trolleybuses, and in turn Bradford opposed the renewal of the company's Bradford-Keighley-Skipton licence. Sensibly the Commissioners granted Bradford's application, whereupon the Corporation withdrew their counter-objection. And when West Yorkshire withdrew their bid to augment their Keighley-Bradford frequency, BCT cancelled their Eldwick application. The dust settled – briefly.

However, when the company's six-months trial of the peak-hour limited-stop Eldwick to Bradford journeys proved unprofitable, they sought removal of the licence restrictions. Determined not to be outflanked, the Corporation revived their rival Eldwick application. Not for the first time, and with Bingley's cordial support, they expressed willingness to take part in a joint service. The Corporation's bid was approved on 12th September 1964. West Yorkshire appealed – vainly – and by June 1965, the names 'Eldwick, Dick Hudson's, Shipley Glen and Shipley Moorhead' had been inserted into BCT bus destination blinds. The intended victim had become the victor.

Bowing to the inevitable, on 20th January 1966, West Yorkshire agreed to accept not only a joint service to Eldwick but also a BCT peak-hour Bingley express and full co-ordination between Bradford and Crossflatts. Bradford's blue buses began to negotiate the steep, winding lanes of Eldwick on driver familiarisation runs.

A feeling of quiet triumph was therefore savoured on Sunday, 6th March 1966, when for the first time a BCT bus, No. 178, rolled into the company's Bradford (Chester Street) bus station labelled 'Eldwick via Ferncliffe, 68A', to the mystification of casual beholders. On its inaugural journey it duly observed West Yorkshire stops as far as the City boundary (Firth Carr) and from Branch to Saltaire, new joint stops being used elsewhere. At Saltaire the depot staff came out to watch No. 178 pass by, but at Bingley Station Square a West Yorkshire inspector came on board to check tickets, which some of the passengers considered a great degradation !

At Eldwick (Beck Bottom) terminus Mr Smith (BCT Traffic Superintendent) observed the safe arrival of No. 178, which then returned to Bradford via Gilstead (68). Continuing the permutations, the bus set out again via Gilstead and Eldwick (68) to the windswept moorland hostelry of 'Dick Hudson's', 812ft above sea level, a familiar resort for hikers and partakers of 'ham and egg teas'.

Safely arrived at Eldwick terminus three inspectors – two BCT and one West Yorkshire – instruct the driver of No. 178 on the intricacies of the route while the conductor poses on the right of Mr J. Copland, contributor of many illustrations in this book.

[Photo: Author

The new service was unusual in several respects:–

(i) It was the first joint operation between BCT and Keighley-West Yorkshire Services Ltd. (who were operating on behalf of West Yorkshire);

(ii) Most of the buses were stabled at depots outside the city (ie Saltaire and Keighley);

(iii) Between Eldwick and Dick Hudson's there were no fixed stopping places;

(iv) The fares were higher than for any comparable route served by BCT, ie,

Bradford to Eldwick 1/8d and Dick Hudson's (8 miles) 1/10d,

Bradford to Leeds (9° miles) 1/-

Bradford to Dewsbury (11 miles) 1/4d

Bradford to Huddersfield (12 miles) 1/9d

– between Bingley and Dick Hudson's company fare scales applied, and at Eldwick two consecutive stops were both fare stages !

The new joint stop signs, attractive in red (for West Yorkshire), blue (for BCT) and white (lettering and border) placed both operators on an equal basis at long last.

The forty-year battle was almost over, though West Yorkshire continued to cajole BCT to sell their operating rights beyond Saltaire – to which the author, when he became a Transport Committee member, invariably retorted, "Over my dead body !" and discussed with Mr Deakin ways of running Bradford buses to Keighley and even Skipton !

The express service to Bingley (26X) was launched on 7th March, again by No. 178, operating four inward journeys at the morning peak and four outward journeys at teatime; the only stops were at Hallfield Road, Park Gates, Frizinghall, Saltaire and Cottingley Bridge. Simultaneously the Saltaire Mills (23) schedule became an all-day facility under its new name of 'Shipley Glen'.

Returning to Chester Street bus station for its first venture to Dick Hudson's, No. 178 is flanked by two West Yorkshire buses – one of them distinctly battered.   [Photo: Author

14 THROUGH ALL THE CHANGING SCENES

An interesting extension of the popular 'See Your City' tours began in the summer of 1966 when by mutual arrangement Leeds Corporation provided tours to Bradford's Bolling Hall and Lister Park while BCT buses conveyed holidaymakers to Adel, Kirkstall Abbey, Roundhay Park and Templenewsam in Leeds.

On the evening of 3rd June 1966, the Hebble Motor Services Queensbury to Harecroft bus made its final run. Locally known as "T' Flyer", it had operated a useful rural service since 1928, working in its heyday from Duckworth Lane to the Raggalds Inn via Wilsden, Black Dyke Lane, Egypt, Walls of Jericho, Rock and Heifer, Back Heights, Thornton, Old Road, Chat Hill, Yews Green, Queensbury (High Street) and Mountain. Providing a delightful ride, especially on a hay-scented summer evening, its passing was greatly mourned, although as Hebble pointed out, it had long since ceased to pay its way.

But as the high uplands of Thornton were now devoid of public transport, Hebble were persuaded by Councillor J. Buffham to attempt a three-months trial with a twice-weekly circular journey to the Hill Top area. Adequate

support was not forthcoming, and Hebble finally withdrew at the end of September, when an appeal to BCT was rejected on the grounds of the difficulty and expense of diverting the Thornton trolleybus route – a truly absurd excuse, as no one would ever have contemplated despatching trolleybuses to such a sparsely populated area – and the high cost (ie unprofitability) of using motorbuses.

Understandably dissatisfied, the villagers requested the attendance of the chairman (Councillor Sissling) at a public meeting where they learned that although in the distant future housing development at Hill Top might warrant a good bus service, at present the area barely merited a taxi service. The protesters could legitimately have enquired why Tong Village with its smaller population qualified for a twice or thrice daily service while Hill Top

An eighteen-year-old Leyland PD2 was not the most inspiring vehicle to replace the Wakefield Road trolleybuses. Number 564 is seen at Tong Cemetery terminus on its first (official) arrival on 2nd April 1967.
[Photo: Author

did not, but in the patient Bradford manner they waited until West Yorkshire agreed to divert an occasional Denholme/Keighley (56/57) bus up West Lane and Hill Top Road, which they began to do on 3rd May 1970.

A year or two later at the request of the author the Committee visited Hill Top Road and the farthest reaches of Thornton Road near Denholme Gate – in a Regent V – before agreeing that the then current arrangements were adequate.

In the meantime Hebble had passed into the hands of the State-owned Transport Holding Company, a move which prompted a request from Halifax to be allowed to acquire the THC's part-ownership of the services in their area. The request received a firm refusal.

For several years the Bradford trolleybus network had been enjoying a welcome reprieve. The urgent need to replace worn-out motorbuses, delays in deliveries of new vehicles and the unwillingness of the Committee to discard the Tong Cemetery/Holme Wood trolleybuses until the reconstruction of Wakefield Road made it unavoidable had obliged BCT to renovate and improve the trolleybus fleet.

However, events beyond their control impelled the Department to recommence the conversion programme. Hardly had the bulldozers and pneumatic drills appeared in Wakefield Road when a major electrical fault rendered the Dudley Hill sub-station hors de combat. From 1st March 1967 motorbuses, usually Leyland PD2s, supplemented the trolleybuses on weekdays. Full licences having been obtained, motorbuses took over both routes permanently on 1st April, vehicles once more being supplied from Bowling depot as in tramcar days.

As the highway works progressed all the Wakefield Road services became subject to alterations, and the road – or what remained of it – was closed from 22nd September 1968 to 3rd May 1970, during which time the Dewsbury (4), Holme Wood (17), Tong Cemetery (18), Adwalton (19) and Tong (20) buses were diverted via Manchester Road, Croft Street, Paley Road and suburban side-streets to Fenby Avenue, Sticker Lane, Rooley Lane and Rook Lane, with various permutations.

Permutations of a different kind befel the Bankfoot-Holme Wood (80) buses in September 1967 when bridges at the extremities of the route – in Beckside Road and Tyersal Lane – were simultaneously declared weak, and for a month journeys were made via Spencer Road/Grange Road and Cutler Heights Lane/Holme Wood Road.

Emergencies resulting from causes natural and unnatural continued to harass the Department. Wishful to be rid of Kassapians' splendid warehouse adjoining Exchange Station, British Railways sought permission for its demolition, but the Corporation, slowly becoming aware of the architectural losses over which it had presided for so long, refused consent. On the night of 17th March 1968, sixty tons of coping stones fell to earth, causing the diversion of all bus services from Hall Ings into Vicar Lane and Church Bank; the Thornton trolleybuses reversed at the Ritz and Britannia House where they connected with a temporary City-Thornbury motorbus service. The warehouse was hurriedly demolished amid rumours that

shadowy figures armed with crowbars had been glimpsed on the parapets. Then on 2nd July a tremendous storm flooded the city centre for two hours; every service had to be curtailed, and trolleybus 734, caught in 'heavy seas' at Bank Street was hauled to dry land by the ever-ready AEC Matador waggon. Shortly afterwards Leyland PD2 567 paid the ultimate price for its superior mobility by suffering decapitation on an unauthorised venture beneath a low bridge in Bowling Back Lane.

By mid-1967 the motorbus fleet embodied an interesting mixture of old and new, dispersed between the six depots:–

Horton Bank Top	: AEC/MCW Regent IIIs 1-4, 7-14, 16-20, 22	= 18
Bowling	: Leyland PD2s 560/1, 572/3, 45/9, 54/7/9, 62/3,	
	Leyland PD3s 241-255, Atlanteans 256-270	= 41
Bankfoot	: AEC/MCW Regent IIIs 24/9, 31/3/5/8/9, 40	
	AEC/E.Lancs Regent IIIs 68, 71/2, 81-6, 90	
	AEC Regent Vs 106-111, 113-121, 139	= 34
Thornbury	: AEC Regent Vs 141-152, 170-180	
	Leyland PD2s 554-9, 562-7, 570	= 36
Ludlam Street	: AEC 'RTs' 401-5, 407-9, 410/1/3/5/6/7/9,	
	421/2/3/5	
	AEC Regent Vs 112, 122-5, 126-138, 140,	
	153-169, 181-225	
	Daimler CVG6s 234-240;	
	AEC Reliances 501/2	= 108
Saltaire	: Daimler CVG6s 226-233	
	Daimler Fleetlines 271-285	= 23
	Total	260

The Reliances had been re-numbered from 301/2 in March 1967 to create space for further deliveries of new stock, and several old Regent IIIs and PD2s were stored for possible rehabilitation. On 25th-27th October 1967, an AEC Swift demonstration single-decker, LYY 827D, was tried on the Holme Wood/Tong Cemetery (17/18) routes, and orders were placed for an interesting variety of vehicle types:–

5	AEC 36ft-long Swift single-deckers	(503-7)
5	Leyland 36ft-long Panther single-deckers	(508-512)
15	Leyland Atlanteans	(286-300)
15	Leyland PD3A/12s	(301-315)
20	Daimler Fleetlines	(316-335)

In anticipation of early delivery, BCT decided not to renew the Certificates of Fitness of the 'RTs', Leyland PD2s and MCW-bodied Regent IIIs when they expired, but the bodybuilders warned that they were so heavily committed to export orders that deliveries could not be guaranteed. Only one tender was received for the single-deck bodies, and at the request of Metro-Cammell the contract for the Fleetline bodies was transferred to W. Alexander and Co (Coachbuilders) Ltd of Falkirk, whose products were as yet unknown in Bradford but who had successfully tendered for the fifteen PD3A/12 bodies. The overhauling of the trolleybuses therefore continued and the Fleetline chassis had to be stored in Thornbury depot for five months.

A trickle of new buses finally began in October 1968 when Atlantean 289 and Fleetline 317 arrived simultaneously and appeared in service on routes not previously served by rear-engined buses. The Atlanteans (286-300) were identical to 256-270 except that engine

Above: Modern motorbus comfort at last. MCW-bodied Leyland Atlantean No. 258 deposits three satisfied customers in Allerton Road on 1st March 1967.   [Photo: Author

Below: Awaiting inspection by the Transport Committee, MCW-bodied Leyland Atlantean No. 292 and Daimler Fleetline No. 321 with its shapely Alexander body were photographed inside Thornbury works by the *Yorkshire Post* in October 1968.

shrouds were omitted and two-piece wide gliding doors were used in preference to the previous four-piece jack-knife type. The Fleetlines (316-335) with their deeply-domed Alexander bodies provided a new standard of passenger comfort, with their Smith's combined heating and ventilation system and extra-wide bodies of the newly-authorised 8ft 2°in dimension.

Justifiably proud of their fine acquisitions the manager and the Lord Mayor, Alderman E. Newby, OBE, despatched Fleetline 335 with suitable destination displays to Bradford's twin city of Roubaix on the occasion of its 500th anniversary in June 1969.

Of the PD3s (301-315) and single-deckers (503-512) there was no sign whatever, and so the few remaining 1949-50 AECs and Leylands summoned up strength for further service to their city.

The fleet now comprised about 260 motorbuses and 74 trolleybuses, of which 227 and 67 respectively were in daily use. Covering up to 800 miles a week, each motorbus received a weekly brake-check and a complete check every 10,000 miles; bodies were overhauled every two years, but most chassis overhauls were now carried out by contractors. The platform staff numbered 547 drivers and 552 conductors, backed by 428 maintenance staff at Thornbury works and the depots – craftsmen, fitters, electricians, painters, coachbuilders, sheetmetal workers, trimmers, etc. It was likely that staff numbers would decrease if one-man-operation – for which the single-deckers were intended – could be introduced as in Halifax, Huddersfield and Manchester, but the unions were taking a cautious attitude. Industrial relations were a little fragile: services were suspended for an hour on 24th July 1968 while the 'busmen' attended a TGWU meeting at which they voted 1,000 to 1

in favour of strike action if national negotiations for a £1 rise were unsuccessful, whereupon the City police warned BCT to place all serviceable vehicles under lock and key at night, with the result that the Works, the 'Tin Shed' and the 'Far West' had to disgorge derelict stock awaiting disposal. The crisis passed peacefully, however, and as a goodwill gesture the Department allowed all motorbus depots except Bankfoot and Ludlam Street to close on Christmas Day, skeleton services being provided until 6.0pm.

Heavy snowfalls some weeks later caused delays and much minor damage; one of the Daimler CVG6s was left stranded in open country above Eldwick where opportunist gentlemen made off with the battery before the bus was dug out next day.

By this time the latest Atlanteans (286-300) had taken up residence at Bowling depot whilst Fleetlines 316-325 were working from Bankfoot on the City Circle (renumbered from 30th March 1969, as route 1 (anticlockwise) and 2–(clockwise); Nos. 326-336 regularly worked the Leeds (72) service on which they were matched by Leeds Atlanteans.

In April the Leyland PD3A/12s ordered eighteen months previously put in a belated appearance. They were in fact the last PD3s ever built and the last forward-engined buses bought by BCT, and with their Alexander bodies, St. Helens-type bonnet and one-piece lower saloon rear windows they were distinctive and unusual. All were

Alexander-bodied Leyland PD3A No. 313 passes Illingworth's factory at Shelf – formerly Victoria Mills where Bradford's last steam tram had been photographed nearly seventy years earlier.

[Photo: Author

allocated to Bankfoot depot, when the last of the 'RTs' retained to cover winter emergencies were withdrawn after a decade of excellent service to their adopted city.

When AEC/MCW Regent IIIs 7 and 13 bade farewell to Horton Bank Top depot in April an era ended, as they were the last survivors of the 1-20 series which had served the Horton routes continuously since the trams were withdrawn twenty years earlier. They were replaced by monocontrol Regent Vs 106/7/8, the first forward-entrance vehicles at Horton Bank Top. Valiant No. 13, the last of a magnificent breed, was finally withdrawn on 25th October when the long-awaited single-deckers arrived.

AEC Swift No. 503, the first service single-decker bought for forty years, made its gleaming debut at an exhibition in Harrogate on 10th August, and No. 505 was launched on the City Tour two days later. The five Leyland Panthers began prowling around the City in October, No. 510 having been glimpsed on test on 5th September. Both types bore Marshall bodies with front entrance and centre

exit, and the floor rose towards the rear where the engine was situated, thus ensuring good visibility for all passengers. As they were primarily intended for stage-carriage work their seats were closely spaced, which caused much discontent to long-legged people, especially when they were used for private hire – indeed, the Corporation's Development Committee returned almost apoplectic from a cramped 160-mile round trip to Blackpool. The Panthers were distinguishable by the wire-mesh grille in the front panel and, unfortunately, by some mechanical unreliability. All were set to work on the Undercliffe-St Enoch's Road (61), Woodside (83) and Haworth Road (27-9, 32) services based on Ludlam Street.

Sadly, even before the single-deckers arrived they were already 'white elephants'. In their quest for one-man operation BCT had bought them with union approval, only to find that one-man operation of double-deckers was now acceptable. Twenty 33ft-long Fleetlines and thirty similar Atlanteans had therefore been ordered; the Fleetline order

'Bradford Means Business' was the motto of the day when AEC Swift No. 503 was proudly displayed at Harrogate in August 1969.
[Photo: Author

Futuristic Provincial House was arising from the wreckage of Thornton Road and Tyrrel Street when Leyland Panther No. 508 set out for St. Enoch's Top on 31st January 1970.
[Photo: Author

was later doubled, leaving only twenty buses still to be bought to bring the era of trolleybuses to a close.

As part of the process of drawing up detailed specifications for the new order the Department borrowed a 33ft Atlantean demonstrator, MTF 665G. With its 79-seat Park Royal front entrance/centre-exit body it was the largest bus hitherto seen in Bradford, and incorporated novel features such as upper-deck periscopes, electronic passenger counter operated by a stair tread, and a public address system, all of which were demonstrated as the unusual bus in its tasteful 'Notts and Derby' blue and ivory livery worked the Dewsbury (4), Bierley (21) and Huddersfield (64) routes.

During the autumn of 1969 the redevelopment of the central area advanced towards the Alhambra Theatre. Victoria Square and lower Manchester Road were superseded by Princes Way, and Regent V No. 144 was the last bus to traverse Town Hall Square before it was transformed into The Tyrls.

From time immemorial (or, in Bradford's case 1926 !) journeys on 'the last bus home' at night had often been enlivened by harmless merriment, occasional bursts of inharmonious song and amateur entertainment such as 'playing the spoons', all of which were the genial sequel to the over-enthusiastic consumption of 'pints, gills and drams' in city centre hostelries. Sadly, towards the end of the 'sixties – the 'Affluent Era' – geniality all too often degenerated into truculence and physical assault.

Understandably unwilling to tolerate attacks on their members the unions decreed a one-month curfew on weekend travel, and from 13th December 1969 all buses returned to depot from 9pm on Fridays, Saturdays and Sundays, which in practice meant, for instance, that the last Brighouse departure was at 7.33pm and the last Wrose departure only seven minutes later. Cinemas, public houses and bingo halls were deserted; the Alhambra Theatre lost £100 a night and the manager of the Victoria Hotel complained that "the place has been like a morgue" (a North American term denoting a mortuary). Many frustrated revellers hitch-hiked home, and by 11pm there was not a taxi to be had.

As a precautionary measure BCT began to fit Pye two-way radios to the buses.

Twin-entrance Leyland demonstrator MTF 665G attracts interest as it leaves for Dewsbury on 19th July 1969. The vacant site on the left was being prepared for the future Interchange.

[Photo: Author

15   HANDS OFF BRADFORD !

Under the heading 'Private and Confidential' the Ministry of Transport circulated a nineteen-page document to transport operators early in 1967 in which the Minister (Mrs Barbara Castle, MP) explained her desire for integrated transport regions in which buses and trains would be co-ordinated and local railway services subsidised by a regional authority which would raise its funds by a compulsory levy (precept) on the local councils.

At the Minister's request a Yorkshire and Humberside Passenger Transport Co-ordinating Committee was established, but the only local authority represented on the Committee was Leeds, and its chairman was a Leeds alderman. Huddersfield, Hull, Doncaster and Grimsby/Cleethorpes were suggested as pilot areas.

In Bradford (and elsewhere) concern mounted quickly, as compensation to existing operators for loss of their undertakings was to be limited to their outstanding capital debt, which in practice meant that Bradford would receive nothing whereas Leeds, having 'piled up a huge debt' as a matter of policy, would be handsomely compensated. Moreover, railway losses in the four 'mini-regions' were known to be about £10,000,000.

Formally publishing her White Paper on 5th December 1967 as a prelude to a Transport Bill, the Minister announced her intention of establishing Passenger Transport Authorities and Executives (PTAs and PTEs) in Tyneside, Merseyside, the West Midlands and the Manchester area and, at a later date, in other areas where transport needed planning and integration. The PTAs were to comprise some local councillors as well as Ministry nominees, and could decide to operate a break-even basis or subsidise services from local rates.

In addition the Minister proposed to:–
 (i)   convert the Transport Holding Co into a National Bus Company,
 (ii) give Exchequer grants of 75% for development and Bus Grants of 25% for new one-man-operated vehicles,
 (iii) allow local authorities to grant concessionary fares,
 (iv) increase fuel tax relief by 3d a gallon and reduce bus drivers' working time by three hours a week.

Not surprisingly in Bradford Councillor Sissling viewed with misgivings the enormous increase in Government intervention in local transport; if a PTA were to be inflicted upon the West Riding, Bradford's rates would have to rise by up to 9d in the £ merely to cover the railway losses. His fears were echoed by Wallace Arnold but not by Ilkley UDC who optimistically believed that as Ilkley's railway was 'now almost breaking even', the question of a subsidy might not arise !

More broadly-based comment came from the 'Bradford Transport Review' whose editor, in an analysis of the proposed PTA/PTEs concluded that:–

'Possibly such bodies may be desirable in the Manchester, Glasgow and Birmingham areas, but the West Riding hardly seems to lend itself to schemes of this kind, as the transport-operating boroughs – Bradford, Halifax, Huddersfield, Leeds, Doncaster, Rotherham and Sheffield – are sufficiently far from each other to have a distinct and separate network of services which would derive no benefit from integration.

Finances and working conditions vary considerably . . . integration would inevitably extend the scope of local disputes. . . . If, however, the outcome was that Bradford, instead of being swallowed up, was given control or joint control of all services radiating from Bradford . . . then some advantage could be gained through the elimination of the wasteful competition which has hampered our municipal enterprise for the last forty years. Perhaps the latter solution is too optimistic, however, and we would echo the Transport Committee's demand – Hands off Bradford !'

Invited to see for herself, the Transport Minister unhesitatingly agreed that the West Riding was not suitable for a PTA/PTE, and the threat vanished.

Spontaneous rationalisation was nevertheless in the air. Concerned by the Government's plans Messrs Samuel Ledgard, operators of services from Bradford to Harrogate via Menston, Bradford to Leeds via Pudsey – etc – and purchasers of the B&B company thirty years earlier, had sold out to West Yorkshire who in turn had resold the Bradford-Pudsey-Leeds service to Leeds Corporation. Unwilling to see a service within their operating area wholly owned by their neighbour, Bradford made a bid for a half share in the route, but Leeds, seizing the opportunity of exacting revenge for Bradford's long-standing refusal to change its half share of the revenue from route 72 to a 5-4 split in favour of Leeds, graciously conceded to BCT the operating rights within their own city but retained the whole of the rights within the intervening borough of Pudsey thereby restricting Bradford to a 1/6th share of the service and 1/3rd of the revenue. (By comparison, the division of revenues on the other joint services were: Route 64 equally shared: Route 68/68A allocated per mileage run: on Route 4 BCT and YWD exchanged occasional journey to balance mileage or overcome staff shortages.)

Ledgard's buses made their last runs on 14th October 1967 and next morning the new joint service (78) opened

Bradford on 4th March 1967 – new Daimler Fleetline No. 283 passes through Cheapside en route for Crossflatts. The background includes the late-Victorian Post Office and the mediaeval Cathedral tower.

[Photo: Author

between Bradford (Chester Street) and Leeds (Park Place) by way of Manchester Road, Croft Street, Vicar Lane, Leeds Road, Galloway Lane, Pudsey, Hough Side Lane and Whitehall Road. The fare was 1/8d and the journey time 47 minutes. As the name 'Pudsey' was initially confined to the destination blinds of Regent Vs 126-135, Bradford's first bus was No. 134, which met its Leeds counterpart (590) in the previously unknown hinterland of Hough Side. Ten months later the Regents were supplanted by Daimlers 234-240 and on 8th September 1968 the two termini were removed to (New) Hall Ings, Bradford, and Leeds Central Bus Station.

A third link with Leeds, called 'Fastaway' opened on 6th September 1971, with four journeys at the morning and evening peak-hours. Originally intended as service X72 it was actually launched as 272 with only eight stops and a journey time of less than half an hour. All the buses were single-deckers, but whereas the LCT vehicles were 'one-manners' Bradford's carried conductors.

Until recent years the traditional shackles on municipal expansion had been firmly maintained. In the Midlands Walsall Corporation had managed to gain 'back-door' access to Birmingham only by linking one of its local

services with that of a private operator, but now the regulations were being relaxed, and wider opportunities were beckoning at last.

An even grander scheme then unfolded. Far away in the south of Yorkshire the little Mexborough and Swinton Company proposed a network of inter-town services along the new M1 motorway which was due to open in the autumn of 1968. Huddersfield and Halifax launched a joint service to Sheffield by virtue of their Joint Omnibus Committee status, although Huddersfield later withdrew from the service as part of a bargain whereby the JOC was sold to the Corporation. A consortium of interested parties was formed, comprising Mexborough, Sheffield JOC, Rotherham Corporation, Yorkshire Woollen, Yorkshire Traction, West Riding and Hebble, and a service from Sheffield to Bradford via Dewsbury was agreed upon. On learning of this, Bradford notified the consortium that as the service would enter BCT's operating area at Birkenshaw, Bradford would have to be admitted as a partner in the venture.

With some reluctance the point was conceded, and Bradford duly received formal consent for operation in such exotic locations as the Rural District of Wortley, the Urban Districts of Dodsworth, Rothwell, Heckmondwike, Rawmarsh, Swinton and Mexborough, the Boroughs of Ossett, Batley, Spenborough and Brighouse and the County Boroughs of Dewsbury, Barnsley, Rotherham, Sheffield, Halifax and Leeds – thus covering every possible permutation of route.

More prosaically the Bradford portion (4 miles)

constituted less than a tenth of the whole; BCT were therefore entitled to not more than one journey per week, and sensibly decided to 'accumulate' mileage until they became entitled to operate a bus for a whole week in place of a Yorkshire Woollen duty. In practice therefore the Corporation contented themselves with issuing joint publicity and a new range of tickets – which with values of up to 6/6d were the highest ever issued by BCT. Nevertheless the names of 'Sheffield', 'Barnsley', and 'Mexborough' duly appeared on the destination displays of all future BCT buses, and as the Department was liable to provide 'change-overs' in case of a breakdown, single-deckers 503-512 were made available and were occasionally used.

'Only twelve bob – 12 shillings (12/-) – return and about 95 minutes travelling time . . . luxury coach comfort and speeds of around 70 mph on the motorway,' enthused the reporter who sampled the trial run on 14th October 1969. Under the title of 'White Rose Express' (X33) the daily service began four days later, the regular operators being Sheffield and Yorkshire Woollen. As the expresses accomplished the journey in half the time taken by the previous stage-carriage facility (ruefully described by a user as 'A bed-and-breakfast affair') they were well received, although patronage was moderate at first.

A new approach to the problem of assaults on bus crews was made in April 1970, when Regent V 144 received cab-controlled klaxons and flashing lamps on its front and rear domes, but when a practical test of the alarms in the middle of Town Hall Square was totally ignored by passers-by, all buses from No. 106 upwards began to receive two-way radios with a short aerial on the front dome.

Although the 1968 Transport Act had largely by-passed Bradford its restriction on drivers' permitted hours took effect on 1st March. On behalf of BCT the Ministry of Labour scoured the district in an attempt to recruit another ninety drivers but their efforts were largely fruitless, and forty-two services had to be reduced outside the peak-hour. The Queensbury (11) schedules were linked with the Stanningley-Buttershaw (9) through workings, and the Clayton services were reorganised with the bus journeys (36) being extended from Thornaby Drive to the top of The Avenue and the trolleybuses (37) reverting from the latter point to their original terminus at Town End on 31st May.

The first of the 33ft-long Daimler Fleetlines were licensed on 1st August 1970. Their striking Alexander bodies with front entrance and centre exit presented an avant-garde appearance; angular 'peaks fore and aft' replaced the traditional curved roof domes; windscreens were recessed, and primrose paint was much in evidence. With one-man operation in view BCT had specified upper-

First municipal successor to Ledgard's buses, Regent V No. 134 stands in Chester Street bus station before exploring the hinterland of Pudsey.
[Photo: Author

deck periscopes and upper-deck seat-availability counters monitored by sensors on the stair treads; the space between the two doors was occupied by luggage racks and the staircase. Initially allocated to Thornbury depot the impressive vehicles took up service on the Holme Wood/ Tong Cemetery (17-18), Bradford Moor-Crossflatts (23-26) and Stanningley-Queensbury/Buttershaw (9-11) services after No. 402 had been exhibited at the Commercial Motor Show. Their arrival was timely, as buses were having to supplement the Bolton Road (40-42) trolleybuses during a temporary spare parts shortage; no less than nineteen Regent Vs were due for re-certification and five Atlanteans were immobilised by transmission troubles and recurring strikes at the Leyland factory – indeed, No. 258 had been off the road for half a year, No. 259 had languished outside Bowling depot for months, and others had been returned to the makers for repairs.

Sadly, the new high-capacity buses did not receive the popularity which they deserved. Passengers disliked the unusually difficult step height; the staff refused to allow the extra standing accommodation and unilaterally altered the interior notices from '18' to a mere '8', and despite previous acceptance of one-man-operation on two-door 33ft vehicles the unions decided that they were too long and that the drivers' view of the exit door was insufficient. 'One-manning' was therefore postponed once more, to the irritation of the Leeds manager who threatened to introduce one-man-operation on his share of services 72, 78 and 272 !

Not surprisingly therefore, the chief business of the Transport Executive Group, post-1967 successors to the Transport Committee, on 5th June 1970 (the first attended by the author) was a careful consideration of tenders for new vehicles ie the twenty buses destined to replace the last trolleybuses. In view of the unions' attitude a reversion to 30ft bodies was clearly necessary, and tenders had been invited from Daimler, Leyland and Bristol Commercial Vehicles, though the last-mentioned had not troubled to quote. Daimler offered chassis with Leyland engines for delivery in 18/20 months or with Gardner engines in 34 months, while Leyland offered Leyland-engined chassis in 30/31 months. Unanimous choice favoured the Daimler, to the satisfaction of the author who, while accepting the inevitability of Leyland engines nevertheless hankered after the fine Gardner 6LX units if delivery dates improved.

AEC Swift No. 506 won a cup for the smartest and most mechanically-proficient vehicle of its class at the Huddersfield Commercial Vehicle Rally on 27th July 1970, to the delight of the Transport Executive Group who had received few cheerful tidings that year. Leyland Panther

Thirty-three feet long Daimler Fleetline No. 404 displays its front entrance and centre exit at Bradford Moor terminus, August 1970; the space between the doors was reserved for luggage and standing passengers. Tailed by 30ft Fleetline No. 272 it is occupying the loading space allocated to the Thornbury-Thornton trolleybuses on services 6 and 7.   [Senior Transport Archive; photo: Robin Hannay

No. 509 was loaned to British Railways a fortnight later.

In support of a demand for a £20 minimum weekly wage the staff staged a series of Fridays-only strikes in September and October, these being the first complete stoppages since 1926. No Leeds or company buses ran into the city, although Huddersfield buses approached as far as Bailiff Bridge; as the strikes continued, West Yorkshire recommenced their services into Bradford but did not pick up. The public were remarkably unperturbed; the weather continued fine, Bingley railway station platforms welcomed unprecedented crowds, and the Aire Valley trains ran 'packed to the doors'.

No sooner had the dispute been resolved with a pay increase of 33/- per week – necessitating another fares application in addition to an increase already imposed on 21st September – than the union presented a further demand for a 17/- increase. In December 1970 the electricity workers reinforced their own claim for a 30% wage rise by imposing selective power cuts without notice, thus randomly disrupting the trolleybus services. Every available motorbus was therefore kept on stand-by, although the old PD2s were no longer available, No 573 having retired with a cracked cylinder on 30th November, thus breaking a link with the C. R. Tattam era, as it was the last tram-replacement vehicle and the last exposed-radiator bus. Sturdy if uninspiring, the PD2s had served Bradford worthily for a whole generation.

'Decimalisation Day' – a D-Day less welcome than its wartime namesake – took place on 21st February 1971 on BCT buses. During the preceding week 'old' coins had to be tendered in multiples of 6d, change being given in 'new' pence. Passengers were obliged to learn new values and colours:–

4d fare now 2p (yellow ticket)	1/2 fare now 7p (red ticket)
7d fare now 3p (green ticket)	1/3d fare now 8p
9d fare now 4d (blue ticket)	1/5d fare now 9p
10d fare now 5p (white ticket)	1/6d fare now 9p
11d fare now 5p (white ticket)	1/7d fare now 10p
1/- fare now 6p	1/8d fare now 10p
1/1 fare now 6d	

with a 1p orange ticket for multiple issues eg two 3p and one penny tickets for a 7p fare.

Broadway, the fine thoroughfare opened 37 years previously as a much-needed link between Forster Square and Town Hall Square, fell prey to the city planners when it closed for pedestrianisation, (a new word which caused amusement to those who encountered it for the first time) on 6th March 1971. The cross-city services were transferred to Market Street which, even in the uncongested days of twenty years previously had been deemed too narrow for buses !

16   **A BUSY WEEKEND**

The long campaign to eliminate Hebble took the form of accidental 'direct action' when trolleybus 724 rammed a Hebble bus in Little Horton Lane in October 1970. Hebble struck back by writing off trolleybus 801 in the same thoroughfare two months later, but these gallant skirmishes were the last of their kind, as Hebble's day was almost done.

Since 1969 the little company had become increasingly dependent on its sister company, West Yorkshire, for vehicles and depot accommodation, and on 3rd May, 1970, West Yorkshire had taken over the services from Duckworth Lane to Bingley and Bradford to Bingley via Allerton and Wilsden as well as Hebble's share of the Bradford-Huddersfield (64) route.

Over in Halifax the enterprising Corporation and JOC manager (Mr G. G. Hilditch) and at least one member of Bradford's Transport Executive Group (TEG) were determined that drastic change should come. Following a discreet exchange of memos the Halifax-Bradshaw-Queensbury timings were adjusted so that scheduled connections could be made with BCT's Queensbury (11) service, and from that moment pressure was exerted. On 28th July 1970 the TEG voted to negotiate with Halifax and Hebble, as the latter were no longer able to guarantee regular services (they were obliged to borrow three Halifax buses a few months later) whereas the Corporations were able and willing – and threatening to provide an impromptu through service by the expedient of 'running on each

other's licences'. A satisfactory agreement was duly announced on 18th January 1971, whereby Halifax JOC was to absorb Hebble and pool the Bradford services with BCT.

Bradford did not wish to share the unremunerative Bradford-Wibsey-Hipperholme service or the peripheral Halifax-Shelf-Odsal-Dudley Hill-Stanningley-Leeds service, with the result that Halifax bus stop signs were erected along these routes; on the surviving joint BCT/Hebble signs Hebble's red was overpainted in Halifax green.

Halifax threw themselves enthusiastically into the huge task of re-planning services, issuing publicity and over-painting Hebble vehicles in the familiar (though not in Bradford) orange, cream and green. Both Corporations sent their drivers to explore each other's territory. Bradford depot allocations reflected the changing conditions: Bankfoot received Regent Vs, 145-9 and two-door Atlanteans 433-5 while Horton Bank Top, in an orgy of modernisation, welcomed not only Regent Vs, 141-4 but also Fleetlines 316/7/9 and smartly-repainted 321-5.

The weekend of Saturday 28th February to Monday 1st March, 1971, was historic and eventful. On Saturday night the Allerton (16) trolleybus service ceased and Atlanteans commenced to work through to West Bowling (16) next morning, the sister service (15) into the Allerton estate being extended to Ayresome Oval on the Monday.

But the focus of attention on that dark, cold Monday

At 2.55pm (according to the church clock) on Saturday 27th February 1971, Hebble Motor Services No. 622 passed a fellow Regent V, BCT No. 106, at Queensbury terminus, but two days later Hebble were only a memory.   [Photo: Author

morning was elsewhere. Bradford's blue and cream buses invaded the streets of Halifax at an hour so early that few were present to see them; the Bradford management had declined Halifax's imaginative suggestion that their respective first buses should meet ceremonially on the hills beyond Queensbury, as the first departure from Bradford was at the uncivilised hour of 5.28am ! Soon Halifax's buses were circumnavigating Bradford City Hall to the wonderment of those who were seeking the now-vanished Queensbury and Shelf buses.

So complete was the transformation that even Bradford's Regent Vs were welcomed with delight, while Horton Bank Top proudly contributed its magnificent Alexander-bodied Fleetlines. The Halifax contingent was a colourful mixture of Northern Counties-bodied Fleetlines, MCW-bodied Regent Vs and, briefly, an ex-Hebble or two. Most bore informative destination displays. BCT displayed 'Halifax' or 'Halifax General Hospital' via 'Shelf' or 'Queensbury' while most Halifax vehicles showed 'Halifax Bus Station' or 'General Hospital' via 'Northowram and Shelf' or 'Boothtown and Queensbury'. BCT buses also had 'Bradshaw' on the 'via' blinds in case further joint services were established.

Bradford provided five buses but Halifax seven, as the latter had sunk into the venture not only the Hebble services (7/17) but also the JOC Northowram-General Hospital (3/4) and Queensbury (40) workings and the Corporation service to Boothtown (24) which survived as a peak-hour working, officially joint service 74. The new service 76 commenced at Bradford's former Queensbury loading-point at Norfolk Gardens (Hall Ings) and proceeded to Halifax Bus Station (Crossfield) via Morley Street, Queensbury, Boothtown and Woodside (not to be confused with Bradford's Woodside, though the later PTE sometimes did). Service 77 started from Town Hall Street, Bradford

(now Channing Way) at the old Shelf loading-point; buses journeyed via Town Hall Square, Princes Way, Odsal, Shelf (Belle Vue), Hud Hill, Northowram Village (where some buses called at the Hospital), Stump Cross and North Bridge, where buses terminating in Halifax proceeded to Crossfield while those continuing to General Hospital paused in Commercial Street before venturing (to the great surprise of local passengers) along Skircoat Road, Heath Road, Skircoat Green Road and Dudwell Lane.

Vehicles travelling outwards via Shelf returned via Queensbury and vice-versa, encountering Pennine gradients and magnificent vistas as they did so. It was now possible to see Bradford, Halifax, Huddersfield, Leeds and Sheffield buses together at the new Jacob's Well roundabout in Manchester Road.

The first day's operation was somewhat erratic, as drivers were negotiating many miles of new territory, and continually-falling sleet was obscuring the new destination displays, but vigilant inspectors provided extra buses to Queensbury and ensured that passengers were not left waiting. The scheduled frequencies were ten minutes at the peak hour, compared with Hebble's 30 minutes frequency (hoped-for but not always achieved !)

Passenger reaction was almost ecstatic. "What lovely buses – you've done us proud !", exclaimed a Queensbury resident to the author, while a joyful Shelf resident wrote,

'As one who has complained bitterly over the inadequate bus services between Bradford and Halifax, may I be one of the first to congratulate both Bradford and Halifax Passenger Transport Departments on the vastly improved service ? At last we have some decent, clean buses to ride on, without breakdowns, and they keep to the timetable, which is a great improvement. May I thank all those concerned, and the bus crews as well. Keep it up, lads – it is appreciated !'

Falling sleet had obscured the new destination displays of BCT Daimler No. 323 when it arrived in Hall Ings on the first day of the through services to Halifax on 1st March 1971 – but it received a warm public welcome nevertheless.
[Photo: Author

The 'lads' did as they were bidden, and the service flourished, despite pleas (firmly resisted) for a journey-lengthening detour via Bradford's Woodside Estate, and a brief outbreak in Halifax of the industrial unrest which had plagued Bradford. During a strike of the Halifax fitters in October 1972 Halifax were unable to fulfil all their duties; at first BCT ran their normal complement of buses with extras to Queensbury and Shelf but then temporarily withdrew to the pre-1971 termini, not having enough spare buses to cover the Halifax workings. On another occasion Regent V No. 224 was loaned during a vehicle shortage, as the partnership was very amicable. Similarly, during July 1973, two buses were loaned to Halifax to 'work off' excess mileage accumulated by BCT on the joint routes; Fleetlines 284/5, Atlantean 296 and Regent Vs 178, 187 and 197 took turns in sharing this brief holiday, but all were manned by Halifax crews.

Captions for pictures overleaf

Upper: Partners at last. In Crossfield Bus Station, Halifax, BCT Alexander-bodied Fleetline No. 323 prepares for departure to Bradford by way of Northowram and Shelf while a fellow Fleetline – Northern Counties bodied Halifax 91 – aims to reach the same goal via Woodside, Boothtown Road and Queensbury.

[Photo: Author

Lower: Over the hills and far away – Bradford Fleetline No. 325 drops down from Crow Point towards Boothtown on the mountainous journey to Halifax via Queensbury on 27th March 1971.

[Photo: Author

Below: With a background of Calderdale hills BCT 144 stands outside Halifax General Hospital on 6th March 1971, before returning to Bradford via Halifax, Northowram and Shelf. The circular object above the destination is an experimental flashing alarm.

[Photo: Author

See previous page for captions

17 ON TO THE END

Here is no abiding city . . . (T. S. Eliot)

The second and final batch of 33ft buses was now ready for delivery. Leyland Motors despatched the thirty Atlantean chassis to Falkirk in April 1971 and on 15th June the Transport Executive Group had the pleasure of inspecting the first arrival, No. 447, which they found to be outwardly similar to the Daimler Fleetlines (401-440) apart from maker's insignia and appreciably lower suspension, a factor which was to prove popular with elderly and handicapped people. Numbers 441-458 were licensed for the Saltaire via Thackley (40), Thackley shortworking (41) and Greengates via Idle (42) routes which they inherited from the trolleybuses on 1st July. Arriving a month later the remainder of the order, 459-470, took over the Clayton (37), Pasture Lane (38), Wibsey (45) and Buttershaw (46) routes from the trolleybuses on 1st August; on which day they also took over the whole of Thornbury depot.

The 'promotion' of former trolleybus drivers to motorbus duties had painful consequences for the modern rear-engine vehicles, which of course were infinitely more complex than their electric counterparts. Long accustomed to allowing their 'trolleys' to coast at great speeds down the steep descent of St. Enoch's Road, the new recruits practised similar feats with the Atlanteans by the simple expedient of slipping them out of gear. The results were dire. The gearbox oil pumps suddenly found themselves disconnected and unable to lubricate the gears, which, in turn, quickly overheated and jammed solid when the clutch was let in at the bottom of the hill. Bent prop-shafts and angry words were the inevitable outcome.

Less controversial was the application of a coach livery to two of the AEC Swifts. On the basis of two coloured drawings submitted for approval by the Executive Group,

Leyland Atlantean No. 445 had been in service only eighteen days when it arrived in Canal Road for one of the popular City Tours.
[Photo: R. Marshall

The network contracts – Saltaire-based Daimler No. 229 was the last BCT bus at Dick Hudson's on 10th July 1971, when a lack of passengers caused the route to be cut back to Eldwick. Only one passenger – a lady – was on board.

[Photo: Author

No. 506 was repainted in all-over primrose with a broad South Sea blue waist band edged in dark blue, whereas No. 504, more colourfully, sported a 'Notts and Derby' blue roof and a matching waistband edged in buff, with primrose elsewhere. Number 504 was voted the more attractive of the two, and within a short while No. 506 was altered to match. Both were regularly lent out for private hire.

Meanwhile the upland hostelry of Dick Hudson's (68/68A) had bidden farewell to its public transport service when BCT Daimler CVG6 No. 229 made its last ascent on 10th July 1971, followed at a later hour by the final three Keighley-West Yorkshire vehicles. 'The bus service which for years took ramblers from Bradford to the gateway to Ilkley Moors is being withdrawn', the press reported, the reason being, in the words of the KWYS spokesman, that "there are no passengers travelling on it – there used to be, but now people have their own transport". The schedules were adjusted so that the frequency of buses to Eldwick (Beck Bottom) remained undisturbed.

A variation of the joint Dewsbury service, numbered 4B, was introduced on 14th August when some journeys were diverted between Birkenshaw Bar and Birstall Smithies by way of Town Street, Old Lane, Birkenshaw Lane, Moor Lane, Bradford Road, Low Lane, Birstall Market Place and Smithies Lane.

Queensbury and Shelf Urban District Council had been discussing the provision of concessionary travel for pensioners living in their district, and at the suggestion of the Halifax manager (who was concurrently manager of the neighbouring Todmorden JOC) a Todmorden-style scheme was agreed upon by both Halifax and Bradford. Accordingly in October 1971, a supply of TJOC tickets valid on both Halifax and BCT buses was sold at full value to the UDC who issued them at half price to their elderly. By this time there were 35,000 permit-holders in Bradford itself, each of whom paid £1 per annum for a pass. The cost of the fare reduction was paid from the rates, as the Transport Department's income had dropped by £93,000 when the scheme was first introduced, and the Traffic Commissioners had refused to allow any fares increases until the concessions were removed from the transport budget.

In July 1971, the Executive Group extended the concession to evening hospital visitors, but not to 'bingo addicts' or to West Yorkshire bus passengers except in areas of the city such as Bolton Woods where no Corporation services ran.

Relentlessly-increasing volumes of traffic were by this time causing traffic jams in the city centre at peak times; bus schedules were seriously disrupted and passengers vociferously critical. Traffic experts suggested vast gyratory systems as a promising solution; the simple bus turning facilities at Tong Cemetery terminus should, they urged, be replaced by a mile-long trek to Westgate Hill returning via North View Road. Fortunately their advice was not heeded. In a more practical vein the Transport Executive Group visited Reading to sample the 'bus lanes' which had been pioneered there a few years earlier; they returned impressed and enthusiastic, though the Chairman and his deputy felt it prudent to conceal the fact that they had narrowly escaped annihilation by a Reading Corporation bus while unwarily venturing to cross a contraflow lane ! Bank Street (Market Street to Broadway) and Market Street (Bank Street-Bridge Street) were recommended as trial areas, but the Transportation (ie Highways) Executive Group blocked the proposal despite debates and questions in Council in 1973.

The approaching close of trolleybus operation, long threatened, was foreshadowed on 15th November 1971, when a few of the latest Atlanteans were despatched to Duckworth Lane trolleybus depot to serve the Duckworth Lane (8) route during repairs to a trunk water main early in December. Recalling the havoc caused by the application of trolleybus driving techniques to the Wibsey motorbuses, the Department decided to leave the Atlanteans in their new home when the water main was renewed, so that all drivers could become accustomed to them. The buses, therefore, appeared in spasmodic service on the Thornton

Now in an attractive coach livery, AEC Swifts Nos 504-506 prepare to convey the civic party from Thornbury works to City Hall after the ceremonial closure of the trolleybus system on 26th March 1972.
[Photo: R. Marshall

to Thornbury (7) route also. The news that the twenty Fleetlines ordered for the final changeover were being delayed by a toolcutters' strike was a nuisance rather than a hindrance, as there was an adequate reserve of buses to cover all trolleybus duties when required.

A miners' strike and consequential shortage of electricity brought considerable hardship to the city. Mills, workshops, offices, schools and homes were deprived of heat and light, and the trolleybuses were placed in store on 10th February 1972. Power supplies were rationed until the end of the month, and trolleybus workings did not resume until 7th March. An interesting by-product of the dispute was the conversion of Regent III No. 82 into a mobile generator bus (0.79) to provide dc power in Thornbury works – a factor which providentially ensured its preservation and its ultimate restoration twenty-two years later.

On the morning of 25th March 1972, the Duckworth Lane-based Atlanteans (451-470) took over the full operation of the services, the few Regent Vs temporarily loaned during the strike having been sent back whence they came. Immediately after the ceremonial closure of the trolleybus undertaking on the following day, semi-coaches 504/506 (and, less formally, one of the trolleybus overhead repair wagons !) conveyed the civic party from Thornbury to City Hall.

His *bêtes-noirs* having been eliminated at last, Mr Christie, the retired Traffic Superintendent, gave public vent to his feelings. Dismissing the trolleybuses as 'quaint hybrids', he attacked the Corporation for having 'wasted so many tens if not hundreds of thousands of pounds merely to satisfy the egotism of a handful of people and others who let sentiment carry them away'. His mathematics were spectacularly wide of the mark and his interpretation of policies and motives sadly inaccurate. The unspoken question still remains: why do transport professionals consciously seek employment in towns and cities to whose transport policies they are diametrically opposed ? In the words of the traditional Yorkshire dictum,

"There's nowt so queer as fowks !"

During the author's brief reign as acting chairman (27th March to 15th May) only one serious problem arose:

the breakage of a track-rod on one of the Horton Bank Top-based Fleetlines necessitated the precautionary purchase of new sets for all the 30ft Fleetlines (271-285, 316-335). The equipment was delivered by Securicor within a week, but one vital question needed to be asked – did the incident warrant the temporary withdrawal of the affected buses from the Halifax via Queensbury (76) route with its potential perilous plunges over precipices ? Shying away from such searching suggestions, the management replied that it did not.

Simultaneously a strong complaint was received from Pudsey Borough Council that BCT had been 'dilatory to the point of rudeness' in continually deferring requests for agreement on concessionary fares. When it transpired that requests had indeed been received in 1965, 1967 and 1968, an offer of a Queensbury-type scheme was immediately made to Pudsey, and also to Shipley UDC.

Following a heartfelt plea from the West Yorkshire company that its part-day service to Esholt, an isolated rural enclave of the city, was incurring a grievous loss of £2,393 per annum, the Executive Group agreed to pay a £190 subsidy, while the Department of the Environment volunteered no less than £1,200 !

A distinctly unusual incident occurred when a City Circle (2) bus tore the radio aerial from the roof of a North-East Gas Board caravan. A prankster had stretched a rope across Killinghall Road and attached it to the aerial; the bus chanced to be the first vehicle to pass by.

A daily journey to Calverley and Leeds Road Hospitals (22) inaugurated on 19th March 1972, proved to be the last new service begun by BCT. Operating on Wednesdays, Saturdays and Sundays only, it was routed via Barkerend Road, Gilpin Street and Woodhall Road.

In the summer Bradford and Leeds advertised joint bus/ canal trips at 75p per adult and (as usual) half-fares for juveniles. The Bradford tours commenced at Rodley and terminated at Saltaire while Leeds operated in the reverse direction. Permitting 2° hours 'on the briny', the voyages were proclaimed to have 'all the advantages of a sail without the problem of seasickness !' – unless, of course, the Regent Vs were used on the land journey !

The newest Daimlers, Nos. 336-355 were regular performers on the Saltaire (40) and Greengates (42) routes when buses took over from trolleybuses in 1971. Number 343 stands at Saltaire terminus (Saltaire Road) on 11th August 1972.   [Photo: J. Copland]

The gradual conversion of Manchester Road into a six-lane highway robbed Bankfoot depot of its forecourt, and a new entrance had to be made in Rathmell Street. At the other end of Manchester Road the City loading-point of the Brighouse/Huddersfield (63/64) services was moved from a highly-inconvenient site opposite the Telephone Exchange to a central venue in the Tyrls, to the satisfaction of the author who had long promised his colleagues that he would 'stand them a pint' when the long-overdue transfer took place. Less pleasingly the Development Committee in preparation to close Tyrrel Street demanded the removal of the Clayton (36/37) and Wibsey/Buttershaw (43-46) loading points to new sites beyond the new Inner Ring Road. The Transport Executive Group stood firm, and when Tyrrel Street closed on 18th February 1973 the queues transferred a mere 100 yards into the Tyrls.

On 24th May 1972, the Executive Group inspected bus No. 336, the first of the 30ft Daimler Fleetlines (336-355) ordered in 1970, and were pleased with their purchase. The vehicles were similar in appearance to the 33ft version (401-440) except in length and absence of a central door; they were neater and lower-slung, with larger windows and vandal-proof interior lighting. With the entry into service of No. 355 on 15th August an era closed, as the management confidently asserted that no additional stock would be needed during the remaining lifetime of the Department, and the registration marks XAK 336-355L were therefore the last issued to BCT by the Bradford Corporation Vehicle Licensing Department.

Older vehicles retired at last – the surviving rear-platform Regent IIIs (68, 71/72, 81, 83-86) as well as non-standard fuel-hungry Regent Vs 121-125, although No. 123 was permitted a brief respite until the following April. Also the single-deckers were relieved of their enforced duties in all-day service to Wrose (34), Saltaire/Greengates (40/42) and Bankfoot (80), leaving them free to venture further afield; Nos. 508/511 visited Wetherby Races on hire to Wallace Arnold during the Spring Bank holiday, and No. 511 also worked a journey to Manchester (X12) jointly operated by Yorkshire Woollen and North Western Road Car when Leyland Leopard 314 belonging to NWRC failed in Bradford and underwent repair at Ludlam Street on 26th May. Some of Bradford's own vehicles were meanwhile undergoing more fundamental repairs – the engine sub-frames of Fleetlines 316-335 (like the Atlanteans before them) were having to be reinforced and measures to strengthen the body structures of Leyland PD3s 241-255 were increasing the overall weights from 8 tons 11cwt 2qrs to an impressive 9 tons 0cwt 3qr.

Bus fares rose once again on 30th April to forestall a £265,000 deficit; 5p and 6p fares were increased by 1p and higher fares by 2p.

Christmas shopping expeditions in 1972 were cheered on their way by Atlantean 264 and Fleetlines 272 and 320

Leyland Atlantean 264 conveys festive greetings to the shoppers of Bradford (and Wrose) on Christmas Eve, 1972.

[Photo: J. Copland

specially painted in a blue and white 'Santa' livery with reindeer, Christmas trees, holly and Father Christmas himself wishing Bradford folk a 'Merry Christmas in Bradford' and (perhaps more to the point) 'Happy Christmas Shopping in Bradford'. The novel venture attracted press and television acclaim.

After years of wrangling a one-man-operation agreement between BCT and Transport and General Workers Union representatives was reached. In response to points raised by the union the Chairman and the author visited Birmingham and were greatly struck by the efficient and trouble-free operation of one-man buses on the Ridgacre Lane and Bartley Green routes. Questionnaires to other colleagues following demands for the abolition of waybills and change-giving revealed that Chesterfield, Doncaster, Grimsby-Cleethorpes, Halifax, Huddersfield, Leeds, Rotherham and Sheffield gave change and Hull did not, while Lincoln issued redeemable vouchers in lieu of change. Only Leeds permitted a 'closed shop' for one-man-operation drivers. The resulting agreement stipulated that (i) the 33ft buses would not be used, (ii) there would be no 'closed shop', (iii) waybills would be retained, (iv) exact fares would be requested but change would be given if needed , and (v) a basic wage increase of £1.25p would apply. The full cost of £122,000 (plus a craftsmen's wage award of £46,684) necessitated yet another fares application.

Horton Bank Top depot's 30ft Fleetlines were therefore exchanged for Thornbury's 33ft versions (411-420) so that No. 316-355 could be made ready. Illuminated panels proclaiming the message 'Pay on Entry – Exact Fare,

please' were fitted to the front dash, with periscopes, radios and a fixed (Ultimate) ticket machine inside. Bradford's entry into the world of one-man-operation began on Sunday 31st December 1972, when 316-335 class Fleetlines took up operation on the Clayton (36-38) services and the new 336-355 Fleetlines took over the Saltaire/Greengates (40/42) routes. The joint Leeds (72/78) workings followed suit on 20th May 1973.

The replacement of Purchase Tax and Selective Employment Tax (SET) by a new Value Added Tax (VAT) on 1st April 1973, had only one profound effect on the fortunes of BCT – in the canteen Roast Beef, Pork, Lamb, Braised Steak, Grilled Liver and Lamb Chop (all with 'two veg') increased from 10p to 11p per portion and Fruit Pie, Jam Roll and Milk Puddings from 3p to 3½p.

After years of indecision Bingley UDC (quickly followed by Shipley) voted to seek a pensioners' fare scheme from Bradford but as they requested a SELNEC-type token scheme incompatible with anything else in the area, the decision was referred to BCT's successors.

Under the startling headline, 'Nauseating Mobile Mess in the name of Gain', an Ilkley resident criticised Bradford's two all-over advertising buses, Atlaneans 287 and 289 which from June/July 1973 began to advocate the virtues

One-man-operation reaches Bradford at last as the driver of Fleetline 325 collects fares from Clayton passengers in The Tyrls on the last day of 1972.

[Photo: Author

of Sharps' electrical wares and certain consumer delights to be found at the Buywell Shopping Centre in distant Thorp Arch.

'While the Queen is on her throne, the bobbies patrol the streets and the familiar and friendly buses trundle along the roads', he wrote, 'one has a warm feeling of security and faith in the good order of things in this blessed plot of ours.

A number of buses . . . however have recently been turned into an offensive and prostituted mess of Picassoesque whorls and convolutions of garish, sickly and nauseating colour. If gain is to be the only yardstick . . . it is not beyond the bounds of reason that they should take it to the utmost limit and paint the heads of bald drivers and the backsides of hapless conductors.'

Happily the crews were never called upon to make this supreme sacrifice, and as children enjoyed riding on 'a rainbow bus', Bradfordians replied that since BCT buses did not run to Ilkley, and Ilkley residents did not pay rates to Bradford, the city should be left to run its own affairs. And when the third and last 'mobile hoarding', Atlantean 288, appeared in cheerful claret and amber advertising Bradford's 'Telegraph and Argus' the only significant protest came from a Bingley ratepayer. Real Bradfordians appreciated that the three buses were revenue-earning, as the advertisers paid the whole cost of painting and restoring to normal livery as well as a substantial rent.

A day of mellow magnificence heralded the Centenary of City Hall on 9th September 1973, when many of the Corporation departments – Waterworks, Refuse Disposal, Fire, Standards, Transport, Housing and Conditioning House – opened their doors for the first (and in some cases the last) time. The Freedom of the City was bestowed upon Bradford-born J. B. Priestley, and a lecture on Delius, a former freeman, was delivered by his amanuensis Eric Fenby. Returning from thanksgiving at the Cathedral the Lord Mayor (Alderman Derek Smith) reviewed a colourful cavalcade of 31 buses in Lister Park, ranging from a 1927 Leyland Lion sent by Halifax to the latest Leeds Atlanteans

and Huddersfield Fleetlines. Bradford's own exhibits were recently-rediscovered Lion 325 of 1927, preserved PD2 No. 59, Atlantean 262, AEC Swift 506 and, most fittingly, No. 355, the last of the line.

The enthralled throngs melted away, and thereafter the scene darkened swiftly.

Mr Edward Deakin, General Manager since 1963, unexpectedly found himself President of APPTO on the sudden death of Mr Albert Burrows, the Liverpool manager. In his speech to the 72nd Annual Conference he noted the anticipated opening of a Channel Tunnel in 1980 as outlined in a Government White Paper, commented that the transport industry's previous worries about Nationalisation had been superseded by new worries about Local Government Reorganisation in six months time, and welcomed Government proposals for subsidies for transport coupled with restraints on private cars in city centres. Sadly the Executive Group convened on 23rd October to discuss yet more wage claims was the last he attended; a few days later he succumbed to the combined pressures of finance, preparations for the PTE, recurrent disputes over school transport and his presidential commitments. Mr John H. Hill, the Traffic Superintendent, was appointed Acting Deputy General Manager on 13th November 1973, leaving the Rolling Stock Engineer (Mr B. B. Browne) in complete charge of engineering functions.

Meanwhile the Transport Department and Executive Group had been planning their own demise, never an agreeable task. A major reorganisation of local government, threatened since 1945, was now taking ominous shape, and for West Yorkshire a Metropolitan County Council superimposed upon five Metropolitan Districts was proposed. In June 1971, the spectre of a County-controlled PTA/PTE had been resurrected; evidently the stake driven through its heart in 1967 had not been of sufficient calibre. The combined county boroughs proposed an amendment whereby the County should control transport planning and finance, delegating the actual operation to district units which would liaise with the District Councils and retain a distinctive livery. At a subsequent APPTO meeting the author argued that if the existing municipal undertakings were to be transferred to a PTE, the local National Bus companies should be commandeered also, as it would be absurd to perpetuate the age-old rivalries (the reactions to this proposal were interesting – the Leeds manager was delighted but his chairman frosty, while the Bradford manager appeared inwardly scandalised !).

Following the passing of the Local Government Act, 1972 the Metropolitan Councils and a PTA/PTE were set up in 1973 and were to assume full control on 1st April 1974. The nascent PTE advocated a uniform fare for the whole County – a logical step but one with tremendous financial implications, as the policy was to embrace NBC fares also.

Up to this point the earlier proposals of the combined county boroughs still found favour with the PTE, and at their request each of the four municipalities painted a bus in a distinctive PTE operating district livery, ie Bradford-blue, Calderdale-orange, Kirklees-Huddersfield red, and Leeds-green, all with a large expanse of 'buttermilk'. Thus Bradford Fleetline 410 emerged from Thornbury paintshop with 'Notts and Derby, blue roof and lower panels with 'buttermilk' everywhere else and 'Metro Bradford' in silver letters. In this guise it transported the Bradford Transport Executive Group and the PTA/PTE around the BCT depots on 6th December 1973 – the only occasion on which both sides ever met formally. But next month the PTA overruled the PTE and resolved on a uniform livery. Red they dismissed as 'common'; orange they considered 'too hard to keep clean' (how had Halifax managed to keep it clean for 40 years ?), blue was 'not durable' (how had Bradford's blue endured 75 years ?) and brown 'dull' – therefore the Leeds 'Verona green' with fawn interior decor was decreed – as cynics had predicted from the outset. The Executive Group patriotically decreed that South Sea blue and primrose should continue to be applied in its paintshop until the last day of BCT.

New Year gales blew in an era of great changes, beginnings and endings. They also imperilled the stability of double-deck buses on the exposed routes to Halifax (76/77) and both undertakings prudently substituted single-deckers on 19th January.

In mid-November 1973 the Executive Group had been alarmed to find itself in the middle of a serious vehicle shortage. No fewer than thirty buses were due for early recertification, a task far beyond the capacity of Thornbury Works, which could process only one bus per week even when fully staffed, which it was not. The situation was aggravated by the complexity and relative unreliability of modern rear engine buses, as well as the long delays in deliveries of spare parts (a whole year for a chassis cross-member).

Several buses had been despatched to contractors such as Lex Tillotson, Isles of Stanningley, Reliance (Brighouse) and Pelican Engineering (Rothwell), but the works staff threatened to 'black' these outlets as they had banned overtime in protest against national pay policies. Moreover a brief Middle East war had brought about a threat of fuel

rationing which had barely subsided when the coal miners struck in opposition to pay policies. The ensuing electricity cuts reduced Bradford's workplaces to a three-day week which paradoxically relieved the pressure on the bus services, but unnecessary lighting and heating had to be banned; Bradford's streets were in semi-darkness and the Christmas street illuminations were not used at all.

The overtime ban was eased on 17th January 1974 but some service reductions could not be avoided. Seaside municipalities were approached for the loan of spare vehicles, but Liverpool had already borrowed all that Southport could spare, and Blackpool could not assist as they carried out all their heavy maintenance in the winter months. Edinburgh were willing to help – at a price – and the ever-friendly Chesterfield manager, Vincent Rigby, promised assistance if needed.

At that juncture Halifax, having overcome their own problems, despatched six buses free of charge, as they owed a good deal for mileage provided by BCT, and Huddersfield, having retrieved seven buses recently lent to Sheffield, were equally happy to assist.

Attention next focussed on the rapidly-worsening financial crisis. In October 1973 the Council had decided not to raise fares to offset wage increases costing £581,000, but by January a further pay award and a fuel price increase had boosted the deficit to £706,000. The Transport Executive Group were unanimous in wishing to hand over a debt-free undertaking to the PTA/PTE, but were overruled, thus exposing a curious paradox – the predominant politics of the PTA/PTE who would unwillingly inherit this unwelcome liability were the same as the outgoing City Council, whereas the incoming City of Bradford Metropolitan Council, of a different political persuasion, would rightly escape the blame. When another wage claim forced the deficit up to the staggering figure of £1,000,000 in a full year, the Executive Group on 17th January 1974 made a final attempt to avert catastrophe. As the Corporation's remaining reserves were insufficient to make good the loss, and as the fares would rise by 23% if BCT's passengers had to meet the deficit in full, the Group voted to bring fares up to the same level as those of their future partners in the PTA and to seek the remainder from the rates. Sadly this last appeal to common sense met the same fate as the others. Inevitably when the four municipal undertakings were handed over 2° months later, a dismal financial legacy was revealed:

Bradford	–	£562,000
Calderdale	+	35,000
Huddersfield	–	234,000
Leeds	–	1,198,000
		– £1,959,000

(Within three weeks of the takeover the PTA had to impose a 16.2% fares increase in Bradford, send a bill to the new Bradford Council for £1,235,000 and levy a £1,000,000 rate for the coming year. Such was the price of irresponsibility.)

The days were now fast dwindling, and familiar

The rustic delights of Tong Village: Daimler No. 355 stands at the gates of Tong Hall during a private visit in March 1974.
[Photo: Author

Neighbours came to the assistance of BCT when a vehicle shortage threatened early in 1974. Huddersfield Corporation's red and cream Regent III No. 189 rests at Bingley Church before journeying to Bradford Moor.
[Photo: Author

Friends of Bradford City Transport hired the newest bus, Daimler No. 355, for a final tour of the municipal motorbus network on Sunday, 24th March 1974. Here No. 355 is seen in Bowling Old Lane re-tracing the long-forgotten route to Horton Bank Top via Ripleyville.
[Photo: Author

Corporation activities were performed one by one for the last time.

Bradford's last delegates to APPTO (Area D, Yorkshire, Lincolnshire and North Derbyshire) at Halifax on 19th February bade farewell to professional and elected colleagues of many years standing. The new Brighouse bus station, the final creation of Brighouse Corporation, opened its doors to BCT buses (service 63) on 5th March, and the last privately-arranged bus tour of Bradford was held on 24th March, when the newest bus (355) visited historic haunts such as Bolton Woods, Tong, Drighlington and Birkenshaw before travelling on the old route 62 via Ripleyville and Bankfoot to Horton Bank Top depot where, uniquely, it was photographed with Leeds 706, preserved Huddersfield 234 and Halifax 366 (on loan to BCT but semi-defunct, barely managing to stagger out of the depot amid clouds of smoke).

Meeting for the last time on 27th March the Transport Executive Group (Alderman Moran, Councillors Dunne and King, the Acting Deputy Manager, Mr Hill, and Secretary, Mr Tidswell), voted £100 for the Transport Social Club and £20 for the Bradford Dance to be held that evening, approved a pay award to the inspectors and cash clerks, shook hands and parted. The splendid Dance, held at Connaught Rooms, was the last official function of BCT, and the presentation of long-service and driving awards on 29th March was the last meeting of management and staff. Inside the works Atlantean 258 and Fleetline 272 were the

last recipients of a handsome coat of South Sea blue and primrose, whilst Fleetline 276 had (no doubt against its will) been adorned in the colours of its future owners.

Sunday, 31st March 1974, was a day of serene splendour. The warm sun shone down upon the City and County Borough of Bradford, the Yorkshire Ridings and countless ancient shires and civic corporations as they bade farewell to centuries of history. Amid splendid pageantry the City Council laid up its standard in the venerable Cathedral; the Police Band proudly played itself out of existence, the Fire Brigade extinguished itself, the Waterworks and Sewage Departments prepared to flow into other channels, and Bradford City Transport's smart blue buses performed their last faithful duties. By the time that many of them had returned to their respective depots in the early hours of the next day they were already in the service of new owners.

"We'll all go riding on a rainbow" – or is it a "nauseating mobile mess" ? Atlantean No. 287 flaunts its 'Picassoesque whorls' in aid of Sharps' electronics at Hollingwood Lane on 30th June 1973.

[Photo: Author

18 THE CLOUD-CAPP'D TOWERS

Bradford's Transport Interchange has often been the subject of criticism from people outside the City, who have derided the design and indeed the whole concept, and have asserted that the project was launched by Bradford Corporation in the full knowledge that it would be paid for by someone else, ie, the future West Yorkshire PTE. This cynical view bears little relation to sober fact.

From 1958 the Transport Department's fleet had been housed in seven (formerly ten) depots of varying sizes, only one of which – Ludlam Street – was anywhere near the city centre. Over the years potential sites at Westgate, Brownroyd and City Road had been considered as suitable locations for a central depot which could supersede the smaller establishments, but it was not until 1967 that the Transport Committee, faced with an unending spiral of cost increases and fare rises, engaged outside consultants to study the whole question of the Department's efficiency. Predictably the consultants recommended a central depot as a means of reducing running costs by about £40,000 a year.

The Corporation therefore acquired the former Bridge Street railway goods depot for £220,000, and on 10th July 1967, Daimler Fleetline 271 conveyed the Committee around their new 11-acre acquisition which was capable of accommodating a six-bay bus station as well as the depot.

By this time British Railways were seriously considering the future of the adjoining Exchange Station, once a thriving rail centre but now visited only by a sad handful of diesel trains. Acutely aware that the loss of railway facilities would jeopardise Bradford's prosperity, the Corporation agreed to investigate the feasibility of constructing a combined road and rail interchange on the Bridge Street site.

The report, presented to the Council on 3rd June 1970 by the British Railways Board architects, revealed a new and unique concept – a centrally-situated transport centre adjacent to main traffic routes which would accommodate

With the exception of Ludlam Street all Bradford's bus depots were former tramsheds, mostly incorporating a stone facade with a glass-roofed interior. Photographed on 2nd April, 1950, 1935/6 Regents Nos. 417, 422 and 395 are standing outside Bowling depot which, as the accompanying dross hill suggests, was built on land bought from Bowling Ironworks. [Photo: J. Copland

local and long-distance bus and railway services, a depot for 200 buses, taxi-stands, a multi-storey car park, a new headquarters for BCT, a hotel and a Post Office sorting-depot. The underlying aim was to reverse the decline of public transport and the growth of car ownership by the provision of well-designed and attractive travel facilities incorporating lifts, escalators and footbridges which eliminated conflict between pedestrians and vehicles.

The Transport Executive Group was not thrilled. "A lot of money, gentlemen !", warned Mr Deakin. Had the railway factor not arisen the author would have preferred a drive-through bus station on the soon-to-be-cleared area in front of City Hall, while Mr Deakin with rare humour but geographical justification professed to prefer the site of City Hall itself ! However, for a combined rail/bus station Bridge Street was the only practical choice, as the railhead could not be extended nearer to the city centre.

An agreement having been signed by the Corporation, the design of the bus station was left to the Transport Executive Group. Three options were available:–

(i) A conventional open-air concourse with glazed passenger shelters;
(ii) An overall glass roof supported by pillars with independent glazed enclosures on each island platform;
(iii) As (ii) but with the overall glass roof suspended from central pillars.

Option (i) was discounted because it was little better than the windswept, cheerless concrete wastelands to be found in most towns, and option (iii) was an untried design which might prove unstable in high winds. The accepted option, (ii), had an estimated cost of £4,303,000 less the resale value of the other depots, and if the tenders could be evaluated and contracts awarded by July 1971, the Interchange could be operational in July 1973.

Following cost-benefit studies compiled by the Department of Transport a Government grant was promised, subject to the provision of a large pedestrian access bridge from Norfolk Gardens, spanning Hall Ings. Tenders were therefore not invited until January 1973, by which time inflation, soaring building costs and delays caused by a builders' strike had boosted the estimated cost to £7,343,000 less Government grant of about £2,300,000 and the resale value of the redundant properties (which turned out to be £200,000 for the smaller depots and £1,100,000 for Thornbury).

Modernisation of the railway facilities had already begun. On 18th January the Lord Mayor (Ald. Audrey Firth, JP) waved off the last train from 'the shadows of the grandiose arches of Exchange Station' while the last late-night connection for Halifax (Halifax bus No. 280) made a less ceremonial departure from the station yard. Next day the first train entered the unpretentious new station on the Bridge Street site where (in the words of the press) the Interchange would 'bring warm feet and other luxurious comforts to train and bus passengers. Its effect on Bradford is likely to be tremendous and well in advance of its time; other towns will have to follow us in providing this sort of facility'.

As an essential part of the project a two-year study of traffic conditions and transport requirements was commissioned jointly by the Corporation and the Department of the Environment, and under the control of Messrs Travers Morgan, consultants, a 20-strong team of civil engineers, traffic experts, transport planners and statisticians began work in August 1973. Meanwhile the site having been cleared and culverts diverted, pile-driving began in January 1974. Bradford had truly laid the foundations.

The impressive Interchange, claimed as the finest in

Duckworth Lane, the last British trolleybus depot, was the home of dual-entrance/exit Atlanteans Nos. 455, 459, 462, 465 and 461 (and others) when this photograph was taken on 10th September 1972.

[Photo: J. Copland

Europe, opened for business on 27th March 1977, with the departure of the 6.38am Buttershaw (via Horton Bank Top) bus. But the bus no longer belonged to Bradford: it wore the green and buttermilk livery of Metro – the West Yorkshire Metropolitan County Council's passenger transport unit. Metro, West Yorkshire, West Riding, Yorkshire Woollen and other National Bus Company subsidiaries' vehicles used platforms A to E and the long-distance coaches platform F, while closed circuit television kept an eye on movements. In the office block framed portraits of all the Bradford Corporation Transport managers from C. J. Spencer to Edward Deakin looked down in polite interest upon the futuristic scene.

The Interchange was briefly considered as a headquarters for the new PTE, but fears that other new Metropolitan Districts might feel slighted if Bradford were chosen as the centre of an important County function ensured that the PTE took up residence in Wakefield, a place where no PTE bus could be seen.

National inflation raised the cost of the Interchange to a crippling £16,200,000 with debt charges of £2,000,000 a year. One of the county councillors, entirely missing the point, bemoaned 'the unnecessary luxury', adding, "We just want to operate buses between two stops without having to worry about maintenance and heating costs."

Following 'Deregulation', ie, the repeal of the 1930 Transport Act, shortlived competition on the streets of Bradford prompted Yorkshire Rider – successor to 'Metrobus' and thus to BCT – to remove a few services from the Interchange, which despite repeated assurances had never been used to its full potential. And when Yorkshire Rider was sold to its employees, the £23,000,000 received by the PTE was not used to liquidate the Interchange debt: opulent new headquarters in the expensive heart of Leeds were purchased instead. Thornbury Works closed when the bus fleet shrank; its functions also were transferred to Leeds. Parts of the immaculate Interchange were converted into a car park, and non-transport uses were considered. The dream had faded – or had been switched off.

Bradford Transport Interchange is, of course, West Yorkshire's most heavily-used bus station.

The last purchases made by Bradford City Transport were twenty Alexander-bodied Daimler CRL6/30s. Number 350 stands in Canal Road outside the Transport Offices on 27th May 1973.

[Photo: J. Copland

APPENDICES

Fleet List of Motor buses

Route List of Motor bus Services

Route Map of Motor bus Services

Bradford's first bus was duly photographed by AEC's staff photographer before leaving the factory.   [Senior Transport Archive; photo: AEC

Fleet Number	Entered Service	Registration Number	Chassis Number	Withdrawn	Disposal
330	21 September 1927	KW 2265	46022	18 March 1939	ARP/GL/H
331	20 September 1927	KW 2266	46026	30 April 1939	ARP/K/R
332	1 October 1927	KW 2267	46027	30 September 1938	ARP/TH/ SH/SS

Bristol B 'Super'; Bristol 34.2 hp petrol engine   Bristol B33F/RD body   Cost £1,300 each

Fleet Number	Entered Service	Registration Number	Chassis Number	Withdrawn	Disposal
333	1 October 1927	KW 2268	46028	12 August 1936	FI
334	9 October 1927	KW 2269	46029	31 October 1938	ARP/GL/H
335	1 October 1927	KW 2270	46030	31 October 1938	ARP/K/FU
336	8 October 1927	KW 2271	46031	18 March 1939	ARP/GL/H
337	7 April 1928	KW 3576	B 243	20 February 1935	MW
338	7 April 1928	KW 3577	B 241	28 February 1935	MW

Leyland Long Lion PLSC3; Leyland 28 hp petrol engine; sliding-mesh (crash) gearbox. Leyland B35F body   Cost £1,366 each

Fleet Number	Entered Service	Registration Number	Chassis Number	Withdrawn	Disposal
339	26 May 1928	KW 3578	46208	20 September 1938	ARP/K/SH
340	5 May 1928	KW 3579	46209	5 August 1936	TI/TE/LA

Bristol B 'Super'; Bristol 34.2 hp petrol engine. Bristol B34R body   Cost £1,317-12-3d each

Fleet Number	Entered Service	Registration Number	Chassis Number	Withdrawn	Disposal
341	3 July 1928	KW 4360	B 315	29 July 1936	H
342	7 July 1928	KW 4361	B 318	5 August 1936	CH
343	5 July 1928	KW 4362	B 325	27 June 1936	MW
344	12 July 1928	KW 4363	B 323	9 September 1936	H
345	11 July 1928	KW 4364	B 320	30 September 1936	H
346	12 July 1928	KW 4365	B 322	August 1934	FO
347	1 August 1928	KW 4366	B 324	27 June 1936	MW
348	1 August 1928	KW 4367	B 321	30 September 1936	H
349	2 August 1928	KW 4368	B316	30 September 1936	B
350	2 August 1928	KW 4369	B 317	5 March 1934	WH
351	1 August 1928	KW 4370	B 319	30 September 1936	H
352	1 August 1928	KW 4371	B326	9 May 1935	MW

Leyland Titan TD1; Leyland 38.4 hp petrol engine sliding mesh (crash) gearbox.
Leyland L27/24RO body.   Cost £1,720-15-0d each.
Re-equipped with Gardner 6LW engines: 355 (1934), 364/5 (1935), 358/9, 360/2/3 (1936). Re-equipped with AEC 7.7 engine: 353 (1936). Loaned to London 1940/1: 358/9. 362/4/5. Loaned to Sheffield 1940/1: 354/6/7. 361/6/7. Loaned to Hull, 1941: 356/7/361/6. Loaned to Middlesbrough, 1945: 354/361/6/7.
The bodies of 355/7 were transferred to 359/363.

Fleet Number	Entered Service	Registration Number	Chassis Number	Withdrawn	Disposal
353	29 August 1928	KW 4500	70310	25 June 1946	M
354	8 November 1928	KW 4501	70326	20 November 1945	SA

MOTOR BUS FLEET LIST

AEC 413 chassis; AEC 35 hp petrol engine United Automobile Services B28R body (ordered as 30 seaters and recorded as such in 1927)   Cost £1,183-18-0d each

Fleet Number	Entered Service	Registration Number	Chassis Number	Withdrawn	Disposal
301	1 May 1926	KU 8601	413050	24 March 1931	C
302	5 June 1926	KU 8602	413052	31 December 1930	MW
303	4 May 1926	KU 8603	413057	26 October 1933	GL/N
304	5 May 1926	KU 8604	413054	31 March 1935	GL/N
305	7 May 1926	KU 8605	413056	19 March 1935	MW
306	15 June 1926	KU 8606	413053	31 December 1930	S
307	15 June 1926	KU 8607	413051	18 January 1935	MW
308	10 July 1926	KU 8608	413059	31 December 1930	D
309	13 July 1926	KU 8609	413055	31 December 1930	GL/N
310	6 July 1926	KU 8610	413058	24 March 1931	SM

Leyland Short Lion PLSC1; Leyland 28 hp petrol engine; sliding-mesh (crash) gearbox. Leyland B31F body   Cost £1,225 each

Fleet Number	Entered Service	Registration Number	Chassis Number	Withdrawn	Disposal
311	13 October 1926	KU 9901	45273	24 March 1931	S
312	18 October 1926	KU 9902	45272	30 July 1936	ST
313	13 October 1926	KU 9903	45274	12 August 1936	ARP/K/SH
314	13 October 1926	KU 9904	45275	12 August 1936	L
315	2 November 1926	KU 9905	45276	24 March 1931	S
316	3 November 1926	KU 9906	45277	12 August 1936	L
317	5 November 1926	KU 9907	45278	12 August 1936	BCED/H

AEC 413 chassis; AEC 35 hp petrol engine; Northern Counties B30FD body   Cost £1,205 each

Fleet Number	Entered Service	Registration Number	Chassis Number	Withdrawn	Disposal
318	29 January 1927	KU 9908	413121	24 July 1934	T
319	10 January 1927	KU 9909	413125	November 1933	GL/N
320	3 February 1927	KU 9910	413122	24 March 1931	SV/N
321	15 January 1927	KU 9911	413124	15 November 1934	GL/N
322	13 January 1927	KU 9912	413126	31 December 1930	SV/H/SH
323	10 January 1927	KU 9913	413127	30 July 1936	H
324	31 January 1927	KU 9914	413123	6 April 1936	P

Leyland Long Lion PLSC3; Leyland 28 hp (43° bhp) petrol engine; sliding-mesh (crash) gearbox. Leyland B36R body   Cost £1,418-6-0d per bus

Fleet Number	Entered Service	Registration Number	Chassis Number	Withdrawn	Disposal
325	7 September 1927	KW 2260	46020	12 August 1936	SW/W/Sy/ WYTM
326	7 September 1927	KW 2261	46021	20 September 1938	ARP/K/SH
327	7 September 1927	KW 2262	46025	12 August 1936	KE
328	7 September 1927	KW 2263	46023	30 September 1938	ARP/K/CO
329	20 September 1927	KW 2264	46024	31 December 1938	ARP/K

MOTOR BUS FLEET LIST

Fleet Number	Entered Service	Registration Number	Chassis Number	Withdrawn	Disposal
355	12 November 1928	KW 4502	70327	31 October 1944	S
356	12 November 1928	KW 4503	70329	26 June 1946	DE
357	1 November 1928	KW 4504	70328	31 December 1943	S
358	12 November 1928	KW 4505	70330	18 April 1947	H
359	12 November 1928	KW 4506	70331	31 October 1947	GL
360	12 November 1928	KW 4507	70332	8 March 1948	K
361	13 November 1928	KW 4508	70333	26 June 1946	DE
362	15 December 1928	KW 4509	70334	17 April 1948	K
363	15 November 1928	KW 4510	70335	20 February 1946	K
364	12 November 1928	KW 4511	70337	4 October 1948	GL/BL
365	12 November 1928	KW 4512	70336	4 March 1946	K
366	12 November 1928	KW 4513	70338	26 June 1946	DE
367	12 November 1928	KW 4514	70339	20 November 1945	SA

Leyland Long Lion FLSC3; Leyland 28 hp petrol engine; sliding mesh (crash) gearbox
Leyland B35F body   Cost £1,317 each

Fleet Number	Entered Service	Registration Number	Chassis Number	Withdrawn	Disposal
368	2 February 1929	KW 5220	47905	28 September 1938	ARP/K/SH
369	2 February 1929	KW 5221	47906	30 November 1938	ARP/K
370	2 February 1929	KW 5222	47907	31 December 1938	ARP/K/HR
371	2 February 1929	KW 5223	47908	31 December 1938	ARP/K
372	1 February 1929	KW 5224	47909	18 March 1939	ARP/GL/H
373	2 February 1929	KW 5225	47910	31 December 1938	ARP

Leyland Titan TD1; Leyland 38.4 hp petrol engine. Vickers L27/24RO body.   Cost £1,845 each.
Re-equipped with Gardner 6LW engines; 1933-376, 1934-378/9, 381/2/4; 1935-374/57/7,383; 1936-385.
Sliding mesh (crash) gearbox. Loaned to London 1940-1: 374/6/7 and to Sheffield 1940-1: 381-5.

Fleet Number	Entered Service	Registration Number	Chassis Number	Withdrawn	Disposal
374	26 March 1929	KW 5320	70618	1945	K
375	28 March 1929	KW 5321	70619	31 August 1948	K
376	30 April 1929	KW 5322	70620	17 April 1948	K
377	30 April 1929	KW 5323	70621	24 June 1948	GL/TA
378	3 May 1929	KW 5324	70622	26 September 1947	K
379	2 May 1929	KW 5325	70623	30 November 1945	K/M
381	9 July 1929	KW 6500	70734	31 August 1948	TO/G
382	6 July 1929	KW 6501	70735	20 February 1946	K
383	6 July 1929	KW 6502	70736	4 March 1946	K
384	6 July 1929	KW 6503	70737	4 March 1946	K
385	17 July 1929	KW 6504	70738	31 August 1948	SP

MOTOR BUS FLEET LIST

Leyland Lioness PLC1; Leyland 28.9 hp petrol engine sliding mesh (crash) gearbox; Roe B26F normal-control body   Cost £1,238. One-man-operation bus. Parcels Department 1932-7; Illuminated vehicle 1937-1959.

Fleet Number	Entered Service	Registration Number	Chassis Number	Withdrawn	Disposal
380	7 May 1929	KW 6025	47768	30 July 1932	PD/SV/RE

Leyland Super Lion LT1; Leyland 4 cylinder 28.9 hp petrol engine; sliding mesh (crash) gearbox; Leyland B35F body.   Cost £1,362 per bus. UW 4t 16cwt 2qr. Relicensed 1/11/42 to 11/8/1945-388, with perimeter seats for 31.

Fleet Number	Entered Service	Registration Number	Chassis Number	Withdrawn	Disposal
386	3 August 1929	KW 6505	50509	31 December 1938	ARP/K/HE
387	3 August 1929	KW 6506	50510	31 December 1938	ARP/GL/H
388	3 August 1929	KW 6507	50511	31 December 1938	MOWT/WA/WI
389	10 August 1929	KW 6508	50512	31 December 1938	ARP/GL/H
390	10 August 1929	KW 6509	50513	31 December 1938	ARP/GL/H

Leyland Titan TD2: Leyland 8.6 litre 46.8 hp oil engine; sliding mesh (crash) gearbox; Leyland L24/24R body. UW 6t 15½cwt.   Cost £1,087-12-6d including hire charges of £612-7-6d. Purchased October 1933.

Fleet Number	Entered Service	Registration Number	Chassis Number	Withdrawn	Disposal
391	3 December 1932	TF 9821	1942	15 March 1948	K

AEC Regent 661; AEC 8.8 litre 49 hp A164 oil engine, indirect injection; pre-selector, Weymann composite H26/24R body (No. CS 23).   Cost £1,854-17-8d including hire charges of £855-18-0d. Purchased July 1933.

Fleet Number	Entered Service	Registration Number	Chassis Number	Withdrawn	Disposal
392	28 October 1932	MV 3749	6612050	24 March 1948	K

AEC 'Q' 761; AEC 45.7 hp 7.4 litre petrol engine, offside-mounted. Metropolitan-Cammell H31/29F all-metal body: Cost £1,800. UW 5t 18cwt 1qr. Possibly fitted with saloon door by BCT in 1935 as 'Q' trolleybus 633. Sold for £250 2/8/1940.

Fleet Number	Entered Service	Registration Number	Chassis Number	Withdrawn	Disposal
393	31 August 1933	KY 5141	761008	7 September 1939	DU/BU TY/BF

Daimler COG5: Gardner 5LW engine 36.5 hp; pre-selector; Weymann H30/26R all-metal body (No. M206). UW 6t 5cwt   Cost £1,648-0-8d including hire charges of £648-0-8d.

Fleet Number	Entered Service	Registration Number	Chassis Number	Withdrawn	Disposal
394	13 September 1934	ADU 471	9226	31 December 1949	KI

MOTOR BUS FLEET LIST

AEC Regent 661; AEC A165 8.8 litre 49.2 hp/90 bhp direct-injection 1800 rpm engine; compression ratio 16:1 : fluid flywheel; Wilson floor-mounted pre-selector. Weymann H27/24R body (395-414), English Electric H27/24R body (415-419) Cost £1,913 each. UW 6" tons. Nos. 415-418 received East Lancs H30/26R bodies, 1944 No. 405 received body from 398, 1949.

Fleet Number	Entered Service	Registration Number	Chassis Number	Withdrawn	Disposal
395	6 Feb 1935	KY9100	06613185	30 September 1950	BI
396	6 Feb 1935	KY 9101	06613182	31 October 1952	RH/TUL
397	6 February 1935	KY 9102	06613174	31 October 1952	GL/AU
398	1 March 1935	KY 9103	06613177	7 May 1949	S
399	19 February 1935	KTY9104	06613192	30 September 1950	B1
400	20 February 1935	KY 9105	06613190	31 October 1952	GL/RO
401	22 February 1935	KY9106	06613183	23 October 1952	GL/BIMBK
402	23 February 1935	KY 9107	06613196	30 September 1950	BI
403	26 February 1935	KY 9108	06613197	31 December 1949	BI
404	5 March 1935	KY 9109	06613198	20 August 1949	BR/BE
405	7 March 1935	KY 9110	06613178	30 September 1950	B1
406	7 March 1935	KY 9111	06613191	30 December 1950	CP
407	8 April 1935	KY 9112	06613187	31 December 1949	BI
408	5 April 1935	KY 9113	06613189	20 September 1949	S
409	8 April 1935	KY 9114	06613195	20 September 1949	BR/BE
410	8 April 1935	KY 9115	06613194	28 November 1952	GL/FF
411	8 April 1935	KY 9116	06613193	21 October 1952	RH
412	8 April 1935	KY 9117	06613180	31 December 1949	BI
413	8 April 1935	KY 9118	06613184	29 November 1952	GL/AU
414	8 April 1935	KY 9119	06613176	13 September 1950	BI
415	8 April 1935	KY 9120	06613181	23 October 1952	GL/AU
416	8 April 1935	KY 9121	06613188	31 October 1952	GL/FF
417	8 April 1935	KY 9122	06613179	13 September 1950	BI
418	8 April 1935	KY 9123	06613175	29 October 1949	BR/BE
419	20 April 1935	KY 9124	06613186	23 October 1951	O/BC

Daimler COG6: Gardner 6LW 8.4 litre 43.5 hp engine; pre-selector. Weymann H26/26R body Cost £1,822.

Fleet Number	Entered Service	Registration Number	Chassis Number	Withdrawn	Disposal
420-	20 December 1935	AKU 181	9517	29 December 1949	BI

AEC 661; AEC 7.7 litre 41 hp 6-cylinder engine; pre-selector; Weymann H28/26R body (421-5); English Electric H28/26R body (426-430) Cost £1,941-2-6d each (421-5) £1,938-17-6d each (426-430). Numbers 428-430 received East Lancs. H30/26R bodies, 1944. UW 6t 14cwt (421-425) UW 6t 15cwt (426-430).

Fleet Number	Entered Service	Registration Number	Chassis Number	Withdrawn	Disposal
421	10 September 1936	AKW 421	06614042	28 November 1952	RH
422	3 September 1936	AKW 422	06614043	13 September 1950	BI
423	2 September 1936	AKW 423	06614044	23 October 1952	RH
424	1 October 1936	AKW 424	06614045	6 August 1953	RH

MOTOR BUS FLEET LIST

Fleet Number	Entered Service	Registration Number	Chassis Number	Withdrawn	Disposal
425	7 September 1936	AKW 425	06614047	31 August 1950	BI
426	1 August 1936	AKW 426	06614041	31 August 1950	CN
427	1 August 1936	AKW 427	06614046	20 September 1949	BR/BE/HU
428	1 August 1936	AKW 428	06614048	12 September 1950	BI
429	2 August 1936	AKW 429	06614049	8 May 1953	RH
430	2 August 1936	AKW 430	06614050	30 June 1953	RH/PR/BI

Daimler COG6: Gardner 6LW 8.4 litre 43.5 hp engine; 3000 rpm; Daimler fluid flywheel; Wilson pre-selector; final drive ratio 6.25:1; Weymann H28/26R body Cost £1957-5-0d UW 6t 14" cwt.

Fleet Number	Entered Service	Registration Number	Chassis Number	Withdrawn	Disposal
431	7 October 1936	AKW 431	9655	14 March 1950	BI
432	1 August 1936	AKW 432	9656	4 August 1950	BI
433	9 October 1936	AKW 433	9657	31 December 1949	KI
434	2 November 1936	AKW 434	9658	31 August 1950	BI
435	16 August 1936	AKW 435	9659	13 December 1949	KI
436	17 October 1936	AKW 436	9660	7 June 1951	B1
437	5 August 1936	AKW 437	9661	20 May 1950	BI
438	1 October 1936	AKW 438	9662	29 November 1952	RH
439	1 October 1936	AKW 439	9663	31 December 1949	KI
440	31 August 1936	AKW 440	9664	31 August 1950	BI
441	1 October 1936	AKW 441	9665	31 December 1949	BT
442	1 October 1936	AKW 442	9666	6 November 1946*	S
443	7 August 1936	AKW 443	9667	31 December 1949	KI/WRP

* Destroyed by fire

AEC Regal 662; AEC 45 hp petrol engine. Weymann B30FD bodies Cost £1,710-10-0 each. Received AEC 7.7 litre oil engines and preselectors February 1948.

Fleet Number	Entered Service	Registration Number	Chassis Number	Withdrawn	Disposal
444	9 August 1936	AKW 444	6622002	25 December 1957	H
445	9 August 1936	AKW 445	6622003	29 May 1957	H

(All buses subsequently purchased had oil engines)

Daimler COG6; Gardner 6LW 8.4 litre 43.5 hp engine; 3000 rpm; Daimler fluid flywheel; Wilson pre-selector; final drive ratio 5.8:1. Turning circle 60ft maximum. English Electric H26/26R bodies (446-455); Weymann H26/26R bodies (456-465) Cost £2,093 (446-455), £2,094-11-6d (456-465). Fitted with CWG5 engine circa 1946-462. Number 450 received body from 455, 1952.

Fleet Number	Entered Service	Registration Number	Chassis Number	Withdrawn	Disposal
446	7 January 1939	CKW 446	10576	18 April 1953	RH
447	2 January 1939	CKW 447	10577	18 April 1953	RH
448	5 January 1939	CKW 448	10578	4 April 1952	NO/SH/AV
449	2 January 1939	CKW 449	10579	31 August 1950	BI
450	6 January 1939	CKW 450	10580	31 October 1952	RH

MOTOR BUS FLEET LIST

Daimler CWA6; AEC 7.7 litre 41 hp engine, pre-selector; UH30/26R bodies Duple compisite (476-9, 482-6, 502-11), Northern Counties all-metal (480/1), UW 7t 9cwt Cost £2,549-10-0d (476-9), £2,561-5-0d (480-1), £2,570 (482-6), £2,650 (502-11). Second-hand upholstered seats ex withdrawn buses 1946-51 (476-486); re-seated H31/25R 1956/7 (480-2), H31/26R 1956-7 (484-6, 502-8)

Fleet Number	Registration Number	Chassis Number	Entered Service	Withdrawn	Disposal
476	DKY 476	11456	1 November 1943	17 July 1958	BI
477	DKY 477	11457	1 November 1943	29 January 1958	BI
478	DKY 478	11473	18 November 1943	12 May 1958	BI/BY
479	DKY 479	11474	18 November 1943	17 May 1958	BI/CG/FL
480	DKY 480	11697	3 May 1944	17 May 1958	BI/SG
481	DKY 481	11698	5 May 1944	17 May 1958	BI/BY
482	DKY 482	11781	8 July 1944	17 May 1958	BI
483	DKY 483	11815	18 August 1944	16 May 1958	BI
484	DKY 484	12000	3 March 1945	31 May 1958	BI/SI
485	DKY 485	12001	3 March 1945	28 February 1958	BI
486	DKY 486	12002	3 March 1945	9 May 1958	BI/DA/BI/SR/CK
502	DKY 502	12102	1 May 1945	31 May 1958	BI/CG/FL
503	DKY 503	12103	1 May 1945	31 May 1958	BI
504	DKY 504	12111	1 May 1945	31 January 1958	BI
505	DKY 505	12112	1 January 1946	31 May 1958	BI
506	DKY 506	12121	1 January 1946	31 January 1958	BI/CG
507	DKY 507	12122	1 January 1946	9 May 1958	BI/DA/BI
508	DKY 508	12123	1 January 1946	9 May 1958	BI/DA/CE/CR/BL
509	DKY 509	12131	1 January 1946	31 May 1958	BI
510	DKY 510	12132	1 January 1946	21 April 1958	
511	DKY 511	12146	1 January 1946	9 May 1958	

Daimler CWA6; AEC 7.7 litre 41 hp engine; preselector; Duple UL27/28R body, composite Cost £2,574-5-0d.

Fleet Number	Registration Number	Chassis Number	Entered Service	Withdrawn	Disposal
487	DKY 487	11894	8 January 1945	29 February 1952	CW/HP
488	DKY 488	11895	8 January 1945	29 February 1952	CW/WK
489	DKY 489	11901	8 January 1945	29 February 1952	CW/WE
490	DKY 490	11902	8 January 1945	29 February 1952	NCT/PO
491	DKY 491	11903	8 January 1945	29 February 1952	NCT/LY/MI
492	DKY 492	11904	8 January 1945	29 February 1952	NCT/LY
493	DKY 493	11905	8 January 1945	29 February 1952	CW/FZ
494	DKY 494	11911	6 January 1945	29 February 1952	CW/WE/WL/CK
495	DKY 495	11912	8 January 1945	29 February 1952	CW/WK
496	DKY 496	11913	5 January 1945	29 February 1952	NCT/HY
497	DKY 497	11914	8 January 1945	29 February 1952	CW/FZ

MOTOR BUS FLEET LIST

Fleet Number	Registration Number	Chassis Number	Entered Service	Withdrawn	Disposal
451	CKW 451	10581	2 January 1939	31 August 1950	BI
452	CKW 452	10582	2 January 1939	29 November 1952	RH
453	CKW 453	10583	2 January 1939	13 September 1950	BI
454	CKW 454	10584	2 January 1939	31 December 1952	RH
455	CKW 455	10585	6 December 1938	18 March 1952	S
456	CKW 456	10586	1 October 1938	29 November 1952	RH
457	CKW 457	10587	31 October 1938	19 August 1950	BI
458	CKW 458	10588	1 October 1938	13 September 1950	BI
459	CKW 459	10589	1 October 1938	13 September 1950	BI
460	CKW 460	10590	8 October 1938	31 October 1952	RH
461	CKW 461	10591	1 October 1938	31 October 1952	RH
462	CKW 462	10592	1 October 1938	31 December 1949	BI
463	CKW 463	10593	1 October 1938	28 November 1952	RH/E
464	CKW 464	10594	8 October 1938	13 September 1950	BI
465	CKW 465	10595	1 October 1938	31 December 1949	BI

AEC Regent 661; AEC A182 8.8 litre 49 hp engine (No. U101898); pre-selector; Weymann H30/26R body UW 6t 13cwt 3qr Cost £2,027-15-0d including hire £728-13-7d. Purchased 1940

| 466 | JML 409 | 06615413 | 10 November 1938 | 30 September 1950 | BI |

Guy Arab I; Gardner 5LW 36.5 hp engine; Strachan UL27/28R body (composite) Cost £2,257

| 467 | DKY 467 | FD25944 | 12 July 1943 | 21 June 1951 | SV/BA/SH |

Daimler CWG5; Gardner 5LW 7 litre 36.5 hp 5-clyinder engine; pre-selector; Massey UH30/26R composite body. Cost £2,555 deach.

468	DKY 468	11311	5 February 1943	17 July 1953	RH
469	DKY 469	11323	5 February 1943	7 May 1953	RH
470	DKY 470	11332	10 March 1343	17 July 1953	RH
471	DKY 471	11359	1 June 1943	10 July 1953	RH
472	DKY 472	11382	19 June 1943	17 July 1953	RH
473	DKY 473	11378	19 June 1943	30 December 1952	RH/RI

Guy Arab II; Gardner 6LW 43.5 hp engine; Weyman composite UH30/26R bodies Cost £2,320 Second-hand upholstered seats 1946/1951

| 474 | DKY 474 | FD 26140 | 13 October 1943 | 11 May 1953 | |
| 475 | DKY 475 | FD 26148 | 13 October 1943 | 31 December 1952 | |

MOTOR BUS FLEET LIST

Fleet Number	Entered Service	Registration Number	Chassis Number	Withdrawn	Disposal
540	20 February 1948	EKU 540	09611735	30 April 1963	HY
541	5 March 1948	EKU 541	09611736	30 June 1961	SV/GS
542	5 March 1948	EKU 542	09611737	30 April 1963	HY
543	5 March 1948	EKU 543	09611738	10 May 1961	SV/S

Daimler CVD6; Daimler CO6 8.6 litre engine; pre-selector. Cost £3,779-15-3d each Brush H30/26R composite body; 26ft x 7ft 6in UW 7t 10cwt. Reseated H33/26R 1955-7.

Fleet Number	Entered Service	Registration Number	Chassis Number	Withdrawn	Disposal
544	1 June 1948	EKY 544	14856	30 May 1959	DI/GB
545	2 June 1948	EKY 545	14857	30 June 1959	DI/GB/BS
546	2 June 1948	EKY 546	14858	30 June 1959	DI/GB
547	2 June 1948	EKY 547	14859	30 April 1959	DI/GB
548	1 June 1948	EKY 548	14860	30 June 1959	DI/GB
549	2 June 1948	EKY 549	14861	30 June 1959	DI/GB/ CW/HY
550	2 June 1948	EKY 550	14862	30 June 1959	DI/GB/BS
551	2 June 1948	EKY 551	14863	30 April 1959	DI/GB
552	2 June 1948	EKY 552	14864	30 May 1959	DI/GB
553	2 June 1948	EKY 553	14865	30 May 1959	DI/GB

Leyland PD2/3; Leyland 9.8 litre 0.600 engine, synchromesh gearbox. Cost £3,732-13-0d each. Leyland H30/26R all-metal body, 26ft x 8ft, UW 7t 10cwt 3qr. Reseated H33/26R 1955-6.

Fleet Number	Entered Service	Registration Number	Chassis Number	Withdrawn	Disposal
554	24 July 1949	EKY 554	492000	30 November 1967	WW
555	24 July 1949	EKY 555	492001	31 August 1969	FF
556	24 July 1949	EKY 556	491999	31 October 1970	SV/HA
557	24 July 1949	EKY 557	491519	30 April 1969	RO
558	24 July 1949	EKY 558	491998	31 January 1968	GW
559	24 July 1949	EKY 559	492070	31 July 1970	AU
560	24 July 1949	EKY 560	492072	30 November 1968	WW
561	24 July 1949	EKY 561	492069	30 November 1967	FF
562	24 July 1949	EKY 562	492074	30 November 1967	BRR
563	24 July 1949	EKY 563	492075	31 January 1970	FF
564	24 July 1949	EKY 564	492071	31 January 1968	GS
565	29 December 1949	EKY 565	492073	28 February 1970	RO
566	24 July 1949	EKY 566	492340	31 January 1968	WW
567	29 December 1949	EKY 567	492370	19 April 1968	BRR
568	24 July 1949	EKY 568	492342	20 March 1965	AU
569	1 August 1949	EKY 569	492371	Late 1965	SV/WYPTE
570	1 August 1949	EKY 570	492079	30 April 1969	AU
571	29 December 1949	EKY 571	492341	28 February 1967	HJ
572	29 December 1949	EKY 572	492570	30 June 1969	AU
573	29 December 1949	EKY 573	492569	30 November 1970	AU

MOTOR BUS FLEET LIST

Fleet Number	Entered Service	Registration Number	Chassis Number	Withdrawn	Disposal
498	8 January 1945	DKY 498	11915	29 February 1952	NCT/BB
499	8 January 1945	DKY 499	11921	29 February 1952	NCT/LY
500	8 January 1945	DKY 500	11922	7 February 1952	S
501	8 January 1945	DKY 501	11923	28 February 1952	NCT/LY/MI

Daimler CWA6; AEC 7.7 litre 41 hp engine; pre-selector; Brush UH30/26R bodies. Reseated H31/26R 1956-8 Cost £2,796-10-0d each

Fleet Number	Entered Service	Registration Number	Chassis Number	Withdrawn	Disposal
512	1 January 1946	DKY 512	12137	31 January 1958	BI
513	1 January 1946	DKY 513	12138	31 May 1958	BI
514	1 January 1946	DK Y514	12139	9 May 1958	BI/CG
515	1 January 1946	DKY515	12140	31 January 1958	BI
516	1 January 1946	DKY 516	12141	31 May 1958	BI
517	1 January 1946	DKY517	12142	9 May 1958	BI/CG

Crossley DD42; Crossley 8.6 litre 48.6 hp 6-cylinder engine; synchromesh gearbox; Crossley H30/26R all-metal body; 26ft X 8ft (first 8ft width)Reseated H32/26R 1956 Cost £3,215-10-0d each.

Fleet Number	Entered Service	Registration Number	Chassis Number	Withdrawn	Disposal
518	2 September 1948	EKU 518	94066	31 July 1958	SV/TA
519	2 September 1948	EKU 519	94072	31 July 1958	TA
520	2 September 1948	EKU 520	94078	31 July 1958	TA
521	3 September 1948	EKU 521	94070	31 July 1958	TA
522	3 September 1948	EKU 522	94069	30 June 1958	TA
523	3 September 1948	EKU 523	94067	30 June 1958	TA

AEC Regent III; AEC 9.6 litre 53.57 hp 6-cylinder engine; preselector; Northern Coachbuilders H30/26R composite bodies, 26ft x 7ft 6in. Reseated H/31/26R 1956-7. Cost £3,365-3s-6d each.

Fleet Number	Entered Service	Registration Number	Chassis Number	Withdrawn	Disposal
524	12 December 1947	EKU 524	09611719	30 April 1963	HY
525	12 December 1947	EKU 525	09611720	30 April 1963	AU
526	12 December 1947	EKU 526	09611721	30 April 1963	HY
527	18 September 1947	EKU 527	09611722	23 January 1961	AU
528	12 December 1947	EKU 528	09611723	28 February 1963	TM/HY
529	2 February 1948	EKU 529	09611724	30 April 1963	HY
530	12 December 1947	EKU 530	09611725	30 April 1963	HY
531	12 December 1947	EKU 531	09611726	30 April 1963	HY
532	12 December 1947	EKU 532	09611727	24 May 1961	TA
533	2 February 1948	EKU 533	09611728	30 April 1963	HY
534	2 February 1948	EKU 534	09611729	30 April 1963	HY
535	2 February 1948	EKU 535	09611730	29 September 1960	S
536	20 February 1948	EKU 536	09611731	30 April 1963	HY
537	5 March 1948	EKU 537	09611732	30 April 1963	HY
538	20 February 1948	EKU 538	09611733	30 April 1963	HY
539	5 March 1948	EKU 539	09611734	30 April 1963	HY

MOTOR BUS FLEET LIST

Daimler CVD6; Daimler CD6 8.6 litre 6-cylinder engine; preselector; Barnard H30/26R composite body, 26ft x 7ft 6in (last new 7ft 6in bodies) Cost £3,737-10-0d each

Fleet Number	Entered Service	Registration Number	Chassis Number	Withdrawn	Disposal
574	3 January 1950	FKY 574	15916	30 June 1959	WM
575	2 January 1950	FKY 575	15917	30 June 1959	WM
576	1 January 1950	FKY 576	15918	30 April 1959	WM
577	3 January 1950	FKY 577	15919	30 June 1959	WM
578	2 January 1950	FKY 578	15920	31 January 1959	WM
579	2 January 1950	FKY 579	15921	31 December 1958	WM

AEC 9612E Regent III; AEC A208 9.6 litre (53.57 hp) 6-cylinder engine, pre-selector; Weymann H30./26R body; all-metal (as a.l subsequent buses), 26ft x 8ft. Later fitted with exhaust brakes and reseated H31/26R, 1956 (1-7,9/12, 26/7, 33) or to H33/26R, 1956/7 (1-40) Cost £4,142-15-0d each

Fleet Number	Entered Service	Registration Number	Chassis Number	Withdrawn	Disposal
1	7 November 1949	FKY 1	9612E 4347	30 November 1968	GS
2	6 November 1949	FKY 2	9612E 4348	30 November 1968	GS
3	7 November 1949	FKY 3	9612E 4349	28 February 1969	GS
4	7 November 1949	FKY 4	9612E 4350	30 November 1968	GS
5	6 November 1949	FKY 5	9612E 4351	30 September 1963	AU
6	6 November 1949	FKY 6	9612E 4352	30 April 1964	WW
7	6 November 1949	FKY 7	9612E 4353	24 October 1969	SV/RO
8	6 November 1949	FKY 8	9612E 4354	31 March 1969	GS
9	6 November 1949	FKY 9	9612E 4355	30 November 1968	GS
10	7 November 1949	FKY 10	9612E 4356	30 April 1969	SV/RO
11	6 November 1949	FKY 11	9612E 4357	30 November 1968	GS
12	7 November 1949	FKY 12	9612E 4358	31 March 1969	AU
13	7 November 1949	FKY 13	9612E 4359	25 October 1969	AU
14	6 November 1949	FKY 14	9612E 4360	28 February 1969	RO
15	7 November 1949	FKY 15	9612E 4361	18 February 1964	AU
16	7 November 1949	FKY 16	9612E 4362	30 April 1969	AU
17	6 November 1949	FKY 17	9612E 4363	15 January 1968	HJ
18	7 November 1949	FKY 18	9612E 4364	26 October 1968	AU
19	1 November 1949	FKY 19	9612E 4365	30 November 1968	AU
20	1 November 1949	FKY 20	9612E 4366	31 October 1968	AU
21	1 January 1950	FKY 21	9612E 4367	30 June 1964	WW
22	1 January 1950	FKY 22	9612E 4368	30 November 1968	AU
23	1 January 1950	FKY 23	9612E 4369	30 April 1964	AU
24	1 January 1950	FKY 24	9612E 4370	31 October 1968	AU
25	1 January 1950	FKY 25	9612E 4371	30 September 1963	J
26	1 January 1950	FKY 26	9612E 4372	31 August 1964	AU
27	1 January 1950	FKY 27	9612E 4373	31 August 1964	AU
28	1 January 1950	FKY 28	9612E 4374	29 February 1964	AU
29	2 January 1950	FKY 29	9612E 4375	31 December 1968	AU
30	2 January 1950	FKY 30	9612E 4376	30 April 1964	WW
31	5 March 1950	FKY 31	9612E 4377	30 August 1968	HJ

MOTOR BUS FLEET LIST

Fleet Number	Entered Service	Registration Number	Chassis Number	Withdrawn	Disposal
32	6 March 1950	FKY 32	9612E 4378	30 April 1964	AU
33	5 March 1950	FKY 33	9612E 4379	30 June 1969	AU
34	5 March 1950	FKY 34	9612E 4380	31 March 1964	AU
35	6 March 1950	FKY 35	9612E 4381	31 October 1968	AU
36	6 March 1950	FKY 36	9612E 4382	31 March 1964	AU
37	5 March 1950	FKY 37	9612E 4383	31 March 1964	AU
38	5 March 1950	FKY 38	9612E 4384	31 October 1968	J
39	6 March 1950	FKY 39	9612E 4385	30 November 1968	AU
40	5 March 1950	FKY 40	9612E 4386	30 August 1968	HJ

Leyland PD2/3; Leyland 9.8 litre engine; synchromesh; Leyland (Farringdon) H30/26R bodies 26ft x 8ft. Cost £3,579-10-0d. each ; reseated to H33/26R 1955/6.

Fleet Number	Entered Service	Registration Number	Chassis Number	Withdrawn	Disposal
41	2 September 1950	GKU 41	502774	28 February 1967	WW
42	2 September 1950	GKU 42	502773	31 May 1966	AU
43	2 September 1950	GKU 43	502940	28 February 1967	RO
44	2 September 1950	GKU 44	502941	31 December 1966	WW
45	1 September 1950	GKU 45	502942	21 March 1969	WW
46	2 September 1950	GKU 46	502775	28 February 1967	WW
47	2 September 1950	GKU 47	502771	28 February 1967	WW
48	13 September 1950	GKU 48	502772	30 June 1969	RO
49	13 September 1950	GKU 49	502955	30 September 1969	RO
50	13 September 1950	GKU 50	502956	28 February 1967	WW
51	13 September 1950	GKU 51	504029	28 February 1967	WW
52	13 September 1950	GKU 52	504031	28 February 1967	RO
53	13 September 1950	GKU 53	504030	31 December 1966	WW
54	13 September 1950	GKU 54	504028	30 November 1969	RO
55	13 September 1950	GKU 55	502954	28 February 1967	WW
56	1 October 1950	GKU 56	502953	28 February 1967	WW
57	13 September 1950	GKU 57	504111	30 June 1967	RO
58	2 October 1950	GKU 58	502952	30 April 1970	RO
59	2 October 1950	GKU 59	504109	31 August 1969	SV/WYPTE
60	2 October 1950	GKU 60	504110	28 February 1969	RO
61	3 October 1950	GKU 61	504245	28 February 1967	SV/WYPTE
62	13 October 1950	GKU 62	504288	30 April 1970	RO
63	14 October 1950	GKU 63	504287	30 June 1967	RO
64	14 October 1950	GKU 64	504289	28 February 1967	WW
65	14 October 1950	GKU 65	504286	31 January 1967	WW

AEC 9613E Mark III; AEC 9.6 litre A218 engine (53.5 hp); pre-selector; East Lancashire H33/26R bodies; 27ft x 8ft. Reseated to H35/26R, 1957 Cost £4,507-14-2d each.

Fleet Number	Entered Service	Registration Number	Chassis Number	Withdrawn	Disposal
66	1 November 1952	HKW 66	9613E 7098	30 September 1966	GS
67	1 November 1952	HKW 67	9613E 7090	31 August 1966	HJ
68	1 November 1952	HKW 68	9613E 7091	30 June 1972	GS

MOTOR BUS FLEET LIST

AEC Reliance MU2RA; AEC 7.75 litre engine; Roe B44F; 30ft x 8ft. Renumbered 501/2 March 1967.

Fleet Number	Entered Service	Registration Number	Chassis Number	Withdrawn	Disposal
301	10 March 1958	OKW 106	MU2RA939		WYPTE
302	3 March 1958	OKW 107	MU2RA940		WYPTE

AEC Mark III 'RT', ex London Transport, Feb–May 1958. (Purchased from Bird, Stratford-on-Avon). AEC 9.6 litre engine; pre-selector.   Cost £1,700 each. Bodies H30/26R: PR (Park Royal), W (Weymann), S (Saunders) PR: 404/6-8/410/2-6/418/9/420/4; W: 401-3/5/9/17/22/3/5; S: 411/21 26ft x 7ft 6in.

Fleet Number	Entered Service	Registration Number	Chassis Number	Withdrawn	Disposal
401	16 May 1958	HLW 141	0961048	30 April 1969	AU
402	16 May 1958	HLW 143	0961039	6 October 1963	HJ
403	2 June 1958	HLW 145	0961155	30 April 1969	AU
404	16 May 1958	HLW 148	0961170	30 April 1969	AU
405	2 June 1958	HLW 149	0961173	6 October 1963	HJ
406	10 May 1958	HLW 150	0961164	6 October 1963	AU
407	2 June 1958	HLW 152	0961024	30 November 1968	AU
408	1 July 1958	HLW 155	0961125	30 November 1968	AU
409	2 June 1958	HLW 158	0961133	19 October 1968	AU
410	10 May 1958	HLW 159	0961047	6 October 1963	RS/FR/ DS/RK
411	1 August 1958	HLW157	0961138	30 November 1968	AU
412	10 May 1958	HLW 161	0961058	29 February 1964	AU
413	6 June 1958	HLW 164	0961020	30 April 1969	AU
414	2 June 1958	HLX 223	0961059	17 December 1964	AU
415	17 May 1958	HLX 229	0961166	30 November 1968	AU
416	2 June 1958	HLX 230	0961045	21 September 1968	HJ
417	1 August 1958	HLX 231	0961160	31 October 1963	AU
418	10 May 1958	HLX 232	0961167	28 February 1967	AU
419	16 May 1958	HLX 233	0961121	31 October 1968	AU
420	17 May 1958	HLX 234	0961153	29 February 1964	AU
421	10 May 1958	HLX 235	0961176	30 November 1968	AU
422	1 August 1958	HLX 238	0961036	31 October 1968	AU
423	2 June 1958	HLX 241	0961070	31 October 1968	AU
424	10 May 1958	HLX 243	0961103	28 February 1967	GS
425	1 August 1958	HLX 228	0961177	31 October 1968	AU

AEC Regent V LD2RA; AEC 9.6 litre engine; epicyclic 2-pedal monocontrol; exhaust brake: Metro-Cammell Orion lightweight H39/31FD body; 30ft x 8ft   Cost £5,662-16-10d. each.

Fleet Number	Entered Service	Registration Number	Chassis Number	Withdrawn	Disposal
106	2 May 1959	PKY 106	LD2 RA 584		WYPTE
107	2 May 1959	PKY 107	LD2 RA 585		WYPTE
108	2 May 1959	PKY 108	LD2 RA 586		WYPTE
109	3 May 1959	PKY 109	LD2 RA 587		WYPTE
110	3 May 1959	PKY 110	LD2 RA 588		WYPTE

MOTOR BUS FLEET LIST

Fleet Number	Entered Service	Registration Number	Chassis Number	Withdrawn	Disposal
69	1 November 1952	HKW 69	9613E 7093	31 December 1966	GS
70	1 November 1952	HKW 70	9613E 7096	31 December 1966	KS
71	1 November 1952	HKW 71	9613E 7094	31 July 1972	SV
72	1 November 1952	HKW 72	9613E 7095	31 July 1972	WYPTE
73	1 November 1952	HKW 73	9613E 7097	30 September 1966	GS
74	1 November 1952	HKW 74	9613E 7113	31 October 1966	FF
75	11 November 1952	HKW 75	9613E 7115	31 October 1966	GS
76	11 November 1952	HKW 76	9613E 7102	31 October 1966	AU
77	12 November 1952	HKW 77	9613E 7101	31 July 1966	AU
78	1 November 1952	HKW 78	9613E 7111	30 June 1966	J
79	12 November 1952	HKW 79	9613E 7103*	31 May 1966	WW
80	1 November 1952	HKW 80	9613E 7120	30 September 1966	WW
81	5 December 1952	HKW 81	9613E 7099	31 July 1972	FF
82	5 December 1952	HKW 82	9613E 7107	30 September 1971	GS
83	1 December 1952	HKW 83	9613E 7110	30 June 1972	SV/
84	1 December 1952	HKW 84	9613E 7108	31 July 1972	WYPTE/JS
85	1 November 1952	HKW 85	9613E 7116	31 July 1972	GS
86	5 December 1952	HKW 86	9613E 7117	31 July 1972	GS
87	13 December 1952	HKW 87	9613E 7122	31 October 1966	GS
88	1 January 1953	HKW 88	9613E 7125	31 August 1966	HJ
89	1 January 1953	HKW 89	9613E 7106	30 November 1966	J
90	1 January 1953	HKW 90	9613E 7092	31 December 1971	HJ
91	14 July 1953	HKW 91	9613E 7109	31 January 1967	SV/GS
92	21 July 1953	HKW 92	9613E 7118	31 October 1966	HJ
93	22 July 1953	HKW 93	9613E 7100	30 September 1966	HJ
94	21 July 1953	HKW 94	9613E 7114	30 September 1966	HJ
95	14 August 1953	HKW 95	9613E 7119	31 May 1966	HJ
96	13 August 1953	HKW 96	9613E 7121	31 May 1966	WW
97	21 August 1953	HKW 97	9613E 7123	30 November 1966	WW
98	21 August 1953	HKW 98	9613E 7089	31 August 1966	HJ
99	2 September 1953	HKW 99	9613E 7112	31 December 1966	HJ
100	2 September 1953	HKW 100	9613E 7127	30 September 1966	FF
101	18 September 1953	HKW 101	9613E 7124	31 January 1967	FF
102	2 September 1953	HKW 102	9613E 7126	31 January 1967	GS
103	3 September 1953	HKW 103	9613E 7128	31 January 1967	FF
104	18 September 1953	HKW 104	9613E 7105	31 January 1967	FF
105	29 September 1953	HKW 105		28 February 1967	GS

* Quoted by BCT as 9613E 7095

MOTOR BUS FLEET LIST

Fleet Number	Entered Service	Registration Number	Chassis Number	Withdrawn	Disposal
111	1 June 1959	PKY 111	LD2 RA 589		WYPTE
112	9 June 1959	PKY 112	LD2 RA 590		WYPTE
113	1 June 1959	PKY 113	LD2 RA 591		WYPTE
114	1 June 1959	PKY 114	LD2 RA 592		WYPTE
115	5 June 1959	PKY 115	LD2 RA 593		WYPTE
116	1 July 1959	PKY 116	LD2 RA 594		WYPTE
117	1 July 1959	PKY 117	LD2 RA 595		WYPTE
118	1 July 1959	PKY 118	LD2 RA 596		WYPTE
119	1 July 1959	PKY 119	LD2 RA 597		WYPTE
120	2 July 1959	PKY 120	LD2 RA 598		WYPTE

AEC Regent V 2D2RA; AEC AV590 9.6 litre engine monocontrol; exhaust brake. Metro-Cammell H39/31FD Cost £5,876 each.

Fleet Number	Entered Service	Registration Number	Chassis Number	Withdrawn	Disposal
121	3 May 1961	UKY 121	2D 2RA 1003	31 July 1972	RO
122	2 May 1961	UKY 122	2D 2RA 1004	31 July 1972	CA/CU
123	5 May 1961	UKY 123	2D 2RA 1005	30 April 1973	RO
124	2 May 1961	UKY 124	2D 2RA 1006	31 July 1972	RO
125	2 May 1961	UKY 125	2D 2RA 1007	31 July 1972	IT/BLL/DF

AEC Regent V 2D3RA; AEC AV590 9.6 litre engine; syncromesh gearbox; exhaust brake (126-195); Metro-Cammell bodies; H39/31FD (126-135), H40/30FD (136-225). Cost: £5,898-14-0d (126-135), £5,806-15-0d (136-165), £5,904-19-0d (166-195), £6,000-0-0d (196-225).

Fleet Number	Entered Service	Registration Number	Chassis Number	Withdrawn	Disposal
A126	18 November 1962	YAK 126	2D3RA 1061		WYPTE
A127	7 November 1962	YAK 127	2D3RA 1062		WYPTE
A128	7 November 1962	YAK 128	2D3RA 1063		WYPTE
A129	7 November 1962	YAK 129	2D3RA 1064		WYPTE
A130	18 November 1962	YAK 130	2D3RA 1065		WYPTE
A131	19 November 1962	YAK 131	2D3RA 1066		WYPTE
A132	18 November 1962	YAK 132	2D3RA 1067		WYPTE
A133	18 November 1962	YAK 133	2D3RA 1068		WYPTE
A134	7 November 1962	YAK 134	2D3RA 1069		WYPTE
A135	18 November 1962	YAK 135	2D3RA 1070		WYPTE
136	1 April 1963	YK W136	2D3RA 1205		WYPTE
137	1 April 1963	YK W137	2D3RA 1206		WYPTE
138	1 April 1963	YKW138	2D3RA 1207		WYPTE
139	5 April 1963	YK W139	2D3RA 1208		WYPTE
140	1 April 1963	YKW140	2D3RA 1209		WYPTE
141	1 May 1963	YKW 141	2D3RA 1210		WYPTE
142	3 April 1963	YKW 142	2D3RA 1211		WYPTE
143	3 April 1963	YKW 143	2D3RA 1212		WYPTE
144	3 April 1963	Y KW144	2D3RA 1213		WYPTE
145	1 April 1963	YKW145	2D3RA 1214		WYPTE

MOTOR BUS FLEET LIST

Fleet Number	Entered Service	Registration Number	Chassis Number	Withdrawn	Disposal
146	3 April 1963	YKW 146	2D3RA 1215		WYPTE
147	1 May 1963	YKW 147	2D3RA 1216		WYPTE
148	1 May 1963	YKW 148	2D3RA 1217		WYPTE
149	1 May 1963	YKW 149	2D3RA 1218		WYPTE
150	1 May 1963	YKW 150	2D3RA 1219		WYPTE
151	8 May 1963	YKW 151	2D3RA 1220		WYPTE
152	1 May 1963	YKW 152	2D3RA 1221		WYPTE
153	1 May 1963	YKW 153	2D3RA 1222		WYPTE
154	1 May 1963	YKW 154	2D3RA 1223		WYPTE
155	1 May 1963	YKW 155	2D3RA 1224		WYPTE
156	1 May 1963	YKW 156	2D3RA 1225		WYPTE
157	1 May 1963	YKW 157	2D3RA 1226		WYPTE
158	1 May 1963	YKW 158	2D3RA 1227		WYPTE
159	1 May 1963	YKW 159	2D3RA 1228		WYPTE
160	1 May 1963	YKW 160	2D3RA 1229		WYPTE
161	1 May 1963	YKW 161	2D3RA 1230		WYPTE
162	1 May 1963	YKW 162	2D3RA 1231		WYPTE
163	3 May 1963	YKW 163	2D3RA 1232		WYPTE
164	8 May 1963	YKW 164	2D3RA 1233		WYPTE
165	1 May 1963	YKW 165	2D3RA 1234		WYPTE
166	2 September 1963	2166 KW	2D3RA 1334		WYPTE
167	2 September 1963	2167 KW	2D3RA 1335		WYPTE
168	5 October 1963	2168 KW	2D3RA 1336		WYPTE
169	5 October 1963	2169 KW	2D3RA 1337		WYPTE
170	5 October 1963	2170 KW	2D3RA 1338		WYPTE
171	5 October 1963	2171 KW	2D3RA 1339		WYPTE
172	5 October 1963	2172 KW	2D3RA 1340		WYPTE
173	5 October 1963	2173 KW	2D3RA 1341		WYPTE
174	1 November 1963	2174 KW	2D3RA 1342		WYPTE
175	1 November 1963	2175 KW	2D3RA 1343		WYPTE
176	1 November 1963	2176 KW	2D3RA 1344		WYPTE
177	1 November 1963	2177 KW	2D3RA 1345		WYPTE
178	1 November 1963	2178 KW	2D3RA 1346		WYPTE
179	1 November 1963	2179 KW	2D3RA 1347		WYPTE
180	1 November 1963	2180 KW	2D3RA 1348		WYPTE
181	1 November 1963	2181 KW	2D3RA 1349		WYPTE
182	1 November 1963	2182 KW	2D3RA 1350		WYPTE
183	1 November 1963	2183 KW	2D3RA 1351		WYPTE
184	1 November 1963	2184 KW	2D3RA 1352		WYPTE
185	1 November 1963	2185 KW	2D3RA 1353		WYPTE
186	1 November 1963	2186 KW	2D3RA 1354		WYPTE
187	1 November 1963	2187 KW	2D3RA 1355		WYPTE
188	1 November 1963	2188 KW	2D3RA 1356		WYPTE
189	1 November 1963	2189 KW	2D3RA 1357		WYPTE

MOTOR BUS FLEET LIST

Fleet Number	Entered Service	Registration Number	Chassis Number	Withdrawn	Disposal
190	1 November 1963	2190 KW	2D3RA 1358		WYPTE
191	1 November 1963	2191 KW	2D3RA 1359		WYPTE
192	1 November 1963	2192 KW	2D3RA 1360		WYPTE
193	1 November 1963	2193 KW	2D3RA 1361		WYPTE
194	1 November 1963	2194 KW	2D3RA 1362		WYPTE
195	1 November 1963	2195 KW	2D3RA 1363		WYPTE
196	2 March 1964	6196 KW	2D3RA 1421		WYPTE
197	2 March 1964	6197 KW	2D3RA 1422		WYPTE
198	6 March 1964	6198 KW	2D3RA 1423		WYPTE
199	2 March 1964	6199 KW	2D3RA 1424		WYPTE
200	2 March 1964	6200 KW	2D3RA 1425		WYPTE
201	2 March 1964	6201 KW	2D3RA 1426		WYPTE
202	2 March 1964	6202 KW	2D3RA 1427		WYPTE
203	2 March 1964	6203 KW	2D3RA 1428		WYPTE
204	2 March 1964	6204 KW	2D3RA 1429		WYPTE
205	2 March 1964	6205 KW	2D3RA 1430		WYPTE
206	2 March 1964	6206 KW	2D3RA 1431		WYPTE
207	1 March 1964	6207 KW	2D3RA 1432		WYPTE
208	2 March 1964	6208 KW	2D3RA 1433		WYPTE
209	1 March 1964	6209 KW	2D3RA 1434		WYPTE
210	2 March 1964	6210 KW	2D3RA 1435		WYPTE
211	2 March 1964	6211 KW	2D3RA 1436		WYPTE
212	1 March 1964	6212 KW	2D3RA 1437		WYPTE
213	2 March 1964	6213 KW	2D3RA 1438		WYPTE
214	2 April 1964	6214 KW	2D3RA 1439		WYPTE
215	1 March 1964	6215 KW	2D3RA 1440		WYPTE
216	2 March 1964	6216 KW	2D3RA 1441		WYPTE
217	1 April 1964	6217 KW	2D3RA 1442		WYPTE
218	1 April 1964	6218 KW	2D3RA 1443		WYPTE
219	14 March 1964	6219 KW	2D3RA 1444		WYPTE
220	1 April 1964	6220 KW	2D3RA 1445		WYPTE
221	10 April 1964	6221 KW	2D3RA 1446		WYPTE
222	2 April 1964	6222 KW	2D3RA 1447		WYPTE
223	14 March 1964	6223 KW	2D3RA 1448		WYPTE
224	1 April 1964	6224 KW	2D3RA 1449		WYPTE
225	1 April 1964	6225 KW	2D3RA 1450		WYPTE

Daimler CVG6/30; Gardner 6LW 10.45 litre engine, Daimatic transmission. East Lancashire (Neepsend) H40/30FD body

Fleet Number	Entered Service	Registration Number	Chassis Number	Withdrawn	Disposal
226	12 September 1966	EAK 226D	30412		WYPTE
227	3 August 1966	EAK 227D	30413		WYPTE
228	10 September 1966	EAK 228D	30414		WYPTE
229	3 October 1966	EAK 229D	30415		WYPTE

MOTOR BUS FLEET LIST

Fleet Number	Entered Service	Registration Number	Chassis Number	Withdrawn	Disposal
230	16 September 1966	EAK 230D	30416		WYPTE
231	1 November 1966	EAK 231D	30417		WYPTE
232	12 October 1966	EAK 232D	30418		WYPTE
233	11 September 1966	EAK 233D	30419		WYPTE
234	1 November 1966	EAK 234D	30420		WYPTE
235	14 October 1966	EAK 235D	30421		WYPTE
236	1 November 1966	EAK 236D	30422		WYPTE
237	2 October 1966	EAK 237D	30423		WYPTE
238	16 August 1966	EAK 238D	30424		WYPTE
239	3 October 1966	EAK 239D	30425		WYPTE
240	1 November 1966	EAK 240D	30426		WYPTE

Leyland PD3A/2; Leyland O.600 engine; pneumocyclic transmission; East Lancashire (Neepsend) H40/30FD body; UW 8t 11cwt 2qr.

Fleet Number	Entered Service	Registration Number	Chassis Number	Withdrawn	Disposal
241	2 January 1967	FKY 241E	L63130		WYPTE
242	2 January 1967	FKY 242E	L63131		WYPTE
243	23 January 1967	FKY 243E	L63132		WYPTE
244	2 January 1967	FKY 244E	L63133		WYPTE
245	1 February 1967	FKY 245E	L63134		WYPTE
246	1 February 1967	FKY 246E	L63135		WYPTE
247	2 January 1967	FKY 247E	L63136		WYPTE
248	2 February 1967	FKY 248E	L63137		WYPTE
249	1 February 1967	FKY 249E	L63138		WYPTE
250	2 January 1967	FKY 250E	L63139		WYPTE
251	1 February 1967	FKY 251E	L63140		WYPTE
252	1 February 1967	FKY 252E	L63141		WYPTE
253	1 March 1967	FKY 253E	L63142		WYPTE
254	1 February 1967	FKY 254E	L63143		WYPTE
255	1 March 1967	FKY 255E	L63144		WYPTE

Leyland Atlantean PDR1/2; Leyland O.600 engine; pneumocyclic gearbox. Metro-Cammell-Weymann H43/31FD; engine shrouds (later removed). UW 8t 12cwt 3qr.

Fleet Number	Entered Service	Registration Number	Chassis Number	Withdrawn	Disposal
256	21 February 1967	FKY 256E	L63107		WYPTE
257	1 March 1967	FKY 257E	L63108		WYPTE
258	1 March 1967	FKY 258E	L63109		WYPTE
259	1 March 1967	FKY 259E	L63110		WYPTE
260	1 March 1967	FKY 260E	L63111		WYPTE
261	1 March 1967	FKY 261E	L63112		WYPTE
262	1 March 1967	FKY 262E	L63113		WYPTE
263	1 March 1967	FKY 263E	L63114		WYPTE
264	1 March 1967	FKY 264E	L63115		WYPTE
265	1 March 1967	FKY 265E	L63116		WYPTE
266	1 March 1967	FKY 266E	L63117		WYPTE

MOTOR BUS FLEET LIST

Fleet Number	Entered Service	Registration Number	Chassis Number	Withdrawn	Disposal
267	1 March 1967	FKY 267E	L63118		WYPTE
268	1 March 1967	FKY 268E	L63119		WYPTE
269	1 March 1967	FKY 269E	L63120		WYPTE
270	1 March 1967	FKY 270E	L63121		WYPTE

Daimler Fleetline CRG6/30LX; Gardner 6LX engine, Daimatic transmission. Metro-Cammell-Weymann H43/31FD body; UW 8t 13cwt 2qr.

Fleet Number	Entered Service	Registration Number	Chassis Number	Withdrawn	Disposal
271	22 February 1967	FKY 271E	61697		WYPTE
272	2 March 1967	FKY 272E	61698		WYPTE
273	1 March 1967	FKY 273E	61700		WYPTE
274	1 March 1967	FKY 274E	61699		WYPTE
275	1 March 1967	FKY 275E	61701		WYPTE
276	1 March 1967	FKY 276E	61702		WYPTE
277	1 March 1967	FKY 277E	61703		WYPTE
278	1 March 1967	FKY 278E	61704		WYPTE
279	1 March 1967	FKY 279E	61705		WYPTE
280	1 March 1967	FKY 280E	61706		WYPTE
281	1 March 1967	FKY 281E	61707		WYPTE
282	1 March 1967	FKY 282E	61708		WYPTE
283	1 March 1967	FKY 283E	61709		WYPTE
284	1 March 1967	FKY 284E	61710		WYPTE
285	1 March 1967	FKY 285E	61711		WYPTE

Leyland Atlantean PDR1/3; Leyland O.680 engine; pneumocyclic gearbox. Metro-Cammell-Weymann H43/31FD; 30ft 6in x 8ft x 14ft.

Fleet Number	Entered Service	Registration Number	Chassis Number	Withdrawn	Disposal
286	17 October 1968	LAK 286G	800144		WYPTE
287	1 November 1968	LAK 287G	800145		WYPTE
288	23 October 1968	LAK 288G	800955		WYPTE
289	14 October 1968	LAK 289G	800956		WYPTE
290	24 October 1968	LAK 290G	800957		WYPTE
291	16 January 1969	LAK 291G	800981		WYPTE
292	1 November 1968	LAK 292G	800982		WYPTE
293	1 November 1968	LAK 293G	801056		WYPTE
294	3 November 1968	LAK 294G	801057		WYPTE
295	2 December 1968	LAK 295G	801058		WYPTE
296	2 November 1968	LAK 296G	801071		WYPTE
297	2 November 1968	LAK 297G	801072		WYPTE
298	8 November 1968	LAK 298G	801073		WYPTE
299	2 December 1968	LAK 299G	801074		WYPTE
300	2 December 1968	LAK 300G	801178		WYPTE

MOTOR BUS FLEET LIST

Leyland PD3A/12; Leyland O.680 engine, pneumocyclic gearbox. Alexander H41/29FD body; 30ft x 8ft x 14ft 5in.

Fleet Number	Entered Service	Registration Number	Chassis Number	Withdrawn	Disposal
301	4 April 1969	LAK 301G	702872		WYPTE
302	4 April 1969	LAK 302G	702948		WYPTE
303	4 April 1969	LAK 303G	702949		WYPTE
304	25 April 1969	LAK 304G	702980		WYPTE
305	9 April 1969	LAK 305G	702981		WYPTE
306	4 April 1969	LAK 306G	703033		WYPTE
307	4 April 1969	LAK 307G	703133		WYPTE
308	4 April 1969	LAK 308G	703134		WYPTE
309	25 April 1969	LAK 309G	703299		WYPTE
310	13 April 1969	LAK 310G	703300		WYPTE
311	14 April 1969	LAK 311G	703414		WYPTE
312	14 April 1969 (or 1.5.69)	LAK 312G	703501		WYPTE
313	14 April 1969	LAK 313G	703502		WYPTE
314	5 May 1969	LAK 314G	703569		WYPTE
315	5 May 1969	LAK 315G	703570		WYPTE

Daimler Fleetline CRG6/30: Gardner 6LX engine; Daimatic transmission. Alexander H43/31FD body; 30ft x 8ft 2in x 14ft 5in (first 8ft 2in wide bodies)

Fleet Number	Entered Service	Registration Number	Chassis Number	Withdrawn	Disposal
316	1 November 1968	LAK 316G	62870		WYPTE
317	18 October 1968	LAK 317G	62871		WYPTE
318	1 November 1968	LAK 318G	62872		WYPTE
319	1 November 1968	LAK 319G	62873		WYPTE
320	1 November 1968	LAK 320G	62874		WYPTE
321	2 November 1968	LAK 321G	62875		WYPTE
322	1 November 1968	LAK 322G	62876		WYPTE
323	5 November 1968	LAK 323G	62877		WYPTE
324	1 December 1968	LAK 324G	62878		WYPTE
325	1 December 1968	LAK 325G	62879		WYPTE
326	7 November 1968	LAK 326G	62880		WYPTE
327	1 December 1968	LAK 327G	62881		WYPTE
328	1 December 1968	LAK 328G	62882		WYPTE
329	1 December 1968	LAK 329G	62883		WYPTE
330	1 December 1968	LAK 330G	62884		WYPTE
331	1 December 1968	LAK 331G	62885		WYPTE
332	2 December 1968	LAK 332G	62886		WYPTE
333	1 December 1968	LAK 333G	62887		WYPTE
334	1 December 1968	LAK 334G	62888		WYPTE
335	9 December 1968	LAK 335G	62889		WYPTE

AEC Swift MP2R; AEC A505 engines; Marshall B45FD body, 36ft x 8ft 2°in; UW 7t 18cwt 0qr; front entrance/centre exit.

Fleet Number	Entered Service	Registration Number	Chassis Number	Withdrawn	Disposal
503	3 September 1969	NAK 503H	MP2R 267		WYPTE
504	13 August 1969	NAK 504H	MP2R 268		WYPTE
505	6 August 1969	NAK 505H	MP2R 269		WYPTE
506	16 September 1969	NAK 506H	MP2R 270		WYPTE
507	15 September 1969	NAK 507H	MP2R 271		WYPTE

Leyland Panther PSUR1R/1, Leyland O.600 engine; pneumocyclic gearbox. Marshall B45FD body; 36ft x 8ft 2°in; UW 8t 11cwt 0qr; front entrance/centre exit.

Fleet Number	Entered Service	Registration Number	Chassis Number	Withdrawn	Disposal
508	24 October 1969	NAK 508H	900043		WYPTE
509	25 November 1969	NAK 509H	900044		WYPTE
510	27 November 1969	NAK 510H	900045		WYPTE
511	1 December 1969	NAK 511H	900046		WYPTE
512	1 December 1969	NAK 512H	900047		WYPTE

Daimler Fleetline CRG6 LX33; Gardner 6LX engine, Diamatic transmission, Alexander H47/29FD body; 33ft x 8ft 2 in x 14ft 6in; front entrance/centre exit.

Fleet Number	Entered Service	Registration Number	Chassis Number	Withdrawn	Disposal
401	14 October 1970	PKW 401J	64323		WYPTE
402	12 August 1970	PKW 402J	64324		WYPTE
403	5 August 1970	PKW 403J	64325		WYPTE
404	3 August 1970	PKW 404J	64326		WYPTE
405	2 November 1970	PKW 405J	64327		WYPTE
406	12 August 1970	PKW 406J	64328		WYPTE
407	7 August 1970	PKW 407J	64329		WYPTE
408	1 December 1970	PKW 408J	64330		WYPTE
409	7 August 1970	PKW 409J	64331		WYPTE
410	11 August 1970	PKW 410J	64332		WYPTE
411	2 November 1970	PKW 411J	64333		WYPTE
412	13 August 1970	PKW 412J	64334		WYPTE
413	13 October 1970	PKW 413J	64335		WYPTE
414	2 November 1970	PKW 414J	64336		WYPTE
415	1 December 1970	PKW 415J	64337		WYPTE
416	2 November 1970	PKW 416J	64338		WYPTE
417	12 August 1970 (October?)	PKW 417J	64339		WYPTE
418	7 October 1970	PKW 418J	64340		WYPTE
419	13 August 1970	PKW 419J	64341		WYPTE
420	17 August 1970	PKW 420J	64342		WYPTE
421	2 November 1970	PKW 421J	64343		WYPTE
422	12 October 1970	PKW 422J	64344		WYPTE

Fleet Number	Entered Service	Registration Number	Chassis Number	Withdrawn	Disposal
423	18 August 1970	PKW 423J	64345		WYPTE
424	12 August 1970	PKW 424J	64346		WYPTE
425	1 December 1970	PKW 425J	64347		WYPTE
426	6 November 1970	PKW 426J	64348		WYPTE
427	7 August 1970	PKW 427J	64349		WYPTE
428	10 October 1970	PKW 428J	64350		WYPTE
429	23 September 1970	PKW 429J	64351		WYPTE
430	1 December 1970	PKW 430J	64352		WYPTE
431	9 August 1970	PKW 431J	64353		WYPTE
432	1 November 1970	PKW 432J	64354		WYPTE
433	1 September 1970	PKW 433J	64355		WYPTE
434	1 December 1970	PKW 434J	64356		WYPTE
435	22 September 1970	PKW 435J	64357		WYPTE
436	6 November 1970	PKW 436J	64358		WYPTE
437	1 November 1970	PKW 437J	64359		WYPTE
438	12 October 1970	PKW 438J	64360		WYPTE
439	2 September 1970	PKW 439J	64361		WYPTE
440	6 November 1970	PKW 440J	64362		WYPTE

Leyland Atlantean PDR2/1; Leyland O.680 engine; Alexander H47/29FD body 33ft x 8ft 2' in; front entrance/centre exit.

Fleet Number	Entered Service	Registration Number	Chassis Number	Withdrawn	Disposal
441	1 July 1971	SKY 441J	7100879		WYPTE
442	1 July 1971	SKY 442J	7100880		WYPTE
443	1 July 1971	SKY 443J	7101002		WYPTE
444	1 July 1971	SKY 444J	7101003		WYPTE
445	1 July 1971	SKY 445J	7101205		WYPTE
446	1 July 1971	SKY 446J	7101206		WYPTE
447	1 July 1971	SKY 447J	7101293		WYPTE
448	1 July 1971	SKY 448J	7101294		WYPTE
449	1 July 1971	SKY 449J	7101405		WYPTE
450	1 July 1971	SKY 450J	7101406		WYPTE
451	1 July 1971	SKY 451J	7101484		WYPTE
452	1 July 1971	SKY 452J	7101485		WYPTE
453	1 July 1971	SKY 453J	7101590		WYPTE
454	1 July 1971	SKY 454J	7101591		WYPTE
455	1 July 1971	SKY 455J	7101739		WYPTE
456	1 July 1971	SKY 456J	7101740		WYPTE
457	1 July 1971	SKY 457J	7101741		WYPTE
458	1 July 1971	SKY 458J	7101742		WYPTE
459	16 July 1971	SKY 459J	7101743		WYPTE
460	1 August 1971	SKY 460J	7101744		WYPTE
461	1 August 1971	TKU 461K	7101745		WYPTE
462	1 August 1971	TKU 462K	7101746		WYPTE

A last visit to Horton Bank Top depot in 1974: a 33ft long Fleetline and several Daimler CVG6/30s flank Halifax No. 366 – on loan but in a poor state of health.

[Photo: Author]

MOTOR BUS FLEET LIST

Fleet Number	Entered Service	Registration Number	Chassis Number	Withdrawn	Disposal
463	1 August 1971	TKU 463K	7101747		WYPTE
464	1 August 1971	TKU 464K	7101748		WYPTE
465	1 August 1971	TKU 465K	7101749		WYPTE
466	1 August 1971	TKU 466K	7101750		WYPTE
467	1 August 1971	TKU 467K	7101751		WYPTE
468	2 August 1971	TKU 468K	7101752		WYPTE
469	2 August 1971	TKU 469K	7101753		WYPTE
470	2 August 1971	TKU 470K	7101754		WYPTE

Daimler Fleetline low-height CRL6/30; Leyland O.680 engine. Alexander H41/31FD body; 30ft x 8ft 2'in (9.5m x 2.5m).

Fleet Number	Entered Service	Registration Number	Chassis Number	Withdrawn	Disposal
336	4 August 1972	XAK 336L	65639		WYPTE
337	1 August 1972	XAK 337L	65640		WYPTE
338	4 August 1972	XAK 338L	65641		WYPTE
339	3 August 1972	XAK 339L	65642		WYPTE
340	9 August 1972	XAK 340L	65643		WYPTE
341	9 August 1972	XAK 341L	65644		WYPTE
342	10 August 1972	XAK 342L	65645		WYPTE
343	4 August 1972	XAK 343L	65646		WYPTE
344	9 August 1972	XAK 344L	65647		WYPTE
345	4 August 1972	XAK 345L	65648		WYPTE
346	3 August 1972	XAK 346L	65649		WYPTE
347	1 August 1972	XAK 347L	65650		WYPTE
348	8 August 1972	XAK 348L	65651		WYPTE
349	3 August 1972	XAK 349L	65652		WYPTE
350	9 August 1972	XAK 350L	65653		WYPTE
351	11 August 1972	XAK 351L	65654		WYPTE
352	9 August 1972	XAK 352L	65655		WYPTE
353	3 August 1972	XAK 353L	65656		WYPTE
354	4 August 1972	XAK 354L	65657		WYPTE
355	15 August 1972	XAK 355L	65658		WYPTE

ABBREVIATIONS – VEHICLE DISPOSALS

A	T. Allen, Hungerford	F	W. K. Fleming	PO	A. Proctor, Nottingham
ARP	Air Raid Precautions vehicle	FF	Fisher & Ford	PR	F. Proctor
AU	Autospares, Bingley	FI	Mrs Firth, Bradford	R	T. R. Renny
AV	Aveyard, Yeadon	FL	Fleet Car Sales	RE	T. Redburn
B	J. Butcher, West Melton	FO	J. Foulds, Bingley	RH	Rhodes, Nottingham
BA	Blamires	FR	J. Fozard, Baildon	RI	Riley, Terrington
BB	Black Bank Salvage	FU	Fulwood	RK	A. Roskoss
BC	Buck, York	FZ	Fitzpatrick	RO	Rollinson
BCED	Bradford Corporation Education Department	G	J. Gage, Cardiff	RS	G. Rhodes
BE	Berresford, Cheddleton	GB	Green Bus Company	S	Scrapped
BF	A. W. Braybrooke & Son, Swaffham	GL	Grit Lorry	SA	Sabena, Brussels
BI	Bird, Stratford on Avon	GS	Goodwin & Smith	SG	Shirley's Garage
BK	Blackman, Halifax	GW	G. Welburn	SH	Showman (unidentified)
BL	Blamire, Bradford	H	Hornby, Bradford	SI	R. Sims
BR	Blair, Manchester	HA	Hartwood Exports	SM	H. Smith
BS	Burns, Brereton	HE	C. Herbert, Redditch	SP	Stevens & Price
BT	Bassett	HJ	Hardwick & Jones	SR	C. A. R. Sergent
BU	Burwell & District	HL	J. Holmes	SS	D. M. Stewart
BY	D. Bayliss, Creca	HP	Humphreys Ltd	ST	J. Standish, Leeds
BIM	Bradford Industrial Museum	HR	Hartwell, Hounslow	SV	Service Vehicle
BRR	Barraclough, Carlton	HS	Hants & Sussex Motor Co	SW	W. G. Spence
BLL	Brakell	HU	S. Hughes, Gomersal	SY	J. D. Say
C	Crabtree, Bradford	HY	Hoyle, Wombwell	T	E. A. Totson
CA	H. Clayforth, Guiseley	HZ	Hartwood Exports	TA	Taylor, Bradford
CE	Cantello, Birmingham	IT	Interaction Trust	TE	H. Tennant
CG	Church Bridge Luxury Coaches	J	Jackson, Bradford	TH	C. Thompson
CH	W. H. Church, Halifax	JS	J. Speed	TI	Tillotson, Burnley
CK	Coppock, Sale	K	Kimberley, Hounslow	TM	Trem, Finningley
CN	Cohen, London	KE	P. Kershaw	TO	H. Thompson
CO	Copcroft	KI	Kingsway, Cudworth	TR	Trent
CP	Cooper	KS	Kaye & Seeley	TU	Turner, Brown Edge
CR	Colbro, Rothwell	L	A. Lockwood, Leeds	TY	Tye Bros
CU	Curran, Edinburgh	LA	W. C. Lawrence	W	Wright (showman)
CW	Cowley, Salford	LE	Lewis, Hanley	WA	Wallace Arnold
D	Davidson, Bradford	LK	J. Leake, Oklahoma	WE	Wesley's Coach Service
DA	H. P. Davis, Birmingham	LY	Lyman, Eckington	WH	Wheatley, Patricroft
De	Devey & Company	M	Mrs Midgley, Hoyland	WI	White, St. Helier
Df	Dunscroft	MI	James Millar, Wakefield	WK	C. C. Wakefield (Castrol)
DI	Diesel Engine Exports	MW	Motor Wreckers, Leeds	WL	J. O. Williams & S. Davies
DS	David Sutliffe	MOWT	Ministry of War Transport 1939-42	WM	Warner's Motors
DU	Dutson, Leeds	N	North, Leeds	WW	Wombwell Diesels
E	Exported	NCT	Nottingham City Transport	WRP	W. & R. P. Bingley, Kinsley
		O	W. C. Oliver, York	WYPTE	West Yorkshire Passenger Transport Executive
		P	Mrs L. M. Phillips	WYTM	West Yorkshire Transport Museum (Transperience)
		PD	Parcels Department		
		PI	F. Pincon		

FINAL FLEET LIST, MARCH 31st 1974

Fleet numbers	Type	Year	Total
106-120	Regent V	1959	15
126-135	Regent V	1962	10
136-225	Regent V	1963/4	90
226-240	Daimler CVG6/30	1966	15
241-255	Leyland PD3A/12	1967	15
256-270	Leyland PDR1/2	1967	15
271-285	Daimler CRG6/30	1967	15
286-300	Leyland PDR1/3	1968	15
301-315	Leyland PD3A/12	1969	15
316-335	Daimler CRG6/30	1968	20
336-355	Daimler CRL6/30	1972	20
401-440	Daimler CRG6/33	1970	40
441-470	Leyland PDR2/1	1971	30
501-502	AEC MU2RA	1958	2
503-507	AEC MP2R	1969	5
508-512	Leyland PSUR1R/1	1969	5
			327

LAST DEPOT ALLOCATION, MARCH 31st 1974

Depot	Fleet numbers	Total
Ludlam Street	117-120, 126-135, 161-225, 408-410, 421-432, 501-510 (and Huddersfield 182, 414, 418)	102
Thornbury	136-160, 286-290, 316-320, 322-325, 332-355, 401-407, 441-451, 511/512	83
Bowling	164-166, 241-255, 256/258/262/267, 291-298, 300-305, 411-414/420 (and Huddersfield 178/179)	91
Bankfoot	106-110, 112-116, 306-315, 326-330, 433-440	33
Saltaire	226-233, 271-285 (and Huddersfield 186/189)	23
Duckworth Lane	452-470	19
Horton Bank Top	234-240, 415-419 (and Calderdale 213/215/218, 312/313/366)	11
		312
Delicensed for Overhaul or recertification	111, 257/259, 260-1, 263-6, 268/9, 270, 299, 321, 331	15
		327
On Hire from Calderdale and Huddersfield		13
		340

All the above vehicles were taken into stock by the West Yorkshire Passenger Transport Executive on 1st April 1974, but the last former Bradford City Transport buses were withdrawn from service on the formation of Yorkshire Rider in 1986. Nevertheless a few continue in use in other parts of the country.

'Yea, even like a dream when one awaketh, so shalt thou make their image vanish out of the City'   (Psalm 73)

SERVICE VEHICLES

Original Fleet No.	Vehicle
303	Grit-waggon 0.25 1933-44
304	Grit-waggon 0.31 1935-44
308	Grit-waggon 0.18 1931-44
313	Stores van 0.37 1936-9, ARP mortuary van, 1939-45
317	BCED school ambulance bus 1936-53
319	Grit-waggon 0.24 1933-44
320	Emergency workshop 0.17 1931-44
321	Grit-waggon 0.28 1935-44
322	Stores orry 0.19 1931-6
326	ARP ambulance 0.57 1939-45
328	ARP ambulance 0.56 1939-45
329	ARP ambulance 0.50 1939-45
330	ARP first-aid post 0.66 1939-44; grit-waggon 1944-54 (0.51 1953-4)
331	ARP first-aid post 0.67 1939-45
332	ARP ambulance 0.51 1939-45
334	ARP ambulance 0.49 1939-45; grit-waggon 0.49 1945-54 (0.52 1953-4)
335	ARP ambulance 0.54 1939-45
336	ARP first-aid post 0.68 1939-44; grit-waggon 0.67 1944-54 (0.53 1953-4)
339	ARP ambulance 0.52 1939-45
359	Grit-waggon 0.94 1948-62 (0.41 1953-62)
364	Grit-waggon 0.91 1949-54 (0.42 1953-4)
368	ARP ambulance 0.53 1939-45
369	ARP ambulance 0.55 1939-45
370	ARP ambulance 0.59 1939-45
371	ARP ambulance 0.60 1939-45
372	ARP first-aid post 0.65 1939-44; grit-waggon 1944-54 (0.54 1953-4)
373	ARP ambulance 0.58 1939-45
377	Grit-waggon 0.92, 1949-62 (0.43 1953-62)
380	Parcels van 0.21 1931-7; illuminated vehicle 1937-59 (0.59 1953-9)
386	ARP mortuary vabn 0.69 1939-45
387	ARP ambulance 0.70 1939-44; grit-waggon 1944-53 (0.55 1953)
389	ARP ambulance 0.71 1939-44; grit-waggon 1944-54 (0.56 1953)
390	ARP ambulance 0.72 1939-44; grit-waggon 1944-53 (0.57 1953)
397	Grit-waggon 0.44 1954-62
400	Grit-waggon 0.45 1954-68
401	Grit-waggon 0.46 1954-68
410	Grit-waggon 0.47 1954-68
413	Grit-waggon 0.48 1954-62
415	Grit-waggon 0.49 1954-62
416	Grit-waggon 0.50 1954-68
467	Driver-training bus 0.60 1951-8
518	Driver-training bus 0.60 1958-9
541	Grit-waggon 0.41 1962-73 (0.64 1971; 0.26 1973)
543	Pole-painters' waggon 0.43 1962-72 (0.65 1971; 0.26 1972)

SERVICE VEHICLES

Original Fleet No.	Vehicle
7	Driver-training bus 0.66 1969-72
10	Driver-training bus 0.69 1969-72 (not used)
556	Driver-training bus 0.67 1970-4 (0.33 1972-4)
569	Driver-training bus 0.61 1966-74 (0.34 1972-4)
59	Driver-training bus 0.68 1971-4 (0.35 1972-4)
61	Driver-training bus 0.60 1968-74 (0.36 1972-4)
71	Driver-training bus 0.37 1973-4
82	Mobile generator bus 0.49 1972
90	Driver-training bus 0.37 1972-3

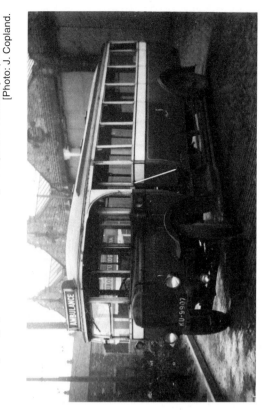

Leyland 'Short Lion' No. 317 survived in post-war livery until 1953 as a schools ambulance, and was photographed on 1st November 1952, in the yard of Thornbury depot.

[Photo: J. Copland.]

BUSES LOANED TO BRADFORD

Fleet Number	Registration	Chassis Number	Entered Service	Returned
Leyland Atlantean Mark II PDR1/1; Alexander H44/34FD body; originally Glasgow Corporation LA91; re-purchased by Leyland April 1963.				
-	SGL 669	623350	August 1964	August 1964
AEC Swift				
-	LYY 827D		25 October 1967	27 October 1967
Leyland Atlantean; Park Royal H47/32FD front entrance/centre exit body.				
-	MTF 665G		16 July 1969	5 August 1969

Leyland TD1 No. 360 and experimental TD2 No. 391 rest wearily outside Ludlam Street depot early in 1946. All are drab and shabby after six years of war.

BUSES LOANED TO BRADFORD

Fleet Number	Registration	Chassis Number	Entered Service	Returned	Withdrawn by LPTB
London Passenger Transport Board Regents; AEC 6-cylinder 95 bhp petrol engines; LGOC H27/21R bodies (ST 362/505/726); Tilling H27/25OS (ST 851/879/966); new 1930/1; hired by BCPT at £25 per month.					
ST 362	GK 3023	6610860	19 October 1942	23 August 1944	8/49
ST 505	GF 7264	6610786	19 October 1942	23 August 1944	7/49
ST 726	GN 2154	6611371	19 October 1942	23 August 1944	12/48
ST 851	GJ 2027	6610579	19 October 1942	30 June 1943	10/45
ST 879	GJ 2055	6610608	19 October 1942	30 June 1943	9/44
ST 966	GK 6242	6611035	19 October 1942	30 June 1943	5/45
London Passenger Transport Board AEC 'RT' loaned to BCPT September 1940; LPTB H30/26R body; 9.6 litre AEC engine; new 1939.					
RT19	FXT 194	6616767			
Leeds City Transport Regents; AEC A152 engines; Roe H30/26 bodies; new 1932					
40	UG 1027	6611935	19 October 1942	March 1943 (although BCPT records show 31/1/1945)	
41	UG 1028	6611936	19 October 1942	March 1943 (although BCPT records show 31/1/1945)	
43	UG 1030	6611938	19 October 1942	March 1943 (although BCPT records show 31/1/1945)	
46	UG 1033	6611941	19 October 1942	March 1943 (although BCPT records show 31/1/1945)	
AEC Bridgemaster, 'chassisless', AEC engine, syncromesh; air suspension on rear axle. Park Royal lowheight 41/31R body; 30ft x 8ft. Also hired by Hull, Huddersfield, Sheffield, Halifax and Leeds; became Barton 805					
-	76 MME	B3RA004	6 May 1958	16 May 1958	
AEC Renown, AEC engine; air suspension on rear axle; Park Royal H39/32FD body					
-	7552MX	U204544	14 April 1964	25 April 1964	
Commercial Vehicles (Daimler) Ltd; Daimler Fleetline CRG6; Gardner 6LW engine; Alexander H44/34FD body; exhibited at Scottish Commercial Vehicle Show, 1963					
-	565 CRW	60613	7 July 1964	21 July 1964	

134

CALDER BUS FLEET OWNED BY BRADFORD, OCTOBER 1st 1928-30th MARCH 1929

Registration	Type	Chassis Number	Seats	Entered Service	Disposal
WU 4576	Chevrolet	RT213703	14	February 1926	?
WU 5562	Chevrolet	7528	14	31March 1926	?
WU 6146	Chevrolet	Y 8313	14	26 June 1926	
WU 6313	Chevrolet	?	14	May 1926	
WU 7090	Chevrole¯	9193	14	June 1926	
WU 6453	Leyland A13	35875	24	1926	Hebble 70
WU 6997	Leyland A13	35876	26	June 1926	Hebble 67
WU8472	Leyland PLSC	45213	31	July 1926	Hebble 59
KU 9303	Leyland PLSC	45217	31	July 1926	Hebble 57
WU 9637	Leyland PLSC	45492	32	14 January 1927	Hebble 58
ED 3278	Leyland A13	?	24	February 1927	Hebble 68
WW 1018	Leyland Lioness	45528	26	April 1927	Hebble 69
WW 1095	BAT	7291	26	April 1927	Hebble 60
WW 2273	Leyland PLSC	45774	31	June 1927	Hebble ?
?	Leyland PLSC	45856	31	June 1927	Hebble 61
WW 3293	Leylanc PLSC	45915	31	August 1927	Hebble 63
WW 3621	Leylanc PLSC	45988	31	September 1927	Hebble 62
WW 3866	Leyland PLSC	46220	36	1 November 1927	Hebble 64
WW 4047	Leyland PLSC	46394	36	November 1927	Hebble 65
WW 4286	Leyland PLSC	46443	36	January 1928	Hanson
WW 7234	Leyland PLSC	46535	31	January 1928	Hebble 66
WR 4375	Leyland A13	?	26	?	Hebble 71
CP 1707	Leyland N	?	32	?	W. Yorks 617
WW 4296	Dennis G	70029	20	January 1928	

(Details courtesy Messrs G. Lumb and J. Copland and the late J. S. Cockshott; extracted from log-books surviving in West Riding County archives, where ownership was recorded as 'Bradford Corporation' but without a date stamp, thus indicating that the buses had been re-sold by Bradford before the first change of ownership had been recorded.)

(All were new to Calder except ED 3278, WR 4375 and CP 1707)

MOTOR BUS FRONT DESTINATION DISPLAYS

	October 1931
BIERLEY	CITY
	DUPLICATE
CUTLER HEIGHTS (Fenby Avenue)	RESERVED
TYERSAL (Via Parsonage Road)	SWAIN HOUSE ROAD
	GREENGATES (Via Undercliffe)
SANDY LANE (Allerton)	APPERLEY BRIDGE
HAWORTH ROAD (Via Toller Lane)	BRIGHOUSE
	HUDDERSFIELD (Via Brighouse)
BANKFOOT	CITY
LISTER PARK	STANNINGLEY
THORNBURY	BRADFORD
CITY	LEEDS
FAGLEY	RAVENSCLIFFE AVENUE
HORTON BANK TOP	FOOTBALL GROUND
WIBSEY	CITY
LITTLE HORTON	
DUCKWORTH LANE	
BANKFOOT (Via Ripleyville)	

(Note: WIBSEY was inserted for use by shortworkings on the Bankfoot-Horton Bank Top service; THORNBURY was for depot journeys and the presence of STANNINGLEY is surprising, as no buses were scheduled to reverse there. HAWORTH ROAD (Via Smith Lane) replaced DAISY HILL shown on 1928 blinds.)

MOTOR BUS FRONT DESTINATION DISPLAYS

March 1974

RESERVED	BRADFORD MOOR	HUDDERSFIELD
SPRINGHEAD ROAD	CITY CENTRE	LEEDS
THORNTON	SALTAIRE	DEWSBURY
THORNBURY	APPERLEY BRIDGE	HALIFAX
FARSLEY	GREENGATES	HALIFAX (GENERAL HOSPITAL)
STANNINGLEY	THORPE EDGE	BRADFORD
BUTTERSHAW	RAVENSCLIFFE	WYKE (GRIFFE HEAD RD.)
CITY CENTRE	HAWORTH ROAD	WYKE (TOWN GATE)
QUEENSBURY	SANDY LANE	SHELF
HOLLINGWOOD LANE	STONEY RIDGE	WOODSIDE
ALLERTON (STONEY LN.)	ECCLESHILL	BAILIFF BRIDGE
WEST BOWLING	HORTON BANK TOP	NORWOOD GREEN
ALLERTON	BUTTERSHAW	OAKENSHAW
HOLME WOOD	WIBSEY	SHEFFIELD
TONG CEMETERY	CITY CENTRE	MEXBOROUGH
DUCKWORTH LANE	WROSE	
ADWALTON	MOORE AVENUE	Deleted:
TONG VILLAGE	FAGLEY	Four Lane Ends
CITY CENTRE	BRIGHOUSE	Ring Road
BIERLEY	UNDERCLIFFE	Newlands
CLAYTON	ST. ENOCH'S ROAD TOP	White Horse
CLAYTON (TOWN END)	TYERSAL	Dudley Hill
SCHOLEMOOR AVENUE	HOLME WOOD	Shipley Moorhead
ELDWICK	BANKFOOT	Dick Hudson's
BRADFORD (CHESTER ST.)	CITY CIRCLE	Thornaby Drive
SHIPLEY GLEN	BOLTON	Heaton
BINGLEY	LISTER PARK	
CROSSFLATTS	CITY CENTRE	

MARCH 1974 'VIA' BLINDS

HEATON	LITTLE HORTON	DUDLEY HILL
TOLLER LANE	ODSAL	BIRKENSHAW
SMITH LANE	WOODSIDE ROAD	FENBY AVENUE
DUCKWORTH LANE	BAILIFF BRIDGE	PARSONAGE RD. TOP
CHAPEL LANE	BRIGHOUSE	SWAINE GREEN
SUNBRIDGE ROAD	NEW WORKS ROAD	LAISTERDYKE
THORNTON ROAD	RESERVED	UNDERCLIFFE
FOUR LANE ENDS	LIMITED STOP	CHURCH BANK
PASTURE LANE	WORKS SPECIAL	HARRIS STREET
BRADFORD ROAD	SCHOOL SPECIAL	FIVE LANE ENDS
LIDGET GREEN	TOUR	THACKLEY
GT. HORTON ROAD	HOSPITAL	CANAL ROAD
EASBY ROAD	SPORTS GROUND	MANNINGHAM LANE
GRANGE ROAD	DEPOT	FRIZINGHALL
CANTERBURY AVENUE	BOLLING HALL	FERNCLIFFE
		GILSTEAD
		PUDSEY
		MEXBOROUGH
		BARNSLEY

Route Names shown in CAPITAL LETTERS	Opened	Route Numbers
BANKFOOT (Red Lion) to LISTER PARK	13th May 1926	72 (1932), 71 (1942)
(Absorbed into City Circle 1st March 1964)		49 (1953)
HAWORTH ROAD (Lynfield Drive)	20th July 1926	69 (1932), 69/70 (1953)
extended to Chellow Grange Road	9th March 1952	29/32/33/35 (1967)
Cross-city service to Greengates etc	8th April 1935	
CUTLER HEIGHTS (Broad Lane)	20th July 1926	65 (1932), 51 (1953)
to Fenby Avenue via Parsonage Road	by January 1928	
Terminus moved from Forster Sq to Hall Ings	8th April 1935	
diverted into HOLME WOOD (51)	12th April 1959	
absorbed into Holme Wood-Bankfoot (80)	6th October 1963	
BIERLEY (Greenwood Arms)	13th October 1926	60 (1932), 21 (1966)
re-routed via Hambledon Avenue	14th May 1956	
extended to Shetcliffe Lane	11th September 1957	
extended to Bierley Lane	2nd June 1958	
FAGLEY (Royal Hotel)	3rd November 1926	66 (1932), 81 (1938)
extended to Falsgrave Avenue (81a), peaks	6th March 1950	73 (1959), 14 (1965)
extended to Falsgrave Avenue (81) full-time	22nd June 1952	
through service to Moore Avenue	7th June 1953	
extended to Flinton Grove	17th June 1962	
DUCKWORTH LANE to LITTLE HORTON	10th January 1927	73 (1932-5, 1942-5,
(South Street)		1957-9)
absorbed into Little Horton (80)	8th April 1935	
(revived 1942-5 and 1957-9)		
{ BANKFOOT (Red Lion) to HORTON	10th January 1927	62 (1932)
BANK TOP	23rd August 1934	
{ extended to Cooper Lane	1st March 1953	
{ extended to BUTTERSHAW		
TONG (Greyhound Inn)	28th February 1927	74 (1932-1949)
(ceased 27th September 1931, revived		No number (1949-1962)
9th August 1933, suspended 10th September		20 (1962)
1939, revived 15th December 1947)		
BANKFOOT (Red Lion) via Ripleyville	7th September 1927	61 (1932), 62 (1934)
discontinued January 1932; combined with		
Bankfoot-Horton Bank Top 23rd August		
1934; reduced to one early-morning		
journey 5th November 1941;		
ceased 5th November 1951		
GREENGATES (via King's Road and Idle)	27th April 1928 }	75 (1932), 76 (1950)
Cut back to FIVE LANE ENDS	21st March 1931 }	
Cut back to SWAIN HOUSE ROAD	13th April 1931 }	
Extended to WROSE	9th September 1932	76 (1932), 34 (1965)
Cross-city Wrose-Fagley/Moore Avenue	7th June 1953	

Route Names shown in CAPITAL LETTERS	Opened	Route Numbers
GREENGATES (New Line) via Undercliffe	12th November 1928	67 (1932), 33 (1966)
Extended to Redcar Road	30th December 1956	
Some journeys extended to		
APPERLEY BRIDGE	14th March 1932	78 (1932), 32 (1966)
Cross-city service to Haworth Road/Sandy Lane	8th April 1935	
LEEDS (King Street)	6th December 1928	71 (1932), 72 (1942)
Extended to Infirmary Street, Leeds	By December 1932	
Extended to Leeds Central Bus Station	7th December 1938	
Cut back to Infirmary Street, Leeds	1st November 1942	
Terminus moved to Hall Ings	13th August 1950	
Terminus moved to Petergate	1st November 1964	
Re-extended to Leeds Central Bus Station	31st October 1965	
'Fastaway' Express to Park Row, Leeds	6th September 1971	272 (1971)
TYERSAL (Arkwright Street)	6th December 1928	65 (1932), 52 (1953)
Terminus moved from Forster Sq to Hall Ings	8th April 1935	30 (1966)
Extended to Tyersal View	30th August 1939	
Some journeys extended to Tyersal Avenue	16th March 1953	
All journeys extended to Tyersal Avenue	13th November 1960	
SANDY LANE (Florida Road)	18th February 1929	70 (1932), 71 (1953)
		29/32/33/35 (1967)
HUDDERSFIELD (Via Brighouse)	31st March 1929	64 (1932)
BRIGHOUSE	31st March 1929	63 (1932)
diverted via Woodside Road	31st December 1956	
Cross-city service to Wrose	18th November 1957	
THORNTON (express to Ashfield Road)	29th May 1929	(No number)
(withdrawn 18th September 1929)		
RAVENSCLIFFE AVENUE (Thackeray Road)	5th January 1931	68 (1932), 35 (1967)
Inward journey via Church Bank	13th April 1955	
FRIZINGHALL (Dumb Mill), BOLTON WOODS	25th September 1931	(No Number)
(withdrawn 7th December 1931)		
DRIGHLINGTON	9th August 1933	77 (1932), 19 (1965)
extended to ADWALTON (Oakwell Road)	9th October 1955	
SHELF (Bottomley's Arms)	20th February 1935	82 (1935)
Cut back to Shelf Hall Lane junction	6th July 1959	
extended to Belle Vue Crescent	28th April 1968	
absorbed into Halifax (77) service	1st March 1971	
LITTLE HORTON (via HEATON)	8th April 1935	79 (Heaton) 1935
extended to BANKFOOT	17th November 1957	80 (1935)
cross-city service to Holme Wood	6th October 1963	
UNDERCLIFFE (via Otley Road, Idle Road	8th April 1935	81 (1935), 66 (1938)
and Northcote Road)		
(Suspended 10th September 1939)		

Left table

Route Names shown in CAPITAL LETTERS	Opened	Route Numbers
DEWSBURY via BIRKENSHAW	30th October 1935	4 (1938)
some journeys via Town Street and Birstall	14th August 1971	4B (1971)
MOORE AVENUE (Poplar Grove) via Canterbury Avenue	22nd March 1939	61 (1939)
cut back to CANTERBURY AVENUE	4th August 1946	
diverted via lower Great Horton Road	1st March 1964	
extended to St. Enoch's Road Top	15th March 1965	
OAKENSHAW (South Street)	1st August 1940	85 (1940)
extended to Oakenshaw Church	15th November 1959	
STANNINGLEY	20th October 1942	90 (1942), 9 (1965)
cross-city service to Buttershaw	14th March 1965	
cross-city service to Hollingwood Lane	28th February 1971	
WYKE (Town Gate)	12th June 1944	86 (1944), 81 (1960)
Extended to Griffe Head Road	4th August 1946	86 (1946)
some journeys via New Works Road	16th August 1965	84 (1965)
BAILIFF BRIDGE (Punch Bowl)	12th June 1944	87 (1944), 65 (1966)
WIBSEY (Acre Lane)	8th January 1945	84 (1945)
ST. ENOCH'S ROAD (TOP)	8th January 1945	83 (1945-1946)
both services withdrawn 23rd April 1955		
MOORE AVENUE (Poplar Grove) via Little Horton Lane	4th August 1946	83 (1946)
extended to Great Horton Road	1st January 1950	
re-routed via Great Horton Road	7th June 1953	91 (1953), 75 (1956)
cross-city service to Fagley/Wrose	7th June 1953	14 (1965)
WEST BOWLING (Avenue Road)	14th December 1947	88 (1947), 15 (1966),
Shortworking to NEW CROSS STREET	19th October 1953	16 (1971)
Extended to Springwood Gardens	12th October 1955	
Diverted via Parkway	22nd March 1964	
Cross-city service to Allerton (Saffron Drive)	26th July 1964	15 (1966)
Cross-city service to Allerton (Prune Park Lane)	28th February 1971	16 (1971)
UNDERCLIFFE (reinstated)	18th July 1948	66 (1948-1964)
extended to Wellington Road	13th July 1952	
extended to Moorside Road	3rd August 1952	
extended to Eccleshill Church	3rd March 1969	
cross-city service to Canterbury Avenue	2nd March 1964	61 (1964)
cross-city service to St. Enoch's Road	15th March 1965	
BRADFORD MOOR (Woodhall Road) (Temporary; withdrawn 3rd December 1949)	24th July 1949	89 (1949)

Right table

Route Names shown in CAPITAL LETTERS	Opened	Route Numbers
QUEENSBURY (Granby Inn)	6th November 1949	73 (1949), 53 (1954) ; 11 (1965)
HORTON BANK TOP (Shortworking)	6th November 1949	74 (1949), 56 (1954)
WHITE HORSE (Shortworking)	6th November 1949	74 (1949), 57 (1954) ; 13 (1965)
Some Bank Top journeys extended to BUTTERSHAW (Reevy Road West)	5th December 1950	74A, later 74 and 54
BUTTERSHAW cut back to Cooper Lane	16th September 1956	54 (1954), 9 (1965)
WHITE HORSE diverted via lower Great Horton Road	25th March 1957	57; 13 (1965)
Cross-city service Buttershaw-Stanningley	14th March 1965	9 (1965)
Cross-city service Queensbury-Stanningley	31st May 1970	9/11 (1970)
Queensbury (11) absorbed into HALIFAX (76)	1st March 1971	
THORNBURY (Roundabout) (withdrawn 1st March 1952)	5th March 1950	89 (1950)
ODSAL (Crawford Avenue)	7th May 1950	75 (1950), 84 (1956)
absorbed into Woodside (83)	14th March 1965	
LISTER PARK to UNDERCLIFFE absorbed into City Circle (50) 1954	10th May 1953	50 (1953)
Heaton Royds/Stony Ridge HOSPITAL	4th October 1953	28 (1965)
THORPE EDGE (Hawthorn Drive)	23rd November 1953	65 (1953)
extended to Northwood Crescent	18th November 1957	29 (1966)
cross-city service to Haworth Road etc	27th December 1962	
NORWOOD GREEN	8th February 1954	No number (1954), 21 (1962) ; 66 (1965)
BUTTERSHAW (via Speeton Avenue)	21st April 1954	55 (1954), 10 (1965)
cut back to Lastingham Green	16th September 1956	
extended to St. Aidan's Church	5th December 1961	
CITY CIRCLE	25th July 1954	50 (1954), 49/50 (1964) ; 1/2 (1969)
WROSE (via Manningham Lane)	22nd November 1954	74 (1954), 63 (1965)
cross-city service to Brighouse	18th November 1957	
Thornton View HOSPITAL	10th June 1956	39 (1965)
WOODSIDE (Lingdale Avenue)	9th July 1956	83 (1956)
extended to Collinfield Rise	14th July 1958	
extended to Edgebank Avenue	4th July 1960	
HOLME WOOD via Fenby Avenue	19th May 1958	59 (1958), 5 (1965)
extended to Broadstone Way	18th August 1958	
extended to Heysham Drive	2nd June 1963	
extended to Egglestone Drive	4th June 1967	
cross-city service to Allerton	26th July 1964	59 (1964) (5) 1965

ROUTES

Route Names shown in CAPITAL LETTERS	Opened	Route Numbers
ALLERTON (Prune Park Lane) (Cross-city -service to West Bowling)	28th February 1971	16 (1971)
ALLERTON (Ayresome Oval)	1st March 1971	6 (1971)
HALIFAX Bus Station (Via Queensbury)	1st March 1971	76 (1971)
HALIFAX Bus Station or General Hospital (via Shelf; some journeys via Northowram Hospital)	1st March 1971	77 (1971)
SALTAIRE via Thackley	1st July 1971	40 (1971)
GREENGATES via Idle	1st July 1971	42 (1971)
FIVE LANE ENDS via Bolton	1st July 1971	41 (1971)
CLAYTON Town End (Via Pasture Lane)	1st August 1971	37 (1971)
SCHOLEMOOR AVENUE	1st August 1971	38 (1971)
WIBSEY (Acre Lane) via Little Horton	1st August 1971	45 (1971)
BUTTERSHAW (Cooper Lane) via Little Horton	1st August 1971	46 (1971)
Leeds Road and Calverley HOSPITAL	19th March 1972	22 (1972)
THORNTON (Cemetery)	25th March 1972	7 (1972)
cross-city service to THORNBURY	25th March 1972	7 (1972)
DUCKWORTH LANE (Infirmary)	25th March 1972	8 (1972)
OCCASIONAL SERVICES		
City Tour		1 (1965-7)
Bolling Hall Tour		2 (1965-7)
Lister Park Tour		3 (1965-7)
Park Avenue (cricket)		47 (1971)
Odsal Stadium (rugby)		48 (1965)

ROUTES

Route Names shown in CAPITAL LETTERS	Opened	Route Numbers
Clayton (THORNABY DRIVE) extended to The Avenue	4th March 1962 / 31st May 1970	36 (1962)
{ ECCLESHILL (Faltis Square) to { ST. ENOCH'S ROAD TOP	18th November 1962	33/44 (1962-1965)
{ City to ST. ENOCH'S ROAD TOP	25th August 1963	44 (1963)
{ City to ECCLESHILL	1st November 1965	33 (1965)
{ extended to BUTTERSHAW/HORTON BANK TOP	14th March 1965	43/44 (1965)
BRADFORD MOOR (Woodhall Road)	18th November 1962	30 (1962), 23-27 (1966)
cross-city service to Crossflatts etc	1st November 1963	
cross-city service to Shipley Glen	5th October 1964	
HOLLINGWOOD LANE via Great Horton Road	27th December 1962	58 (1962), 12 (1965)
cross-city service to Stanningley	28th February 1971	
ALLERTON (Saffron Drive)	2nd June 1963	35 (1963), 15 (1966)
cross-city to Holme Wood/West Bowling	26th July 1964	
BIERLEY via Dudley Hill (withdrawn 1971)	5th June 1963	22 (1965)
FARSLEY (Newlands)	16th September 1963	91 (1963), 10 (1965)
CROSSFLATTS (Micklethwaite Lane)	1st November 1963	24 (1963)
BINGLEY (Church)	1st November 1963	26 (1963)
SALTAIRE (Roundabout)	1st November 1963	25 (1963)
FRIZINGHALL (Ashfield Avenue)	1st November 1963	27 (1963)
Cross-city service to Bradford Moor	1st November 1963	24-27 (1963)
ALLERTON via Bell Dean Road (cross-city service to Holme Wood)	26th July 1964	5 (1964)
SHIPLEY GLEN (Saltaire Mill)	5th October 1964	23 (1964)
WROSE-WIBSEY via Odsal	14th March 1965	34 (1965)
ELDWICK (Beck Bottom) and DICK HUDSON'S (via Gilstead or Ferncliffe) (Dick Hudson's discontinued 10/7/1971)	6th March 1966	68/68A (1966)
BINGLEY (Limited Stop)	7th March 1966	26X (1966)
HOLME WOOD (via Knowles Lane)	2nd April 1967	17 (1967)
TONG CEMETERY (via Dudley Hill)	2nd April 1967	18 (1967)
LEEDS (via Pudsey) New termini at Hall Ings and Leeds Central Bus Station	15th October 1967	78 (1967)
SHEFFIELD (White Rose Express) (via Dewsbury and Barnsley)	18th October 1969	X33 (1969)

COATS OF MANY COLOURS

Preparing for its long journey to Bradford via the Great North Road, No. 466 exhibits its elegant Weymann body and smart 'Ultramarine' dark blue and cream at the AEC works, Southall, in November 1938.
[Courtesy G. Welburn; photo AEC Ltd

In its drab wartime khaki camouflage No. 466 acquired a liking for the Stanningley route, being photographed in Hall Ings in 1946/7 with Thornbury tramcar No. 189.
[Courtesy A. A. Townsin; photo R. A. Mills

Photographed on 12th July 1949 and still serving the Stanningley route, No. 466 now wears the cheerful postwar livery.   [Photo: R. Marshall

BRADFORD CORPORATION PASSENGER TRANSPORT DEPARTMENT

NOTICE TO PASSENGERS

ODSAL SERVICE

Commencing Sunday, 7th May, 1950, tramcars on the Odsal service will be substituted by motor buses, Route No. 75. For frequency, see new timetables.

Route and fares will remain as at present, except that the Odsal terminus will be extended to Crawford Avenue. Passengers are requested to note alterations to certain stopping places.

The Horsfall Playing Fields service will be withdrawn.

C. R. Tattam, M.Inst.T.,
General Manager

11, Forster Square,
Bradford. 21st April, 1950.

T3422.50.450

Traffic Notices informing passengers of impending transport changes in their city were sometimes more significant than at first sight appeared. The Odsall service conversion actually marked the end of the trams, for Bradford's tramcars were withdrawn on 6th May 1950, whilst the trolleybuses were destined to become the last in public service in Britain, finishing on 26th March 1972. The author has produced a companion volume to this one, covering the trolleybuses, and intends to do likewise for the tramway system.

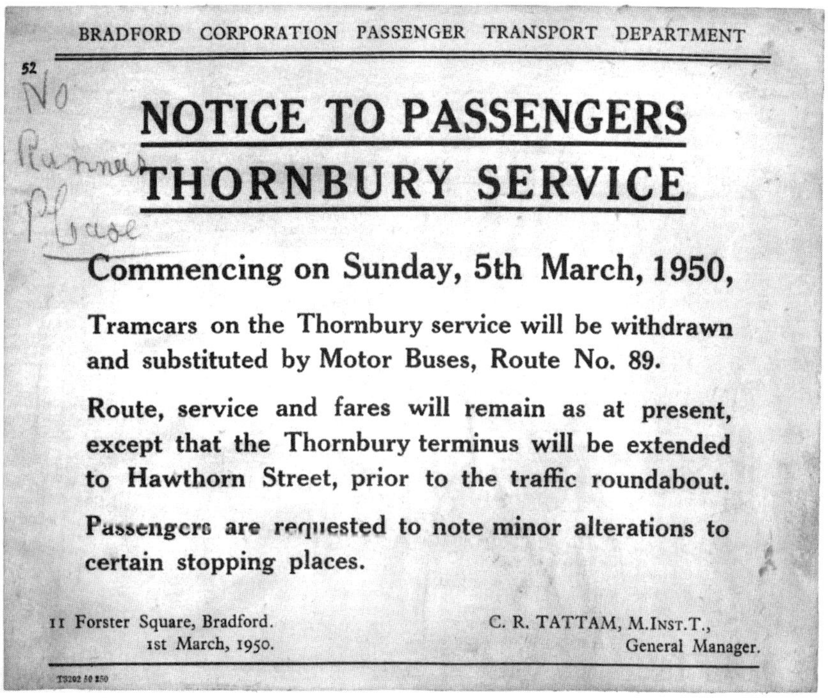

BRADFORD CORPORATION PASSENGER TRANSPORT DEPARTMENT

52

No
Running
Please

NOTICE TO PASSENGERS

THORNBURY SERVICE

Commencing on Sunday, 5th March, 1950,

Tramcars on the Thornbury service will be withdrawn and substituted by Motor Buses, Route No. 89.

Route, service and fares will remain as at present, except that the Thornbury terminus will be extended to Hawthorn Street, prior to the traffic roundabout.

Passengers are requested to note minor alterations to certain stopping places.

11 Forster Square, Bradford.
1st March, 1950.

C. R. TATTAM, M.Inst.T.,
General Manager.

TS202.50.250

BRADFORD CITY TRANSPORT

CITY BOUNDARY ——·——
(R - Ripleyville)

SCALE IN MILES

CIRCLES GIVE DISTANCES OF HALF A MILE FROM CITY HALL.

A Copland study of poles – traction, telegraph and barber's – together with a
1934-style bus and trolleybus sign, provides a suitable epitaph.

The End